"Isaac's book is pure gold. Trying to make your dreams come true in life and business can feel impossible and disheartening. Not with this book by your side! *Just Get Up* WILL empower you to answer your call to greatness no matter what personal or financial challenges you've faced. It's written by a powerful trainer, speaker, and spiritual leader who obviously cares deeply about the hundreds of people he's helped over his career. This book will help revolutionize your mindset to think like a winner and gain the valuable confidence you need to transform your dream (against all odds!) into reality."

—**Marlene Elizabeth, M.Ed.,** #1 International Bestselling Author of *MONEYWINGS™*; Spiritual Life and Certified Money Coach

"Just Get Up is a riveting account of strength and survival that will inspire you and leave a lasting impression. Isaac takes you on a journey inside the stark reality of poverty in America, while also exposing possibilities that most people aren't aware of. His story of overcoming is a well-rounded and proven transformation process of how to successfully achieve your goals and dreams, no matter your circumstances!"

—**Carmell Pelly,** International Best Selling Author, Podcaster, and Recovery Advocate

"I am in awe and blessed to have been able to narrate Isaac's book, *Just Get Up And Manifest Your Inner Genius*. After personally reading his book and narrating the audio version of his unique story, I know now, based on his advice that anything is possible!"

—**Anthony Pica**, Husband and father of 2, Educator and coach for over 20 years, Full time voice over artist

"Isaac Miller demonstrates how discipline and internal motivation can allow you to achieve whatever goals you set for yourself. His first major work, *Just Get Up* tells his personal story of self-accomplishment and success despite a childhood of poverty and family disfunction. His story is one that will resonate with anyone working to achieve their dreams. *Just Get Up* sets the stage for Miller's future contributions for those committed to living a full life, and we can only look forward to his forthcoming books."

—**Robert Lancaster**, LSU Law School Professor

Just Get Up
and Manifest Your Inner Genius

by Isaac Samuel Miller

ISBN 978-1-63393-874-8

Published by

köehlerbooks™

210 60th Street
Virginia Beach, VA 23451
800–435–4811
www.koehlerbooks.com

JUST GET UP

AND MANIFEST
YOUR INNER GENIUS

ISAAC SAMUEL MILLER

VIRGINIA BEACH
CAPE CHARLES

TABLE OF CONTENTS

DEDICATION

I DEDICATE MY MOTIVATIONAL GUIDE to all of the true dreamers who know and understand the irrefutable truth that imagination is everything. I look forward to hearing all of the great stories after you realize the same thing that I have personally discovered: that all humans have unlimited potential. I'm excited for you to discover and finally learn how to use your true gift of value. This will be one of the most exciting journeys that you will ever embark upon. So many people in the world today are breathing corpses because even though they're alive, they're dead because they don't have the courage to be who they truly are and pursue their goals and dreams.

Furhermore, there are some people who do have the courage, but they don't know how to get started, how to discover their gifts, or how to use their gifts. I pray that my *Just Get Up* program helps you to live your dreams. My book will most certainly dig up your gifts, but only if you wholeheartedly and precisely follow my program's format. You have an inner genius inside of you, and I grant you that if you make a full commitment to tap into and release your inner genius, your life will never be the same! So prepare your heart and prepare your mind to discover the truths that only a few throughout the history of humanity have had the inspiration, will, and the courage to explore. I wish I could tell you exactly what you will discover, but I don't believe in spoiling the self-discovery process. However, I'll say this: "You will discover a plethora of treasures that will make you an unstoppable force, and all of your goals will be at your mercy." But you must learn and apply the invaluable tools of *Just Get Up: And Manifest Your Inner Genius* to truly appreciate what I'm saying. Your adventure has begun and after you discover your true gift of value, you'll be amazed where it's found.

FOREWORD

EVERYONE NEEDS "A HAND" FROM time to time. Sometimes it is a literal hand to pull you up when you have taken a fall. As embarrassing as it might be, the care and compassion shown in that act of kindness and the acceptance of help gets you back up and on your way. Sometimes it is words of encouragement that provide motivation to continue a difficult task. That little nudge you needed to remind you of the importance of seeing something through to completion. Sometimes it is as innocuous as someone finding one piece to the jigsaw puzzle or one word in the crossword puzzle that changes the visual just enough for you to see how other pieces fit in. That one piece or word had a hand in seeing the big picture.

For us, Isaac Miller was a hand up when we needed one. We are old enough to be his parents, indeed we have a son his age and one a decade older. We are successful and highly motivated people in most facets of our lives. We have advanced degrees, work in careers we love, and have created a work/life balance that is satisfying. But as age has crept in, we begrudgingly realized we needed to do something to keep our bodies moving and functional.

One of us is a former athlete, one is not. We had purchased an elliptical machine that got intermittent use. We walked and ran around the neighborhood when the weather was good. We stretched, rolled, and did yoga poses when we remembered to. We came to three conclusions: (a) we needed to do this together to have any hope of consistency, (b) we had to stick to a plan of working out before the sun came up, and (c) we needed someone to guide us and hold us accountable. We joined a local gym, signed up for a personal trainer, and Isaac precipitously became part of our lives. Lucky us!

We have spent our lives as teachers and mentors, encouraging and motivating students to keep the end in mind, work hard, and strive for success. One thing we understand is that motivation often has to come from outside before it comes from inside. Our early days training with Isaac were difficult – physically because our bodies were out of shape and mentally because we had not adjusted to our new routine. And if we have to be honest, although we enjoyed hearing Isaac muse about life, what did a young man in his early twenties at the time have to offer us regarding an experienced and proven strategy for pushing us to accomplish our goals? As it turns out Isaac has a lot to offer and we can wholeheartedly attest to this fact. We have vigilantly lived this book with Isaac as it has come to fruition. Three times a week in the waking hours of the morning we have sweated, breathed hard, and listened to his thoughts on actualizing one's dreams. As five-plus years have flown by, we look forward to our early morning workouts interspersed with commentary by Isaac. We have come to appreciate his thoughtful approach to relationships, his wise-beyond-his-years view of life's challenges, his omnipresent belief in himself as the key to his success, and his many smiles. We can attest to the fact that he lives by the words he writes, and has only begun to tap into his potential.

Isaac Miller's compelling life story is the place from which his credibility flows. Most of us will never know the type of roadblocks he overcame to become a college graduate, adoring husband, highly sought-after professional, home owner, respected preacher, spoken word performer, poet, and published author. How did Isaac, the tender child and wide-eyed adolescent, make such courageous decisions to set himself on a path of success? In *Just Get Up*, Isaac's entrepreneurial spirit coupled with strong faith and a commitment to life-long learning are evident. His book will inspire you to get to work on yourself . . . being the best you can be and reaching your dreams!

Just Get Up shares the path of Isaac's own personal journey while motivating and teaching you how you can join him as you pursue your journey to success. Isaac's book demonstrates how life is meant to be an exciting discovery that's full of true purpose along with an unyielding will to succeed. Isaac's experienced strategy demonstrates that it doesn't matter whether you're young or old, because you can rewrite your life's script, and be all that you were designed to be. We are all a work in progress and his book, *Just Get Up And Manifest Your Inner Genius* may just be the "hand" you need!

JANE CASSIDY

Senior Vice Provost

Louisiana State University

JAMES BYO

Director, School of Music

Louisiana State University

PREFACE

IF YOUR LIFE WAS A TV series, would it be legendary? If your life was a TV series, could it be used to inspire someone? Or would your TV series be cancelled after the first episode because it's a waste of airtime? How you decide to use your airtime every day, to showcase your life to the world, is a reflection of how you see yourself. So, before your life airs its final episode, you owe it to yourself not to have the painful regret of living your entire life as a puppet for someone else's dreams.

Life is truly unpredictable, and no one can guarantee your longevity on this planet! So, in order to become a true legend in life, if you truly desire to maximize your unique potential, you must learn how to demonstrate a life that airs like a topnotch TV series. Are you currently living a legendary life? To help guide your heart to answer these questions, simply ask yourself this question: Have you discovered your gifts and chased the dreams that are tucked away in your imagination?

If you truly desire for your life to be legendary and reflect the manifestation of your gifts, then you must manifest your inner genius! To unearth your untapped potential will mandate an intense but rewarding journey of self-discovery. If you're wondering why it's a necessity to manifest your greatness, then here is the answer: if you become the greatest version of yourself, you will unlock your inner genius, and it will literally amaze you, the world, and your family and friends.

To unlock your inner genius and dig up your gifts, you must master how to defeat the greatest threat to your success. At some point along your journey, the greatest threat to your success will become evident to you. My *Just Get Up* program will train and prepare you for the inevitable adversities that you will face as you're pursuing your goals. I personally have lived a life of unfulfilling events, and I know firsthand what it feels like to fight for what you believe in, especially when no one believes in you! *Just Get Up* is my real-life guide of a dreamer fighting his way into living his dreams. My book is a self-help book that briefly analyzes my unique story and how my inner genius was manifested over time. Once I discovered how to manifest my inner genius, I was able to become an entrepreneur at seventeen years of age. When I was eleven years old, I set out on a mission to escape the gripping teeth of poverty, and during my pursuit to greatness I was fortunate to discover a plethora of truths I can share with you that will change your life forever! My life's adventure unveils the path for discovering the true meaning of success.

My book was designed to help you avoid living a life of serendipity, because it's easy to lose your motivation to fulfill your dreams, especially if you haven't discovered the key steps of how to win in life. I'm ready for you to win, and I know you're ready to win, too! My book is just right for you! *Just Get Up* was engineered to cure procrastination, passivity, lack of motivation, lack of self-belief, and unfulfilled goals. *Just Get Up* offers a science to how you can attain your goals and change any unfavorable circumstances that come your way. Although my book isn't a memoir, Chapters 1-3 relive my journey of how I began to manifest my genius after I experienced a life-changing epiphany. Chapters 1-3 introduce my life's experiences, and the many struggles I faced. Chapters 4-13 are designed for motivation, self-development, discovering your personal legacy, manifesting your inner genius, developing a winning strategy, and how to achieve your goals.

As you journey throughout your *Just Get Up* experience, at some point along your adventure, you will begin to discover your life's true treasures. You will be wondering: what are these treasures? They must be discovered, and they will lead to an impactful life that will produce a true sense of value and meaning in life. However, to properly use the many gems you will find requires a successful completion of each chapter.

Throughout each chapter, you must diligently search for *Holistic Discoveries*, which are major keys that you will need to successfully complete your adventure. *Holistic Discoveries* represent lifelines and these lifelines symbolize any type of device or system that's used to help someone stay afloat. For example, suppose you were drowning in the Atlantic Ocean, and someone threw you a floating device to save you from a potentially life threatening situation, although you could probably still survive without this extra assistance depending on your swimming ability. But, regardless of your swimming ability, I'm sure you would appreciate the assistance! Furthermore, *Holistic Discoveries* are similar; but, they're slightly different in this way: I designed these discoveries to help you while making it easier for you to foresee a potential slum or to escape one. So view *Holistic Discoveries* as your guardian angel to help you remain on track as you're traveling to your dreams!

Although the *Holistic Discoveries* you will discover are emblematic, you'll begin to notice that as you're exposing your true potential, *Holistic Discoveries* will help you overcome any setbacks or adversities that you're destined to encounter. Here is a preview into an example of a *Holistic Discovery*: before you move forward, you must accept that your commitment to manifesting your true passions can only come through you! Some of these chapters will contain exercises that are essential for you to unveil your gifts and manifest your true genius.

If you truly want to be successful, I'm promising you, success is within your reach! If you have been sitting around and hoping for good things to happen, I suggest you stop hoping immediately! Remember this: As long as you're still breathing there is always an opportunity to put in the hard work that will eventually lead to your success! Once your inner genius has been excavated, it most certainly will lead to you living your life's dreams. We all are geniuses, so you must view yourself as a genius! For now, if you don't view yourself as a genius yet, that's forgivable: your journey will unearth facts that will prove beyond a doubt that your mind is as beautiful as the mind of an Albert Einstein! If you properly follow my *Just Get Up* program, you will discover *The Octagon Way, The Limelight Spot Effect, Numbers Don't Lie*, and my proven *27-Month Plan*: these concepts will train you and clearly demonstrate how to pursue and unlock your true passion's identity, which will revolutionize your life! After you read each chapter, immediately start applying the things you're learning!

I was inspired to write this book to help you discover your talents, and to show the world that when we put our minds to something, we, as a human race, most certainly can do what the average mind thinks is impossible! For years, I've wanted to write an incandescent book to help people, but I didn't know where to start. However, that drought ended in Pensacola, Florida in May of 2017. I was walking with my wife, and the thought crept into my mind, whispering *"Just Get Up!"*

I have a college degree in Therapeutic Recreation and Leisure Studies, along with a minor in Physical Education. I have years of experience with motivating many people. I have been an entrepreneur for over a decade, and I work as a full-time Fitness Trainer, Certified Therapeutic Recreation Specialist, and a Strength and Conditioning Specialist. I'm also a spoken word artist, sales coach, motivational speaker, writer, and a minister. I have personally trained well over 1,000 people and helped a lot of people to make important changes in their lives. I'm constantly motivating people by helping them to get in shape, inspiring them to manifest their geniuses, delivering motivational speeches for various organizations, and encouraging people to draw closer to God. I've managed personal training sales teams, along with teaching people how to successfully grow their businesses. *Just Get Up* was written between May 2017 and October 2018 in Baton Rouge, Louisiana and in Houston, Texas.

Your *Just Get Up* adventure will culminate in your life becoming a legendary TV series, and your life's channel will finally air the real dreams that are in your imagination! *Just Get Up* will motivate you to believe and to achieve, so manifest your inner genius and go live your dreams!

CHAPTER 1

TURN ON YOUR LIFE'S CHANNEL

MOST PEOPLE HAVE ASKED THESE questions at some point during their lives: "What are my talents and how do I discover my gifts?" "How can I become motivated?" and "How can I stop being a procrastinator?" It's human nature to ponder these questions; however, you must identify your own true passions to unlock the secrets to these questions. Have you identified your most valuable gift and its connection to your purpose in life? It's possible that you haven't used all of your talents, or maybe you haven't discovered the true potential of your inner genius. Just like a car, you have unique features and abilities, but in order to maximize the performance of your life's vehicle, which represents you, you must investigate and challenge your abilities in order to identify the potential that is buried alive inside of you. You have a gift, and after you complete this necessary adventure with me, you will discover things about yourself that will literally make you unstoppable!

You are privileged to be one of the approximately 7.7 billion people who are still alive on our planet! Out of these billions of people, what is your life's role? Do you know? You must identify your life's role in order to discover your gift of value. Your gift of value holds the key to discovering your true passions in life, and living your dreams!

So don't make a settlement with your life by pursuing a life that's not a part of your dreams. If you make a settlement with your life, it will produce a state of recurring discontentment, and feeling unfulfilled will often surface at the most inopportune times during your life. Living an unsatisfying life can easily be traced back to an individual's failure to discover their life's true identity. Remember, all of us have goals and dreams. In fact, without goals and dreams, our lives would be empty and depleted of the growth that's needed for us to feel competent, and happy in our own skin.

No human who has ever walked on this planet, has successfully mastered how to run away from the passions that constantly pull at our hearts. So remember this: "Success is an opportunist, and every time you're reminded of the things that only you know and desire, whether you're aware of it or not, your heart is beating to remind you to create an opportunity to wholeheartedly pursue your passions." Look at it this way: there are over 7.7 billion channels for the universe to operate through. You may be wondering, what is your channel?

You have something that you were born to do, and if you're not tuned in to your channel, you will miss out on your life's journey of discoveries. However, it's important for you to know that no one can tell you what your channel should display because it is a personal discovery process. However, I can show you how to begin to tune in to your life's channel.

When your life's channel is fully manifested, you will know! How will you know? It will lead to wealth, riches, happiness, fulfillment, inner security, joy, peace, love, confidence, greatness, wisdom, and rewarding relationships. How much you discover about your channel depends on how much time you spend watching it. Remember, there are twenty-four hours in a day, and the amount of time you spend tuned-in to your channel will dictate how much you discover about yourself.

Our universe is like cable TV, and the universe provides us with a plethora of channels, so many that we could never watch them all! What channel is your life currently on? Is your life even turned on, or have you powered it off? If you're spending large amounts of your time watching other peoples' channels, please stop immediately! You have too much to learn about yourself. Your goal, moving forward, is to reactivate your life's channel or upgrade your channel. You're capable of adding new phenomenal episodes and stories to your life's channel. Your life's channel should reflect a legendary TV marathon!

Not to sound harsh, but any one of the 7.7 billion TV series being aired today, can easily cease to exist at any moment. If your life's journey ended today, would you be overwhelmingly satisfied with how far you've traveled in your life? Your life's journey could come to an end within the next two minutes, two hours, two months, or two years. So, before your life airs the final episode, you owe it to yourself to manifest your inner genius, which will lead to your life being legendary!

However, before you can fully explore the discoveries throughout your *Just Get Up* experience, it's important for you to take a tour through my life's journey to manifesting my geniuses. It's imperative for you to digest the gems from my first three chapters before your journey intensifies. My experienced strategy of overcoming adversities has equipped me with the faculties that are needed to help you. Your adventure has begun, and I want to take this opportunity to thank you for tuning in to start my *Just Get Up* program.

My Path To Just Getting Up

My name is Isaac Miller, I'm six years old, and I live in Baton Rouge, Louisiana. My family calls me "June" and I don't know why. I thought my nickname was June because I'm a junior, but I was wrong: my Dad's name is Carter. One of my missions is to get to the bottom of why my nickname is June. But in the meanwhile, I'll see if my big sister Brittany wants to play sock volleyball. It's a game she created, and we basically toss and hit a balled-up sock back and forth to one another. My sister and I are beginning to realize that our lives are very different from other kids. My sister is two years older than me, and I'm certain she knows the answer to why we don't go anywhere, or have family dinners like I frequently hear other kids talking about all the time.

Also, I'm trying to figure out what it means to be "tucked in" at night by your Mom and Dad, because I honestly can't answer that question for my friends at school. All I know is that I'm tired of pretending like I know what they're talking about. If they didn't make it seem so juicy, like I should definitely receive tuck-ins at night then I would just tell them that I don't have a clue what being tucked-in means.

I have these inner conversations at least once a day, but today I guess I'll give my mind a break, since I'm excited about being seven years old. I made my seventh birthday today on July, 19, 1995; however, I'm sad because I just returned from my first summer visit with my Dad. My summer visit is over, and I can't remember the last time I saw my Dad, and I'm scared I won't see him again. Maybe something is wrong with my memory because I can't seem to remember anything in my life before I turned six. The only childhood memory I have is when I was five, and I was sleeping on a mat in my kindergarten class during naptime. I miss those days because I got my best sleep, and I didn't have to worry about waking up to roaches crawling on my face. When I was in kindergarten I felt like I was somebody because the kids were kind to me, but that all changed once I got to the first grade. I'm not looking forward to starting my second grade school year in a few weeks because I know I'm going to be teased about my shoes, hair, clothes, and the way I talk.

I hope my little buddies Jim and Mike don't remember when I peed on myself last year because that was embarrassing. I asked Mrs. Martin to let me go use the restroom and I begged her to let me go. She claimed I needed a doctor's excuse indicating that I had a bladder problem. That's the craziest thing in the world; why did she need a silly note when I was dancing around trying my best not to pee-pee? So the inevitable happened and I peed on myself, and my pants were full of urine, and the whole class laughed at me. I just wanted to disappear and go play with my Teenage Mutant Ninja Turtle toys. To make a long story short, Mrs. Martin called my Mom, and she came to pick me up, but I made sure I informed the guidance counselor of what happened! Mrs. Martin was mean, and I wanted her to pay for ruining my second grade year. But, I'll be honest: she is a very pretty lady, so I eventually got over it. Maybe she was being mean to me because she liked me? I don't know. My seven-year-old mind believed in anything, I guess, but I do believe that I can be somebody one day, despite the reality that I'm currently a loser.

My Second Grade School Year

It's August of 1995, and my second grade school year is about to start. I've been practicing on my speech with the school's speech therapist, and I'm trying to build my confidence to speak in front of others. I'm embarrassed that my tongue doesn't roll like normal people, and I have a hard time saying words that start with "str," and "scr." I'm sure there are more words I have trouble with, but I haven't discovered them yet in second grade. The kids tease me a lot, and they say I talk funny, and the girls call me ugly. I like some of the girls, but who am I kidding? They think I'm ugly. I honestly wish I was someone else, and I'm embarrassed that I'm the only kid who is being picked up after school in a raggedy car. I'm sick of being teased, and I just wish I could grow up, and go make my own money. If I was a grownup, then I could get the things I want for me and my big sister.

It's so hard for me to focus when I'm at school because I'm drowning inside of my imagination. I often wonder whether or not death would produce a better way of living for me? I'm dreading each day of school because I'm tired of being teased for wearing raggedy shoes. I'm desperately trying to stay afloat because I'm sinking inside my life's river of poverty. I can't live inside of my life's prison anymore and I'm tired of my sleepless nights being disturbed by gunshots. I'm worried sick whether or not I'll live to experience another day of life's abuse. I don't have a single baby picture to validate my existence, and I'm tired of crying and wondering "why not?" I truly want to be successful, but I don't know where or how to start the process of capturing my life's dreams. I'm beginning to wonder if mediocrity was engineered for me. The only thing that's keeping me alive is my hope that one day, my dream of discovering what life really has in store for me will come true. Those were my thoughts today for my first day of school, and daydreaming helps me to cope. Honestly, I enjoy talking to myself because I know that I care about my feelings.

At school today my teacher told us that we can be whatever we want to be, but my dreams seem impossible because I don't have anyone who believes in me. However, I must admit it's quite comforting to visualize myself becoming a person who is loved. My biggest dream is to provide for my Mom and to pay for my Dad to beat on someone other than my Mom. I don't know what an average seven-year-old desires, however, I just want to know what it feels like to go to the movies. I'm sick of my sister telling me lame bedtime stories, and I'm tired of dreaming about being rich. I don't know what my Mom or Dad do for a living, and I'm tired of not being able to answer that question at school. I thought my Mom's job was selling food stamps, but I remembered when Mrs. Martin said: "Sweetie, that's not an occupation. That's a government-assisted program for people who have low income." I responded to Mrs. Martin's stupid statement by saying, "Well, I know my Mom gets a welfare check, so that means she works at the fair, right?" Mrs. Martin was trying to play me, so I told her, "My Mom gets paid $150 a month, we have a lot of money, and we don't need any assistance." I lied and told Mrs. Martin, "My Mom is so rich that our rent is free and I'm certain she paid for it all upfront." I remember that when I got home that day, I asked my Mom what she did for a living, and she said she was trying to get my grandmother to get her a job doing sitter's work. So I said to myself, "What is sitter's work?"

My Mom told me that sitter's work was when you sit with old people and attend to their needs. After she told me the meaning of the job she was trying to get, I felt accomplished, but my Mom never became a sitter. So now I'm beginning to wonder: maybe it's my role to provide for my Mom and my big sister Brittany. Because my Dad is nowhere in sight and I just found out that I have a half-sister whose name is Dana. What is a half-sister, anyway? I know my Mom didn't give birth to her, so what does this mean? So I approach my Mom and I ask her why my Dad is never around? Also, I ask my Mom if my Dad loves us. My Mom replies by saying, "I don't know what's wrong with your Dad." So I reply to my Mom's statement by saying, "Well, Mom, I love you and I'm going to get us out of this slum." At this point I just remember falling asleep, and my life flashed before my eyes as I woke up, three years older.

I Fell in Love When I Was Ten

It's 1998 and I'm watching the Chicago Bulls play the Utah Jazz in the NBA finals. My Mom loves Michael Jordan, and I wish Michael was my Dad because he seems like a nice guy. Wait a minute, maybe I should be an athlete, and that will be a way to provide for my Mom. I'll go tell my Mom that I'm the next Michael Jordan! But she's distracted with my sister who just walked in and says, "I'm being bullied by this girl who made me eat grass today." Shockingly, I'm actually thrilled to know this because I thought I was the only one being teased and picked on. So I decided to tell my sister it's ok, because I was teased today about the scar that's on my nose. The kids tell me that it must represent my super powers and to be honest I hate it. I wish I could make my scar go away! When I make it to the NBA I'll get plastic surgery and I'll have it removed. Anyway, it's time to do my homework and get ready for bed because I'm beginning to enjoy my dreams more than my real life. I wonder what I'll dream about tonight?

My alarm goes off and, darn, it's time to go back to school already. So I get up, and my sister and I get dressed, and then we catch the bus. I actually like riding the bus because I get to watch the other kids who are riding with me without looking weird. I often wonder how God created people because seeing people move around is truly amazing, especially Tiara Foster. I think she is a true queen and I would love for her to be my princess. *Ok, Isaac, you need to man up and tell her that you like her; it's obvious she wants you!* At least, that's what I'm saying to myself. I have been doing pushups every day so that my chest will looks big, if I ever get my chance to talk to my queen. I love watching Tiara get off of the bus, and I'm so happy that she gets dropped off before me. Wait, I just overheard her saying that she lives across the street from the candy lady, but why is she telling this to Marcus? She couldn't possibly like that jerk-looking guy over me! I love flowers and I'm going to play in the NBA, so if she knows what's best for her, she will look my way.

It's my stop and I get off the bus, but I can't stop wondering whether or not Tiara likes Marcus. *I must make my move quickly before I lose my woman.* Could my big brother Travis give me some advice? My brother was living with my grandmother and he just moved in with us. I had overheard that my Mom couldn't afford to take care of my brother, so my grandmother had offered to raise him. My brother is the oldest and he is so cool, I wish I had his swag. So I walk up to my brother and I tell him about Tiara Foster. And to my surprise, my brother talks on the phone with her big sister. I'm super pumped because I know this is my way in, and my brother can put in a good word for me. So I tell my brother to ask Tiara's big sister if Tiara knows who I am. My brother tells me, "Yes, she knows who you are!"

I'm beyond excited, so I tell my brother to ask Tiara's sister if Tiara likes me, but my brother comes back with some bad news: Tiara said she thinks I'm ugly. After hearing this bad news, I decide to run to my room and close the door. I turn on the stereo and I put on a love song as I'm looking in the mirror trying to convince myself that I'm handsome. I begin to talk to myself and say, *I can't believe this! She thinks I'm ugly! I know what I'm going to do: I'll walk around the corner to the candy lady's house, and if I see Tiara I'll just confess my love.* "Hey, Mom, do you have fifty cents?" My Mom replies by saying, "Boy, what do you need fifty cents for?" "I want to get a Dixie cup from the candy lady." My Mom says, "Okay, but come right on back, you hear?" I reply, "Yes, ma'am" as I silently say to myself, *Tiara, your man is on his way!* So as I'm walking through the woods I proceed to prep myself to confess my love to Tiara. Suddenly I see my woman and I walk up to her, but I freeze because I'm nervous. Tiara says, "Isaac, what do you want?" At this point I'm having a silent conversation in my head saying, *I love you and I want to marry you. Darn, Isaac, get it together! This is your only opportunity.* Unfortunately, my mouth is frozen and my lips aren't moving.

Tiara asks me again, "Isaac, what do you want?" Unfortunately, at this point all of my courage has totally dissipated. So Tiara walks off and I follow her like a lion hunting his prey. Tiara walks to her friend's house just a few houses down, so I stand my ground as I wait for her visit to end. Tiara's friend asks her, "Why is that weird boy just standing there looking at us?" Tiara says, "I don't know, but he's starting to annoy me." After hearing this, I silently say to myself, *Darn, Isaac this isn't going as planned, it's now or never! You must be a Ninja Turtle and go get your woman.* I take a deep breath and I begin my walk toward true love, but Tiara runs away, and I say, "Get back here! I have something to say!" But Tiara runs home and goes inside and closes the door. After this I say to myself, *Oh no my only chance is gone.* So I knock on her door and her Mom comes outside, and she tells me, "Go home, baby." I walk off with my head down, playing the love song in my head that I just listened to a few hours ago, after my brother told me the love of my life thinks I'm ugly. *Darn, Isaac, you blew it!* I can't go to school tomorrow and face the walk of shame.

At school the next day I avoided Tiara by all means. I was embarrassed and I never got my chance to confess my love. I told my cousin Anthony about it once I got home from school and he simply said: "You have to get your heart broken at least once in your life, June." I was determined to figure out how to win a girl's heart. So I asked my other cousin, Michael, "What should I do to win a girl's heart?" He replied, "If you can write some good poetry, then you can have any girl you want." I love the sound of that, and I'm excited to write my first poem. After I finished writing my first poem I ask Michael if he'll read my poem. Michael says, "Okay, I'll read it, June." After he reads my poem, he says, "June, you have a gift." Michael is seventeen and I'm ten, so I figure he knows what he's talking about. After Michael tells me he thinks I have a gift, I started to feel something inside, and my heart agreed with him. Suddenly I feel like I want to be a writer, and I begin to say to myself, *Maybe this is the meaning of the dream I keep dreaming.* So I ask Michael if I can make a living writing and he says, "Yes." He mentions how I can write songs for people and be an author.

So at school the next day, I decide to start writing poems every day, and I feel like I know what my new mission should be. I must figure out how to become a writer and an athlete. To my surprise, during class time my fifth grade teacher asked the class, "What do you want to be when you grow up?" It's my turn to stand up and plead my case, so I stand proudly and say, "I want to be an entrepreneur who writes for people." I inform my fellow students that "My life's dream is to get out of poverty and provide for my family." I tell my classmates that "I'm okay with being different and I think I'm a genius." I conclude my speech by telling the class that one day I'm going to be a famous writer. After class, I rush home because I know I have discovered my gift. I have been trying to figure out my calling for four years now and I've finally discovered my gift. I know I must investigate my newly discovered gift because I know this is a sign from God. So I say to myself, *I will remember 1998 as the year I began to dream about different ways to escape being poor.* I feel like my imagination is the most valuable thing I have, and it is the only exciting thing in my life.

CHAPTER 2

WHEN THE GENIUS IS MANIFESTED

IT'S NECESSARY FOR ME TO relive the moments when I decided to take action to create a better future for myself and my family, before I reveal how the meaning of my inner genius gradually came into fruition. When I turned eleven years old, I made this declaration to my future self: "One day, I'm going to wake up and reminisce about my unwanted past as I recall the unfamiliar roads that I had to travel before I became a champion in life." As a child, I didn't know how I was going to do fulfill my dreams. But I knew I was done living my nightmares.

My Mission to Discover My Dreams Begins

My mission will become evident to you as you're reliving my dreams' retrospective past. So please, dream with me as I relive the moments from my past when I began to chase my dreams. Also, as you're reading and reliving my goal to eventually living my dreams along with its details, I hope your heart's desire to win is fully unleashed as you preview my life as a young boy before my desired future of achievements became my reality. As a kid, I often wondered what my life's adventure would be like once my childhood dreams were fully understood as I progressed into adulthood. As a child

I imagined that my dreams were previews of my future life, and I was determined to envision a path that would eventually lead to me living my dreams. So as we move forward, it's fitting for you to know that you are officially walking inside my childhood and my young adulthood dreams.

It's 1999 and I'm excited to share with you the dream that I had last night. I dreamed that I have a mission to fulfill. What's my mission? I'm wondering, too. Maybe it's in my future, because I still can't fully comprehend the purpose of my dreams. All I know is that my dream's mission is very vivid: I can visualize myself accomplishing something great. So I must investigate this mission to see if it will lead me to experiencing the type of life that only a dream come true can produce. So, I'll get right into how I discovered my life's mission.

Well, it all started after I constantly heard my teachers saying, "Believe in your imagination." I heard that all the time, and it gave me a reason to trust my imagination, and eventually I became convinced that I could live the dreams that were in my head. During the early stages of chasing my dreams it was hard to explain my dreams and my vision: all I knew was that my dreams gave me hope, and I was willing to stake my existence on discovering if it was possible for my dreams to come true.

Real Dreams Include Adversities

When I was a child, I made up my mind to oppose the ideology that I was destined to remain in poverty or progress into mediocrity. Throughout my life, I discovered that gifts and dreams aren't immediately developed and manifested. As I began to fully understand that dreams and gifts have to be nurtured, similar to a newborn, it helped me to change my viewpoints on pursuing my dreams. I use to overthink the outcome by focusing on it. That sounds contradictory, but it's not! Obsessively focusing on the outcome was detrimental for my growth as an individual, and it was harmful for the fulfillment of my dreams.

Furthermore, I discovered that you need these four tools to start the process of digging up your true gift of value, which will lead to you living your dreams. 1. Wholeheartedly believe in yourself and that all things are possible with God. 2. You must be inspired and love what you are pursuing, which also means that you need to have a burning desire to do what you're pursuing. 3. You must have the proper perspective and invest in your mind every day while you're engaging in your mental investment. Simply approach investing in your mind like an exercise program by accumulating an eclectic knowledge base in the area you're seeking to master. 4. You must work hard and adjust your strategy and have faith and creative patience as you travel toward your destiny. Creative patience means to plant all kinds of seeds in different areas. This method will effectively increase your chances of one of the seeds growing. Whatever you do, do it massively and recognize that several of the billions of people that we have on this planet will be interested in investing in your gifts, but only if you make a full commitment to develop your gifts.

My Journey Begins

When I was eleven, I devoted myself to search for ways to revolutionize our planet. My inspiration to revolutionize our planet came from my desperation to escape my life of poverty. Growing up, I didn't have much and I grew up in Section 8 housing. Under the Section 8 program, my Mom's starting rent was $25 a month. Eventually she had to pay $75 a month, and that's all she could afford when I was a child. I was born on July 19, 1988, and during the early stages of my semesters of poverty, I didn't know exactly what Section 8 represented. I refer to my experiences with poverty as semesters because most adversities are just like school: my learning process seemed rough at first, but as I began to adapt and learn, eventually I was able to pass on to the next grade. As a kid, I had a strong desire to pass on to more productive stages in my life, and I believed strongly that a life without poverty was possible for me and my family.

When I turned eleven I began to fully understand the meaning of poverty. Once I comprehended the meaning of poverty, I just remember feeling like I was attacked with an epiphany. Figuratively speaking, it was similar to a heart attack. I just remember it being a traumatic experience for me. The realization of what poverty represented literally attacked my emotions, my spirit, my heart, and my mind. I just remember feeling extremely ashamed and angry. I was angry because I knew poverty wasn't what I wanted for me or my Mom. In retrospect, this was the moment in my life where I started to feel a personal code of standards resonating within myself. The standards I felt developing started to convince me of a rewarding journey for my life.

Although I was optimistic about my future, fear stressed me, and I felt hopeless. I just remember seeing duct tape on my Mom's floors covering up the holes in our house. At night I would turn on the kitchen lights and hundreds of roaches would scatter. I became accustomed to seeing this and felt like it was normal. During my childhood I thought that life consisted of roaches and fantasizing about delicious meals. I remember sitting around with my cousins and dreaming about eating the foods that we saw on some of the commercials. We used to say to one another, "Boy, I would surely like to have some Domino's Pizza."

In addition to wishing for what I considered fancy meals, I can recall people contacting my Mom to trade their money for her food stamps. I remember going grocery shopping with some of these people, and my Mom would pay for their groceries with her food stamps, and then they would give her cash afterwards. Basically, I thought that selling food stamps was my Mom's job. I thought that food stamps was a higher form of money, since I saw so many people exchanging their money for food stamps. Furthermore, I use to hear my grandmother talking to my Mom about getting off of welfare and finding a job. I thoroughly appreciated whenever my grandmother did that. As a young boy, I always had an appreciation for working hard and earning my own way. As a boy, I didn't know why and how I developed my tenacity so young, but as I grew into a young entrepreneur I figured it out.

There's Beauty in Being Uncommon

I can recall seeing some kids at school during lunchtime paying for their food, so I became curious about why I didn't have to pay for my food, too. So, I decided to conduct my own personal investigation by asking some of the kids why they had to pay for their lunch. And eventually I found out! It was because their parents made too much money, or their household income was above the rate, to qualify for free or reduced lunch expenses. I wanted to be one of those kids, because it would mean that my Mom wasn't poor and that I wasn't poor either. Sometimes I lied to the other kids by telling them I paid for my lunch and I said things like, "I paid for my lunch account in advance." The kids would ask questions to find out whether or not you paid for your lunch. To avoid being teased, I lied and, of course, I'm not proud of that! I was teased a lot when I was in school and I hated that my shoes "talked." "Talking" shoes simply means your shoes are split in half and are extremely raggedy. My shoes were in poor condition, and every time I walked, it literally looked like my shoes were talking.

Being teased and bullied often made it hard for me to focus when I was at school. My bullies' names were Ryan Jones and Clarence Piper. In 1999, I was in the seventh grade at Prescott Middle School along with Ryan Jones who was in the eighth grade. Clarence was seventeen years old in the seventh grade, and he threatened to kill me. He showed me his gun one day at school and he said, "If you tell anyone, I will kill you." I was terrified, and my friends Mark and Henry were, too. These big guys bullied the three of us every day, so I hated going to my fifth hour class. Those three jerks literally took our food every day, so most of the time at school, I was hungry. However, one day I got sick and tired of being bullied, so I attempted to stand up for myself and my friends. I'm sure you can visualize what happened after I did that: yes, they beat me up! I told my band teacher Mr. Theory, but he didn't do anything because he was scared, too.

I decided to start lifting weights and taking karate classes so that I could get stronger and be able to beat up Ryan and Clarence. The school offered free karate classes, so I wanted to take advantage of these classes. However, I only attended one class because as I was kicking during one of the classes, the other kids noticed my toenails were painted purple. My silly sister had painted my toenails while I was asleep, and I didn't have a clue until karate class. The kids in my class laughed at me, so out of embarrassment I quit and never returned. But I did practice every day on my own, so I was self-taught, and how skilled I became is up for debate, but I think I was pretty darn good. In fact, I anxiously anticipated an opportunity to use my newly acquired skills on any bully who came my way!

Ryan and Clarence were a grade or two ahead of me, so I didn't see them again. However, shockingly, once I entered high school, Ryan Jones was in my Physical Education class, and we were on the basketball team together as well. During our basketball weight lifting workouts, it was clear that I was the strongest one on the team, and I had developed an ostensible muscle tone as well. So I decided to confront Ryan during one of our basketball workouts. When I did, he pretended like he didn't remember bullying me; but even though Ryan refused to admit to bullying me I was happy I confronted him because it made me feel accomplished. Subsequently, after my heroic experience of finally standing my ground, I began to abandon my thoughts of taking my life. Prior to this courageous act of finally standing my ground I often wondered as a kid, *Is my life worth the hassle?*

The Second Time I Stood Up for What I Believed In

This may seem unbelievable and possibly pompous, but when my Mom used to ask me to go to the store to pick up groceries with the food stamp card, I always refused. She would say, "If you don't go, I'm going to whip you." My reply to that was, "Well, Mom, I guess you're going to have to whip me because I'm not using a poor people's card." Now, I don't look down on poor people and I don't think money makes you rich. However, to the contrary, I think you can be poor while being rich because money shouldn't be the only barometer to define success. I just didn't want to use the food stamp card, so I refused to use it. I use to get spankings for my refusal to use a food stamp card. I'm not proud of my disobedience, but it felt like it was the right thing to do, and I remember feeling so strongly about it that I was willing to be whipped over and over again. I had no clue that taking such a stand would have transitioned into my adulthood, ultimately helping to shape me into the entrepreneur I am today. There is nothing wrong with standing up for something, even if it seems insignificant to others. However, don't be disobedient to your parents, unless it's the clear and absolutely moral thing to do. Always show respect for your elders! However, I did learn this from my food stamp experiences: if you can't stand up for what your heart truly believes in, then how will you stand up to yourself when doubts begin to surface? Of course, you will experience doubts as you're trying to make your life's channel legendary, so remember that doubts are normal. I discovered that doubts simply are an indication that you're trying something that you have never done before. I discovered that trying new and exciting things, even if you've failed at it several times, is a blessing and not a curse.

I'm not bragging by any means, but it's important for you to understand the essence of what I'm about to say. This may seem unbelievable, but it's definitely the truth: it's been over nineteen years and counting and I still haven't used a food stamp card. Today, as a result of my mindset, I'm an established entrepreneur. In retrospect, I could have used the food stamp card and still attained success as well, because it's not the act of using it that would have defined me. The principle for me was to know who I was and what I stood for. That's why I decided never to use food stamps as a child or as a man. That's my personal standard and I know taking a stand when I was eleven has truly helped me. I used to tell my Mom, "I'd rather work and make some money to buy my own food."

I Didn't Accept Any Limitations Placed On Me

I didn't like being a product of my environment, and I know for a fact that standing my ground and refusing to use government-assisted programs was beneficial for me. Standing up for what I believed in helped to make me mentally strong, which led to my resolve to value my self-worth.

To manifest your inner genius, you must take a stand for something that you know is worthy to you, even if it appears insignificant to others. I discovered that this is extremely important for the development of courage. Everything in life matters and how you focus your life's reflective lens is how you will see yourself. So focus your life's lens to reflect an individual that respects him or her self. My motto is to aim to have zero mental quits inside my mind's résumé. When fear surfaces and doubt shows its ugly face, I discovered that if you can excavate a memory of standing up for something in your past, then it can be used to give you the impetus you need to fight back! Remember this: *"The more courageous acts you add to your psyche, the harder it is to quit. I discovered that it's okay to redirect your thinking, but never quit thinking about how to conquer an adversity".*

Although, my childhood experiences could have potentially endangered my self-esteem, I decided to use my painful experiences as my deepest motivation. I remember telling myself, "I have to take on the responsibility to get out of poverty." So I started to search for ways to get my family out of poverty. I would spend days, sometimes nights, conjuring dreams that I hoped would produce money for my family. I hated going to the housing authority to witness my Mom sign papers to remain on Section 8. At times, I became exasperated with my Mom because I felt like she had the power to control the outcome of her own life. My Mom was pretty and young, so from my eleven-year-old perspective I felt like she could do whatever she wanted to do. I remember asking her why she didn't start a career or go to school. I asked out of respect because I love my Mom dearly. My Mom would reply to my question by saying, "School wasn't for me and I wasn't smart enough." I didn't think much of that because I had never heard an adult say that before. Henceforth, I began to feel like school was only for really smart people, which made me feel like my Mom was robbed of her treasures. It was during that moment that I accepted the full responsibility of trying to figure out a way, from no way at all!

In retrospect, I was developing a mindset that would one day produce in me a relentless drive for success. Those emotions gave birth to a winner's mindset and an appetite for accomplishment. My newly discovered feelings created a desire to end the government assistance that my family and I received. So I told myself at that time, *If I accept the mentality to remain on government-assisted programs, I won't see a problem with it as I grow older.* It was during this semester of my life that I realized human beings are constantly faced with decisions and choices about how we live our lives. Meanwhile, despite my personal code of ethics, I couldn't immediately change the fact that I was poor.

I hated every moment of being poor and I was determined to do something about it. I went to bed cold during the winter nights because I didn't have a comforter. I discovered the meaning of a comforter at the age of twenty-six when I was dating my wife, Erika. She came to visit me at my Mom's and stepdad's house, and she asked, "Where is your comforter?" I told her that it was on my bed, and she said, "Those are sheets!" And then she said: "Wait a minute, you don't know what a comforter is?" I said "No, I thought the sheets were the comforter." My Mom knew what a comforter was, but I guess because of financial issues she never purchased one for me or my sister Brittany. So I had never seen or heard of a comforter until I met my wife.

I was poor during my entire childhood, and whenever I watched TV, I noticed that the fictional families on the programs had family dinners. But my sister and I never had family dinners growing up, and I often wondered, *why not?* I'm assuming it was because my Mom didn't enjoy this family tradition during her own childhood, so it was understandable why she couldn't carry it on with her children. However, as a kid I thought this was normal as well, until I became an adult. Once I became an adult, I began to peer into my Mom's family, and I realized she was mimicking what she saw as she grew up.

My biological Dad was alive and he entered my life, sporadically, until I was seven years old. After that, he disappeared and I didn't see him for four years. My Mom told me that the only thing he ever bought for me was a pair of diapers. The main memories I have of my father were of him chasing and beating my Mom. I didn't like the fact that my Dad wasn't around and that he hit my Mom. My Mom told me that he was on drugs, and I reasoned that maybe that was why he hit my Mom and abandoned us.

My Only Summer Visit With My Dad

When I was seven, in 1995, I begged my Mom to allow me to stay with my Dad for the summer in a small town called Independence, Louisiana. It's about fifteen or twenty minutes outside of the city of Hammond, Louisiana. My Mom finally agreed to let my sister and me stay for the summer with my Dad, and I was very thankful. My Mom was always a sweet and down-to-earth person, so she was easy to talk to. Unfortunately, my sister nearly died during her summer visit with my Dad because she became malnourished and developed intestinal worms.

My Dad had found my sister as she lay unconscious, and he

carried her to the hospital which was a few miles away. I remember walking with them because my Dad didn't own a car, so we had to walk. Subsequently, my sister was treated by the doctor and the doctor said to my Dad, "If you had waited another day before you brought her in, she would have died." So the doctor gave my Dad some specific instructions and he followed them. Eventually, the implementation of the doctor's remedies helped my sister feel better after a few days.

Also during my summer visit with my Dad, I realized that I had two mentally ill cousins. One of them would undress himself until he was partially nude, and he would utter these really disturbing noises, and the other one would just stare at you. I also met my half-sister during my sojourn with my Dad, but it was weird because her mother was my Dad's cousin. I just remember my Mom saying, "Your Dad should be ashamed of himself, getting his own cousin pregnant." During our summer stay with my Dad, we didn't go anywhere; we just walked from trailer to trailer. However, I still enjoyed my visit because I loved being around my Dad, and I desperately wanted to feel loved by him.

My Mom came and got us after the summer was over, but I pleaded to stay for another week, so my sister left and I stayed. I still laugh about my sister's statement as she was leaving to go back home with my Mom. My sister was so happy to return home with my Mom. As they left, my sister said, "June, you must be crazy to stay for another week in this slum." My sister's statement didn't bother me because I just wanted to be with my Daddy by any means necessary. My father asked his uncle to take me home when my additional week was over, and that was the last time I felt like my father showed me that he loved me. After that, I didn't see my father again until I was eleven years old.

My Mom and Dad had separated when I was about four or five. My Mom told me she parted ways with my Dad because he was beating her and he refused to work. My Mom informed me of an incident that took place when I was a baby. She said: "Your sister, you, and I were almost killed by a drug dealer because your Dad owed him money and he wasn't able to pay." My Mom informed me that she came up with the money at the very last minute, so she was able to spare our lives. When I learned about this, I was like, *Dad almost got us killed*! Honestly, at the time I still didn't care because I loved my Dad and I just wanted to feel loved by him. So whatever he gave me in life or death was a form of endearment to me. However, in retrospect I appreciate my Mom being a soldier, and I'm thankful for her heroism and quick thinking to save her babies.

Immediately after I returned home from my summer vacation with my Dad, my Mom had a nervous breakdown. I just remember that my sister and I had to stay with one of my aunts. My sister and I were transferred to three different elementary schools when I was in the second grade after my Mom had her breakdown. The story I have always heard of how my Mom had her nervous breakdown is this: I overheard other family members at the hospital saying that she was pulled over by a cop, and she was driving around with just a robe on, based on what the cop indicated, she told the officer she had taken an 8-ball drug. My Mom was hospitalized for a month, and was diagnosed as a paranoid schizophrenic when I was seven. When my Mom was discharged from the hospital, I was very happy to see her!

After that, my Mom spent seven years trying to receive a disability check called SSI, which she eventually received when I was fourteen. During the time that my Mom was fighting to receive SSI, I began to search for ways to make money, because my Mom couldn't work and we only had our welfare check to provide a way of living. During this era of my life I began to question my Dad's love because I hadn't seen him in four years, and I wondered why he didn't come to rescue us. I thought my Dad was my hero, but when we needed support, he was nowhere to be found.

There were moments when I felt like my Mom was learning helplessness because she was so determined to receive SSI. Initially, the doctors said that she didn't qualify and the program turned her down. They said she was capable of working, but my Mom insisted that she wasn't. Honestly, I think that my Mom could have worked at first and might have made a full recovery. However, in retrospect, I wasn't qualified to adequately judge the situation: but those were my thoughts as child. And I do think that my Mom's condition got worse after so many years of taking all of those psychotropic meds for stabilization and anxiety. This may seem ironic, but as a kid I pleaded with my Mom to fight back, and I told her that she could recover if she tried. I really believed that during my childhood.

I just couldn't understand why my Mom didn't see herself the way that I did. But my Mom took care of my siblings and me the best way she knew how. During this semester of my life I was battling with all types of emotions. I felt deserted and ignoble after discovering how sad my life was. I remember saying to myself, *My Dad isn't around and now my Mom is sick.*

I Often Wondered If The Teasing Would Stop

I was teased a lot about my haircuts during middle school because my Mom's boyfriend cut my hair, and he wasn't a barber. But my Mom couldn't afford to get me a haircut, so she did the best she could. The haircuts my Mom's boyfriend gave me were definitely not professional. The kids laughed at me and said I had a "bowl cut" which meant that my haircut looked like a bowl without an aesthetic look. It was bad! I just wanted to end my miserable life. I was so embarrassed when my Mom picked me up from school in her car. The seats literally looked like a hundred cheetahs had run through the car. The outside of the car looked like it had been through World War I and II. There were several bullet holes in the car from gunshots in the neighborhoods where we lived. People were murdered all the time and my neighborhood was bad. I grew up in four different areas in North Baton Rouge, and one of those areas was Glen Oaks, but the "hood" name for that area was Zion City. I lived in three different other hoods as well and their hood names were Boot Town, Ghost Town, and Brooks Town.

Life's Panorama

My sister and I don't know how we looked as babies. My older brother, Travis Miller, was the only one of us who was fortunate enough to have a baby picture. My grandmother helped my Mom raise Travis. He stayed with my Mom until he was seven, and then my grandmother took him, with my Mom's permission, and raised him until he was fourteen. Travis only had one baby picture that my grandmother had paid for my Mom to get developed. My brother was five years older than me and three years older than my sister, so I am the baby. Travis moved back in with our family when he was fourteen and I was nine.

Daddy Drama

After the summer that I stayed with my Dad, I didn't see him again until I was eleven. During this encounter my Dad picked me up, gave me two dollars, and bought me a burger from McDonalds. I thought this was amazing because all I really wanted was for him to show me love! So, any attention he showed me I thought was incredible. However, my Dad did call me once a year to tell me "Happy Birthday."

I remember reasoning with myself during that time: *Maybe my Dad was my way out*? But it dawned on me at that moment that he probably wasn't, because although he always talked a good talk, I never saw any action. I often pondered: *Why did he stop loving me and why did he abandon me?* And unfortunately, I still don't know, however, as you're reading this book please remember this quote: "Reason logically with your emotions and control your emotions or your emotions will force you to give them permission to govern you." So, I reasoned with my emotions, and I was guided to tell myself a different story, despite the evidence during that semester of my life.

The next time I saw my Dad, I was fifteen. And it seemed like seeing my Dad every four years was a pattern. He still called me once a year to acknowledge me and my sister's birthdays. But for some unexplained reason, he stopped calling to wish us "Happy birthday" when I turned seventeen, and he never called to acknowledge our birthdays again. Although I felt deserted by my Dad, I still looked for ways to commend him. So I said to myself, *At least he called to tell me happy birthday for seventeen years.* I mention that to establish that you can always find something good to say about someone, so don't be negative on your path to greatness. But be honest in your expressions, and be honest with how you feel. You can't overcome strongly entrenched experiences unless you're honest with how you feel about them. I didn't agree with my Dad's or Mom's choices in life, but putting others down actually puts you down, so if you do this, please stop! As you begin to manifest your inner genius you must respect life, and accept that what's good for you may not be good or great from another's perspective.

My next encounter with my Dad was when I was twenty years

old, and he came to my dream job at that time. It had been five years since I'd seen him, and I began to notice that his distance was growing. I had just started working at a major gym called Bally's Total Fitness. During his visit I was somewhat excited, but I was tired of the sporadic visits. I use to tell myself, *It'll be another seven years before I hear from or see this man again.* I was extremely hurt; I couldn't understand why a father would abandon his only son. After his visit I reached out to him, but I could never get in contact with him until he called me back years later. I didn't know exactly where he lived in Hammond, Louisiana, because I had only been there once when I was seven, and then he had moved to another place. I constantly battled with asking my Dad why he didn't love me. But I never asked him because I was afraid to hurt his feelings.

At various moments throughout my young adult life I battled my feelings of resentment toward my father because he didn't put forth the effort I wanted him to. I felt in my heart that he owed something to me. I didn't see or hear from him for another seven years after our encounter at my gym. I tried to invite him to my high school and college graduations, but he didn't come, and didn't put forth any effort to remain in my life. So during that semester in my life I felt like I didn't have anyone to look up to.

My father's absence during all of my milestones in my life still hurts me deeply. However, it gave me motivation to *Just Get Up!* It wasn't until I was twenty-seven that I decided to track down my Dad after his many years of absence from my life. It took me three weeks, but I found him. My fiancée and I went to see him. She is now my beautiful wife, Erika Miller. When I went to visit my Dad he seemed happy to see me, but I still didn't get what I wanted to feel from him. I gave him my phone number at the end of our visit, and that was in the summer of 2016, and I have never heard from him again. The pain from that encounter added to my many years of feeling abandoned continues to torment my heart up until this day. I have accepted the *de facto* of what my father is to me, and I've made attempts to contact my Dad since then. But even though I haven't received a call back, I will never give up hope for us to have a relationship one day.

I constantly battled with what to tell my father if he ever called me. A part of me use to look forward to his call, but I knew I wouldn't receive one and it was for the best because I would have told him during that time, "Don't ever call me again." This thought use to comfort me, and it distracted me from the reality that he wasn't calling me, and that he had moved on with his life, as if his only son never existed. But despite the fact that I never had a chance to really get to know my father, I can honestly say I still love him. I discovered that love is a powerful tool to use to your advantage, especially when people let you down. I decided not to become a victim in life by following my generation's past. I had to redirect my life and refocus my mind by moving forward and creating change. By doing this, my negative experiences became like my shadow or my past. My negative experiences will always be part of my life's memories, but I don't allow my negative memories to be present in my future. To this day, I weep when I see a son with his father, no matter the age of the child and his father. Just witnessing a father and son together affects me deeply! I wanted the father-and-son relationship more than you can ever begin to imagine. In fact, these words were penned with tears, while writing this to you! The tears on this page could never adequately represent my sadness. Figuratively speaking, I have cried enough to own my own ocean of tears.

I Learned Never To Blame Others

I used to blame my Mom for my Dad not being in my life. I used to feel like Mom shouldn't have picked my Dad as a mate, and she should have made better decisions with her life. Honestly, I was angry with my Mom because I felt like she was at fault for my Dad not being around. As I grew older, I realized that he chose not to be around. However, I constantly wrestled with being angry with my Mom because I felt like she shouldn't have had a kid by a man who clearly demonstrated to her that he didn't want anything out of life. As you're reading, start thinking about grudges you're holding, and forgive, and let go! You cannot manifest your inner genius by holding on to your past emotions. Looking back, I see my Mom was a product of her environment, and she did the best that she could with her mental instability. Eventually, I abandoned my resentful thoughts and I moved on, but doing so didn't immediately bring an end to my adversities as my journey will continue to reveal.

Garbage Bag and My Disney World Trip

In tenth grade, when I was fifteen, I was fortunate to be able to experience a field trip to Disney World. My Mom's boyfriend at the time, who eventually became my stepdad, paid for my trip. One of the more interesting things about my trip was an embarrassing discovery I made. I didn't know that it was proper etiquette to pack my clothes in a nice luggage bag. So I showed up with all of my clothes in a big black trash bag. I didn't think anything was wrong with that, and from my vantage point that was the right thing to do. But during the trip I began to realize I was the only student who had trash bags for luggage, and I began to feel extremely ashamed.

The next year, I received a proper set of luggage. My grandmother enjoyed the fact that I was taking my relationship with God seriously, so she purchased me a nice luggage set after she discovered that I had packed my luggage in trash bags for my trip to Disney World. I really appreciated my grandmother helping me out.

The Beginning Stages of My Process To Escape Poverty

As a kid I began to be careful of who I associated with, because I learned from my bible studies that my friends would have an effect on me. I really enjoyed learning about God, and my Bible studies really helped to keep me morally clean. Here is an obvious gem that I discovered: if you have people in your life that don't want anything out of life, you must appropriately distance them from your journey to greatness. I'm referring to the people who are trying to stop you from achieving your goals, even if they're close relatives and friends.

By *Just Getting Up*, you're adopting the role of a leader. Sometimes the path to greatness is a lonely road. However, if you want it bad enough, I can promise you that you will run that lonely road with a smile. You have to use your seemingly doomed state of mind as your motivation. One of the things I used to help me to *Just Get Up* was reflecting on this fact: there's always someone, or even a whole nation of people, who have a tougher situation than you do. So always reflect on the world's scene, and you will find people who are winning even tougher battles than yours.

As you begin to manifest your inner genius it will always start with your imagination! I discovered that if you can't see what you want to be in life, it won't happen! You have to walk into the future and see what you desire to do, come back to the present, and start working on it immediately. My first real insight into how I was going to *Just Get Up* and make some money was during my sixth grade English class. My English teacher instructed the class to write about different journal topics every day for five minutes. For some reason, I would take all of my topics, convert them into poems, and then read them to the class.

My second poem that I was inspired to write during my sixth-grade English class was about an eight-grade girl, and it was entitled "Wind Beneath my Wings." After I read what I wrote, there was something special about the poem and it was as though I invented my own language that spoke to the hearts of people. So after that classroom experience I started writing poems every day for my journal topics. I use to hold myself to this standard: I had to write the poems in seven minutes or less. I didn't consider it a success unless I could fill up my whole page with words within those few minutes. That became the precedent for me, and if I couldn't fill up a page in seven minutes, I would stop writing. I would think of a title, and write whatever came to my mind, and the poem was always something special.

It was then that I was reminded that writing was my gift, and I said to myself, *I'm going to be a poem writer, novelist, screenplay writer, and an author of horror books.* I was a young man dreaming, and my writing dreams didn't transpire exactly as I thought. Still, I knew that aspirations like the ones I mentioned would one day make me successful. I entered talent shows and I performed at spoken word poetry events. In 2002, I wanted to compete in a Washington D.C. poetry contest, the winner of which would have the opportunity to work with a publisher. I didn't have enough money to go to D.C., so I asked my grandmother to help, but I guess she was skeptical, so she didn't support that endeavor. Still, my grandmother was a good person and she did a lot of other things for me during my late teens. I'm assuming my grandmother's upbringing and experience resulted in her having a limited view of possibilities, so she said to me, "I do not desire to pay all of this money for you to go all the way up there and not win." I knew at that moment that she lacked faith in my abilities. However, I believed in myself and that's all that mattered! I was about fourteen years old during that semester of my life.

I also began to realize during that time frame that I should not take it personally when people don't support me. Sometimes it's nothing against you; there may be other things going on in people's lives that prevent them from supporting you. So, always look to see if the people who you may need support from have helped you in other ways. Subsequently, I started to organize my support systems, so that I would know who to come to, and for what purpose. The implementation of analyzing my support systems led to a significant discovery: don't become discouraged if you don't receive support from people that you thought would support you.

"*When others doubt you, it's okay, because it's your dream to pursue, not theirs.*" Remember, it's your dream and no one else's. It's your responsibility to make it happen! However, during this era of my life I submitted to the negativity, so I postponed my writing dreams and I decided to pursue something else. But reader: learn from my mistakes! Don't postpone your dreams, the time is now! Do not allow others to project their fears onto you because they aren't courageous enough to pursue their dreams!

Your Talents Are Exposed Early In Your Life

In retrospect, I discovered that your talents are exposed to you during your childhood and early adulthood. What was special about you as a child? Don't listen to any negative self-talk that you might be experiencing. You have abilities and possibly more than what you can ever begin to imagine. Your life depends on it, so put in the thoughts. That sounds interesting, doesn't it? To put in the thoughts! *Put in the correct thoughts and the correct actions will follow.* It doesn't start with putting the physical work in, it starts with doing the mental work. How many books have you read lately that are related to your talents, skills, abilities, and your dreams? Will a baby ever become an adult if it never eats? Most importantly, will it ever become a healthy baby if it continues to eat the wrong things? What are you feeding your genius?

I was determined to succeed at whatever I put my heart into. As the years progressed I continued to write and pursue my dream of going to the NBA. When I was eleven, I pursued three dreams: writing, going to the NBA, and becoming a martial arts master. I was a big fan of Bruce Lee and I wanted to be like him. I took karate classes and I practiced every day on my moves. I figured that if I pursued several of what I considered my talents to be that I would excel in one of them, or possibly all of them. I knew it was important to pursue several dreams that were associated with the things I liked, and I discovered I had to do this until I figured out the one I was most passionate about. I discovered dreams don't enter our imaginations fully developed. So, I had to take several steps, including the first step, to eventually attain clarity regarding my dreams.

Don't Overlook the Things That Come The Easiest To You

I liked the amount of money that athletes made, so I figured that was the way to go. I discovered that the things that seemed easiest to me were clearly the gifts I should pursue and nurture. Some people abandon their gifts and learn other perplexing skills that distract them from their dreams. Do you remember everything that you learned in school? Of course not! It's similar to your gifts: if you don't nurture your gifts, you will lose them. Your gifts will always be inside you, but you won't be skilled at them unless you nurture them. As a child, you had gifts given to you, and all you have to do is simply develop the gifts you were born with.

What if your gifts weren't apparent to you as a child? You still know what you enjoy doing, so begin to bring those feelings back to your heart's surface. That's what I did; I never pursued a career or stayed at a job that I didn't like. If I couldn't see myself working at the job forever with a smile, I started making plans to leave. However, if I could see myself doing the job for a while, then I always asked myself, *In what ways can I expand and grow with this job?* I solved my own problem by deciding to take control of my own destiny and I became an entrepreneur. In Chapter 9, I will provide insight about why it's important to give birth to three dreams that are associated with your true passions. Chapter 9 will develop this concept in detail.

However, in the meanwhile, just make sure all of your dreams, along with the three different ways that you're cogitating to pursue them, are associated with your strong skills and your natural gifts.

I Learned Everything I Could
Possibly Learn About My Dreams

I reasoned that if I went to the NBA it would certainly end my impoverished state. I liked that athletes were fit, and as a kid I desired to have the fit look. I knew if I became a professional athlete that I would conquer my life of poverty. So I began to watch NBA TV every day and night. That was in 1999, and I began to learn about players from the 1950s, and the founder of basketball, Dr. James Naismith. I had an interest in the pioneers of whatever construct or professional practice that was well established. I knew that someone had to start the process, and I said to myself, *One day I'm going to be a pioneer and revolutionize the world.* So as a kid I studied all the greats. This is the best way that I can explain it; I instinctively knew that in order to be the best, you had to know what your predecessors, those who were considered the best, were doing. It may seem unbelievable, but no one told me to study the pioneers of an organization! I just figured it out, so I know that God was directing my steps.

As a child, I learned and practiced discipline and consistency without fully understanding the benefits, however, cultivating these two habits led to the discovery of the power that's embedded into forming discipline and consistency. I always desired knowledge, so I relentlessly studied the things I wanted to do. I encourage you to be a big kid again and let your mind run wild with your dreams. But you have an advantage that I didn't have; you will have the blueprint for being great. By the grace of God I was able to develop wisdom and receive His blessing. My brain wasn't developed enough to understand the science behind the things I was doing. I just believed in the power of my imagination, and that my dreams would come true. I encourage you to believe in yourself and use your imagination as well. I had no proof of how my dreams would work; I just knew I was special, and that my inner genius would eventually be exposed. As a kid I had low self-esteem, but I did believe in myself, although my belief system wasn't as strong as it is now. Believing in yourself is very important and it helped me to conduct myself in a special way. How do you conduct yourself? Do you behave in a way that demonstrates that you already have your dreams? If you're not doing this, you need to start behaving like a champion as soon as possible because you are a *CHAMPION!!!*

In my endeavors to learn everything that I could about the people who were doing the things I wanted to do, I discovered that all of the legends worked hard toward the skills that they were trying to develop. This evidence was also displayed in martial arts; for example, Bruce Lee out-worked all of his contemporaries. So I said to myself that whatever the greats are doing, I have to do that and more. For example, if they ran 6 miles a day, then I told myself that I had to run 12 miles. I didn't actually run 12 miles a day as a child, but I'm mentioning this to establish that whatever the greats were doing, I made it my goal to do just a little more. I was clueless about how to work out at this stage in my life. I can recall seeing my brother and cousins lifting weights, so I asked them a series of questions regarding fitness, and I mentioned to them that I wanted to look like Bruce Lee. So my brother and my cousins gave me the best advice that they could.

When I was eleven I made up my mind that I would lift weights three times a week for an hour at a time. I didn't have a weight set at the time, so I took the drawers out of the small nightstand that was in my bedroom, and I lifted the nightstand. It wasn't much, but I used what I had. I used to press the nightstand over my head, and I curled the nightstand as well. All I could think about was getting out of poverty, and I was determined not to stop until I found my way out! Even though I didn't have weights, I figured out another way. You have heard the saying before, "Where there is a will, there is a way." Please believe in this saying, because it's true!

This may seem unbelievable, but that was over nineteen years ago, and I haven't lived a single week without lifting weights at least three times a week. I have exercised for three days a week or more since I was eleven years old, and I have never missed a single week. I would have had to be totally incapacitated to justify missing my exercise! Nowadays, I lift weights five to six days a week. I'm not lifting nightstands anymore; I'm lifting real weights at a real gym! I didn't realize that my will and determination would eventually lead to me developing the skills that I needed for my career as an entrepreneur.

I eventually realized and fully understood that all of my adversities were necessary. This life-changing epiphany happened when I turned twenty. At twenty I appreciated and realized that my previous nine years of exercising was connected to my journey as an adult.

I became a fitness trainer at seventeen, but I didn't realize how much I would gain by just deciding, as a kid, to work out at least three times a week. The self-discovery process is really amazing to me, and I firmly believe that you don't have to know everything to get started. All you need is a clear vision regarding where you truly desire to take your life, and how you're going to get there will gradually be unearthed, once you fully commit to starting your journey of self-discovery. Even if you don't know exactly how to get there that's okay, trust me—the path will be unveiled! However, this is only applicable if you have a determined mindset and a plan of action. Your plan of action must be full of passion and it must be aligned with your true genius. You don't have to take years to figure it out like I did. Simply and wholeheartedly trust the self-discovery process, and you'll start to enjoy watching your life's channel along with all of its built-in adversities.

My desire to win was unyielding and I refused to be denied. I was fully committed to winning my war against poverty and changing my Mom's outlook on the possibilities in life. So I did whatever I felt was necessary, although I didn't know exactly how I was going to win. I just knew my desire to win was all I needed! I can recall the days when I jumped rope in the rain; I wanted to win so badly that I refused to miss my weekly prescribed exercise regimen regardless of the weather or any adversities that unsuccessfully attempted to wage war with my will to win.

In retrospect, I would have appreciated a coach, but I didn't have one But I am fortunate because I intutitively knew that I needed to force my own hand, so I got up every day, and I did whatever I thought was necessary to become the best. I remember my Mom saying, "Boy, get your crazy behind in this house, you're out here in all of this rain." I said, "Mom, I am destined to be great, I'm sorry, but I can't come inside until I have finished exercising." I jogged around a grocery store called Save A Lot with my shirt off. I felt that taking my shirt off created a more intense mindset. I know that is foolishness now, but foolishness is tied up in the heart of a boy. It was the little things I noticed I did, like taking my shirt off, that helped to motivate me. People passed by me in their cars saying, "You have to run harder than that, young man." Statements like that gave me fuel, so I told myself that as long as I work hard at whatever I do, I will be successful.

In addition to exercising, I played basketball every day and challenged the best players in the neighborhood and at school. If at first I couldn't beat them, I figured out how! I kept personal records of how many times I won and lost against each opponent. I worked on my dreams every day! I never owned a game system as a kid, but I played a few video games sometimes. But I always preferred doing things in reality. I was obsessed with trying to figure out how to make money. I contemplated selling drugs because that's what a lot of the kids around me were doing. I would see them in their cool cars with their cool shoes, and with pretty girls. I can recall saying to myself, *I want that!* However, my love for God compelled me not to take that route. I wanted to take pride in what I did, and the Congregation of Jehovah's Witnesses was very helpful in teaching me about God. My grandmother was a witness, so I was familiar with the witnesses, and I always had an appreciation for God's Word. I'm thankful my grandmother had a solid spiritual foundation because it prepared me for my adversities that I will reveal in Chapter 3.

CHAPTER 3

PANORAMA OF MY GENIUS

My Discovery Process Intensifies

I started high school in the ninth grade when I was fourteen, and I had been practicing for three years, and the time finally arrived for basketball tryouts. The first portion of tryouts was the conditioning aspect. I was the strongest and most explosive person trying out. Maybe my three years of training at that point was paying off. I had no clue that I would be the kid who was in the best shape. I made the team and my physical fitness was extraordinary. However, my weaknesses were exposed during some of the basketball drills—I couldn't do a left hand layup properly—so the coach told me I was going to be the water boy. He put me on another court and I practiced by myself with another player. This frustrated me, but I used it as an opportunity to show the coach that I was better than he thought.

After that day, I went home every day after basketball practice and I practiced for two hours. Eventually the coach allowed me to practice with the team again after he noticed my improvements, or should I say he was forced to allow me to practice with the team. My efforts got me noticed! What does your current effort say about you? Is it getting you noticed? You don't need talent to outwork everyone else! I remember the coach saying, "This boy is outworking all of y'all and he has become the most explosive player on the whole team." I wasn't the most gifted player, but I always aimed to be the hardest worker. Remember this: While you're outworking everyone, most people will mistakenly depend on their gifts alone, but as James 2:24-26 says,"Faith without works is dead." Remember this: Consistent action is unavoidable; your gift by itself sometimes isn't enough! Eventually I learned how to do a proper left hand layup! I never gave up on myself! I never accepted mediocrity. I had a choice to change whatever I was deficient in or choose to create the necessary changes. And of course, I chose the latter.

People in the neighborhood started to notice my efforts and I received some support. One of my neighbors was a nice man who played in a basketball league and he eventually became my barber. He noticed me dribbling the ball up and down the street where I lived. So he asked me one day, "Young man, what are your goals?" And I said, "I want to go to the NBA." He replied, "I can see that you're hungry for it, so let me give you a few pointers." I started to play him one-on-one and he worked on some drills with me. I was never able to beat him, but I definitely became a much better player with his help. As the basketball season progressed, I started to fall behind during practice. During the running drills I noticed some of the other kids were faster than I was, so I went home after practice and I ran some more. Honestly, I knew why I continued to fall behind; it was because I didn't want to fully compete under uncomfortable situations. To be honest, I was afraid to give it everything I had. I was worried about how it would make me feel, if I still came in last place after giving it my all. So I unconsciously guarded my maximum potential so that I could say to myself, "Well, they only beat me because I wasn't giving it my best effort." I had to learn to be honest with myself and eliminate my excuses. I wanted the struggle not to hurt!

However, I continued to fall behind and nothing changed, until I got sick and tired of losing. One day during practice I outran the entire team. After that, the coach said to me: "Don't hold back, Miller, you should have been doing this." That statement stuck with me and I realized that I had been holding back. The coach was right! I was holding back out of fear of being last. Do you do this? How can you possibly know how far you can go, if you aren't willing to at least risk going too far? A motivational speaker, Les Brown, says, "When you argue for your limitations, you get to keep them." It's true! You must give it your all or you won't be successful!

Understand The Law of Attraction and
Raise Your Level of Awareness

I really love this fact based ideology and it's imperative that I share it with you. When you're vibrating at an uncommon frequency people will notice and you will begin to stand out! When you think about something that vibrates, it's something you can feel or hear, but this concept actually goes deeper than just feeling and hearing vibrations. Our minds and our level of awareness operate from vibrations and frequencies as well. The law of frequency and vibration is true, so make a full commitment to digesting its concepts! For a moment, think of thunder, lightning, gunshots, explosions, and tons of other things. Now, for a few minutes hold these vibrations and frequencies in your mind while I briefly and simply apply the irrefutable concepts of the law of vibrations and frequencies. A stronger or more forceful vibration will produce a higher frequency, which will also produce a wider frequency that travels farther. Remember this: *A frequency can only match the level of the vibration and the vibration will only attract the frequency of its vibration and vice versa.* This is why a shotgun sounds louder than a BB gun, and why its frequency of sound and vibration can be felt from a farther distance away. This concept briefly summarizes the law of attraction, which is absolutely true!

So, when you're exerting yourself and laying it all out on the line, people will notice you, and you will eventually receive the support that you need. However, this will be based on the effort you consistently display! You must begin to vibrate and raise your consciousness or awareness frequency to your desired goal's frequency, if you truly wish to achieve your goals. Einstein once said: "Raise your imaginative and conscious frequency to your desired dream's frequency and you can have and do anything that you want". I strongly encourage you to read upon the law of attraction, vibrations, and frequencies. Everything in life operates from a vibration that attracts the frequency that matches its vibration. This is a scientific principle that is well established in physics. If you invest in fully understanding this concept as well as cybernetics and paradigms, I grant you that your life will never be the same! Here is the point: Based on the intensity of any vibration, it can be sensed, felt, and heard from many miles away, and it will attract the frequencies that match its vibrations. For example, if you want to attract billionaires than study billionaires and think like a billionaire. *You will only attract what you are, and if you want to attract something new then you must renew your mind and raise your level of consciousness. Read Romans 12:2 every day!* Here is a fun fact: You won't find positive people who are determined to advance in life hanging with negative people who are determined to remain at low levels, which will absolutely lead to advancements in higher degrees of mediocrity.

How do you know when you're vibrating at an uncommon frequency? When you begin to stand out by separating yourself from the crowd, it'll be obvious you're becoming a different person because you'll begin to do uncommon things. Your nature will attract other unstoppable people, and the pigeons will know that you're an eagle, and the pigeons won't be able to fly as high as you're flying. This is the law of attraction and I discovered from personal experience that this is absolutely true! Another important law to remember is one of Newton's Laws of Motion: Every action has an opposite and equal reaction. So act the way that you want the world to eventually respond to your work ethic and your intense effort!

Remember this principle: *If you're capable of vibrating at an uncommon frequency, then you're certainly capable of vibrating at a common frequency.* How do you know if you're vibrating at a common frequency? The simple answer is, if your life continues to consistently be filled with pigeons, which represent people who aren't trying to fulfill their dreams, or the people who have become complacent with their lives, that's one immediate way you will know. However, I'll be fair, you will always have a few pigeons knocking at your door, but that doesn't mean that you have to invite them inside your mind. But humbly give them a chance to show change from a respectable distance, however, if they're having a negative influence on you, then you know what you must do. You must protect your mind if you truly want to fulfill your dreams. People who are pigeons are no longer experiencing a journey in life; in fact most of their lives have become a mere horror film. However, eagles are capable of flying very high in comparison to other birds. An eagle is the king or queen of its domain, and if an eagle flies across another bird during its peak of flight, it will definitely be another eagle or a Rüppell's griffon vulture.

The concept of flying like an eagle will be developed in more detail in Chapter 13: *The Octagon Way*.

Always Prep Your Mind For Adversities

When I had my dream to play basketball, I never thought of the adversities that I would face. I only focused on the things that would go well. When you start to pursue your dreams, prepare your mind for everything to possibly go wrong. However, do not overly obsess on the things that can go wrong. "Expect failure while expecting success from failure." To illustrate: if you were stuck between two rocks and the person who was trying to help you escape decided to just give up and walk away, would you be okay with that? How would that make you feel? Would you want them to give up and leave you to die? Or would you want them to keep helping until you were free? Most likely, you wouldn't tell them to stop and let you be. You would probably offer suggestions regarding how they could help to set you free. I view dreams in the same way, and I feel at times that our dreams are begging us not to leave them stuck between the rocks, and our dreams are saying to us, "Please don't leave us here to die with you." My question to you is, what are you going to do? Are you going to leave your dreams stuck between the rocks, and walk away from them, while they're begging you for freedom from captivity? Only you can hold your dreams down and drown your true passions!

A Turning Point During The Discovery
Process of My Dreams

In high school, during tenth grade, I started to take my relationship with Jehovah God seriously, so I set a personal goal to read the Bible every day. I mentioned in Chapter 2 that I started studying the Bible at a young age. In high school I started to fully implement the spiritual aspects I was learning, along with pursuing careers in basketball and writing.

I became fully committed to my relationship with my creator when I was fifteen. I believe God is the ultimate genius and He was the key to unlocking my true genius, so don't leave Him out of your life's equation. A year before I became serious about my spiritual path, I discovered I had a photographic and eidetic memory, when my geography teacher asked me to read a poem for Black History Month. All of my teachers, from grades six through twelve, knew that I wrote poetry, and I read a poem every day in English class during those years. But even though I read poems in my classes, I was too shy to perform them in front of large audiences during that time in my life.

During my preparation for my Black History performance, I noticed it took me thirty minutes or less to memorize my two-page poems. I was able to recite poems of 500 to 1,500 words after reading them only a few times. I tested this ability several times and found I was able to do it with everything I wrote. Unfortunately, I ended up not performing my poem for Black History Month because of fear. Are you noticing how my genius was built over time? My genius didn't come out fully formed. I had to develop it! All you have to do is genuinely start and you will eventually produce fully developed dreams by nurturing your gifts.

I Learned To Refocus My Strategy When Necessary

When I was fifteen, I finally started to attend the Christian meetings or religious services, and I had the privilege of speaking in front of the congregation I was attending. I started giving Bible discourses and fulfilling assigned Bible readings. This helped me overcome my trepidation of speaking in front of others. I remember being ashamed about the clothes I had on during that semester of my life. I wore the same outfit every time I attended the services until my grandmother purchased me a suit. Remember this: Genuine people will notice your efforts, and they will start to assist you if you stay committed to your self-discovery process. After attending the services for a while, I eventually engaged in the field ministry.

The field ministry consisted of door-to-door work, and preaching to whomever I came across in the assigned territory. The field ministry helped me to adapt to being adroit at any given moment, and engaging in the ministry conquered my fear of speaking in front of others. Finally, after five years of studying God's word I decided to dedicate my life to God, and I got baptized on November 13, 2004 at the age of sixteen.

Courage is Necessary

Becoming a spiritual man unleashed ideas and character traits I didn't know I had, so I started to change my associations and stop hanging around anyone that wasn't on a similar path. I became an eagle and I only wanted to be around other eagles. Deciding to change my associations was based on I Corinthians 15:33, which states, "Do not be misled: bad association spoils useful habits." Also, Proverbs 13:20 states, "The one walking with the wise will become wise. But the one who has dealings with the stupid will fare badly." I respected God's word and I grasped that whatever it contains is true and applicable to my life.

During my senior year in high school I was asked again to perform a poem for Black History Month, and this time I was ready! I entitled the poem "All Creation is Beautiful." I wrote that poem when I was seventeen, and "All Creation is Beautiful" was my first performance. Your dreams will keep giving you opportunities; you just have to be connected to your dreams to notice your opportunities. When you decide to *Just Get Up*, it will start with small victories that are sparked from courageous acts.

The praise I received after my performance confirmed that I should be a writer. Looking back with eyes of nostalgia, this was a defining moment when I felt like I had discovered a crucial feature of my genius. During this time I still didn't know exactly what I was going to do with my life, but I knew it needed to deal with inspiring people, and using my gift with words. After the performance, I began to reenter talent shows and I competed with other writers. I wouldn't have discovered the extent of my abilities if I had remained afraid. So, after ten years of trying to discover my genius, along with all of the doubts from friends and close relatives, the proof was clear that I had a gift. Shortly after my first real poetry performance, I discovered that I could rap and freestyle as well.

Honesty is The Only Policy

Eventually, I retired my dream to go to the NBA. I felt like that wasn't for me because the games were going to take me away from my weekly congregation services. I picked God over that career, but the reality was I didn't have the height or the skill set. However, don't interpret that as me giving up on my dreams because I learned something valuable during that semester of my life: *"Never give up by never starting things you aren't truly passionate about."*

If the road to success starts to get extremely tough while you're manifesting your genius, you must reevaluate your strategy, and get smarter about how you're pursuing your dreams. Do not neglect the other important responsibilities that you may have in your life. When it's family time, focus on family; and when it's work time, focus on work; and when it's play time, focus on play time! *"A scattered mind during the execution of any task can be deadly."* To illustrate: Imagine someone who is driving and having an argument via text message as they're driving. Their mind is distracted, which can easily result in a wreck. You must be balanced and I had to learn to this as well. You have to know when to let things go that you know aren't internally apart of your mission in life. I can promise you that the things you need to release will be obvious as you're manifesting your inner genius. You cannot doubt yourself: If you're willing to put in the work, who has the right to tell you what you can't do? It's your dream, so always remember that!

When Things Started to Fall Into Place

For years, I argued with my Mom and her boyfriend, who later became my stepdad, about being in the Section 8 program. I know that seems ironic: a child upset with his Mom and her boyfriend for accepting their conditions. Remember this: It doesn't matter how old you are, when you're vibrating at an uncommon frequency, you will be able to shed light that no one knew existed. Are you doing this? Are you standing out in the crowd or are you hiding? Once you fully commit to elevating how you see yourself, you will begin to have a vision that exceeds what you thought was possible!

My relentless efforts to get my Mom to see that she could own her own home eventually paid off. My Mom eventually started to believe in herself and I'm happy God used me to help reignite her flame. When I was nineteen, my Mom and stepdad finally got off of government assisted programs and purchased a house. My Mom didn't have a job, but she pushed my stepdad to do better. So my stepdad searched for several jobs and he didn't stop until he found one. You have to be relentless! They both eventually believed that they could own a home. They did it and I moved into their first home in 2008 when I was twenty years of age. I'm not taking credit for my Mom deciding to get off government assisted programs. But I know I was used by God to inspire her, because I reminded her frequently that she didn't have to be on those programs, and that she could own her own home. I was obsessed with reminding my Mom of her potential, and it began to feel like I had OCD because I couldn't help myself. I refused to accept the situation I was born into, and just knew, within my heart, that the realities I held so dearly within my mind could and would eventually come true!

My stepdad was afraid he couldn't afford a mortgage, so he made me promise that, if he got the house, I would help him pay the mortgage. I didn't actually help him pay the mortgage, but I did help him pay some of the bills because I decided to be selfish, and focus on going to college. I worked full-time, so I couldn't take care of his responsibilities, while trying to prepare a future for myself. Remember this: Sometimes you have to look out for yourself because there will be times when no one else will. Do not neglect your dreams and don't make it harder to fulfill your dreams by agreeing to responsibilities that will create stress for you. You have to protect your resources, your time, and your mind. It's important to develop a health plan as well, so that you can be balanced in the five domains of life. Don't be scared to tell people no!

I was determined not to accept unfavorable conditions. And finally, I had the joy of seeing my own determination inspire others. I'm proud of my mom and stepdad, and I give them full credit for finally deciding to end the housing program that we had been on for two decades. My Mom and stepdad will tell you that I was relentless and determined for them to terminate any handouts they received. So, I know within my heart there is greatness to be seen from all of the 7.7 billion channels that are being aired every day. Remember this: No matter your current circumstances, you can revolutionize any situation that you're fully committed to changing! Remember this powerful quote:

"Man is not a creature of circumstances but circumstances are creatures of man."

—Benjamin Disraeli

I Learned to Expect Tragedies and
The Possibility That Everything Can Go Wrong

After high school I matriculated into college when I was eighteen. I knew I wanted to do something with writing; however, I sat out for a semester after I finished high school, to relax. I have no idea why I did that, but that move ultimately revolutionized my world. Deciding not to immediately enroll into college after high school is what led to me becoming an entrepreneur at age seventen. Very sadly, during my discovery process, my brother was tragically killed when he was twenty-two. He was at a nightclub celebrating one of my cousins' birthdays. The road was dark and my brother's eyes were really bad, and he walked into the street and was accidentally hit by a car. My brother's death report said that, "he was thrown 50 feet into the air and when his head hit the pavement he died instantly." I can remember it like it was yesterday. I can remember my Mom rushing into my room at one a.m. in the morning and crying, while saying, "Travis is dead!"

One of my cousins who was there had called Mom to deliver the bad news. I remember feeling shock and in disbelief. That was the first time I had lost someone close to me. I was seventeen. About two hours after my cousin delivered the devastating news about my brother; a policeman knocked on the door, and asked if Travis Santell Miller lived here. He delivered the bad news to me because I was the one who answered the door. I was the only one who heard the officer deliver the bad news. The police visit is what confirmed the bad news for me. A few hours later, my family and I drove an hour away where my brother's body was being held. I remember riding in the car and my uncle-in-law was driving. I was still in shock and I didn't want to believe that my big brother was dead. I remember arriving at the hospital, and the doctor took us in a room that looked like a chapel. He said, "We tried everything that we could, but we couldn't save him." My Mom fell out in a clamor, and the pain I felt from seeing my Mom cry was overwhelming. The doctor then said, "Can someone come and identify his body?" My Aunt Barbara, my sister, stepdad, Mom, and uncle-in-law were all there. My Mom couldn't stand the sight of her dead son in a body bag, so my uncle-in-law and Aunt Barbara and I went to view the body. One of the hospital's personnel opened the body bag, and my aunt fell out. I remember just looking at him and wondering when he was going to move. I could see the bloodstains on his head that came from hitting the pavement. My uncle-in-law came to me and he just held me for awhile. Eventually, my sister and I went outside, and we began to cry: we both were in disbelief that our big brother was dead.

My brother had survived a bad car wreck as a kid. He was hit by a car when he was five, and nearly lost his life back then. The car wreck he experienced as a child is what caused him to have such bad vision. My brother went through a lot, and he was a cancer survivor as well. He developed a tumor in his arm during his late teens, but the doctors caught it in time, and they removed the cancer. Now, my brother's death was a blow to me, but it taught me a valuable lesson in life: I realized that people cope with things differently, and I didn't have to stop living to honor his death. In other words, I intensified my efforts so that life wouldn't get me down. I worked out the same day my brother was killed, and I went to my congregation's services as well. I remember the people there asking me, "How did you find the strength to come to the service?" I hadn't told anyone, but they found out somehow before the service ended. But I was determined not to break my regimen.

On the day of my brother's funeral, I remember the hearse picking us up. The ride to the funeral hall was a complete state of dysphoria. Once we arrived at the funeral hall, the funeral director lined the family up in the order that he wanted us to walk out. My Mom walked out first, and she cried as soon as she got midway toward his casket. I performed a poem at my brother's funeral entitled "The Real Life" and, amazingly, I didn't get choked up. However, when they opened the casket for the final viewing, the reality set in that my big brother was gone. I attempted to run out of the building, but my three friends, Tyras, Tony, and Frederick, chased me down and comforted me. I turned my back to them and put my face in the corner because I didn't want anyone to see me cry. A part of me appreciated the solace from their presence, but a part of me wanted to be alone as well.

I remember going back home after the funeral and reading some of Travis's letters that he had written to God. In his letters, I discovered that he was making plans to rectify his relationship with God, and his letters made me cry even more. I used to always hear my brother come home at night and get in his bed next to mine. So after his death I would wait up at night to hear him walk in, but it never happened. The week afterward, one of my aunts came over, and took my brother's car, since he had titled it in her son's name. My Mom begged her sister to leave the car, because that was the only thing she had to remind her of her son. Unfortunately, my aunt was more concerned with getting her son a car than she was with her sister mourning her son. I didn't like that, and I developed resentment toward my aunt because of that. No one really checked on my Mom, and my grandmother blamed my Mom for my brother's death. I remember her saying, "If you hadn't taken him from me, he would still be alive, so it's your fault Travis is dead." I know my grandmother meant well, but she was out of line with that comment. I guess she was hurt, so she didn't season her words with love. My brother's death was a turning point in my Mom's life, and I know my Mom never recovered after my brother passed. Subsequently, my Mom became very fearful of death, it became so bad until she didn't want me to go anywhere, out of fear that something very bad would happen to me.

The Experience That Changed My Life

My stepdad purchased a car for me in the summer 2006, before I started my first year of college in the spring semester of 2007. The agreement I made with my stepdad was that I had to find a job to pay my car insurance. I found a job at BREC as a fitness attendant—I was still seventeen at the time. The position required me to open a small fitness facility in the morning, and close it up at night. Some of my job duties included showing the members how to use the equipment, and performing first-aid/CPR. One day when I was at work, a man entered the gym and proceeded to take someone through an exercise routine. He guided them throughout the entire workout for an hour. I had never seen this before, so I thought it was amazing. A few months after that encounter, an older lady approached me at work, and she proceeded to make an expression that sparked a turning point in my life, so she said to me, "I think you would be a great personal trainer." So on that same day I researched what a personal trainer was, and I then talked to Lee Cohn about being a trainer. He was the fitness trainer I observed instructing the client through a fitness regimen.

Retrospectively, that encounter taught me to seek out people who were doing the same things that I desired to do. So, never waste your time talking to people who haven't done anything other than discourage divine pathways. Lee Cohn gave me guidance, and I found an online personal training certification program. I liked the thought of working for myself, I always thought of myself as a CEO, and I always wanted to be in control of my own destiny. After I made up my mind that I was going to work for myself, I decided to inform my Mom and others about my aspiration to become a personal trainer. I guess, out of their fears of the unknown, they discouraged me. I remember them saying, "You will need to get another job at some point because you could lose your clients, and the money isn't guaranteed."

For years, I battled with the fears that others instilled into my head, but I decided to stick to my guns, and I continued my pursuit to become a personal trainer. However, I still went to college, while pursuing my dream of working for myself, and becoming my own boss. I used to tell myself that I have gifts and that I'm the jack of all trades. I learned to believe in myself even when no one else did. My mother didn't believe in me during this time and neither did other people who I looked up to. My family and friends repeatedly said things like, "Personal training doesn't create a stable income, and what are you going to do if you lose all of your clients?"

Do What's Required and Not What's Admired

"Do what's required and not what's admired." During this era of my life, I wasn't knowledgeable about the different personal training programs, or that it even mattered. In fact, after receiving my online certification I tried to get a job at a gym and that gym didn't accept my certification. As I walked out of the gym, one of the gym's personal trainers saw me leaving, and ran outside to catch up with me. He said, "Hey, how old are you?" I answered, "I'll be eighteen soon." Then he said, "You want to be a trainer?" And I said: "Yes!" The trainer who stopped me began to tell me of the best personal training certification bodies to become certified through. He said, "The gyms won't accept or respect a certification unless it's accredited and provided by one of these agencies." He also suggested that I go to college and get a degree related to the field. He suggested that I have an alternative plan, as well.

The older trainer could sense my determination and my uncommon frequency vibrating! I'm telling you, when you go after your dreams and goals like your life depends on it, others will notice. People can sense greatness, and you're a part of the greatness that the billions of people in this world will begin to sense, so don't second guess what I'm saying! Own it and know it! Most importantly, after being denied a job opportunity, I didn't look at that as a failure; I simply said to myself, "OK, what certifications do I need? It doesn't matter how much it cost or what it takes, I'm going to get the certifications and the education I need." At that time I was training a few people at BREC, but I knew I needed to move on to something better. I had two clients that I was working with during that time, and I wasn't satisfied with just two clients because I knew I wanted more! *"Always be hungry! You must have an insatiable appetite to eat success!"*

So I researched the National Strength and Conditioning Association, which is one of the most respected personal training certifications to have in the world. I ordered their books and studied their material. However, I realized that I needed two years to study for it because I didn't have any knowledge of anatomy and exercise physiology during that time. Remember this: don't look at how long it takes to gather the knowledge you need! Just make sure you're learning something new about your dreams every day! *Just Get Up!*

I worked at BREC for two years, and then I studied all that time, and then took the personal training exam with NSCA, and I passed. I started to realize I was special at personal training, and I was only twenty years old. I had been training people for two years at BREC, and at a personal training studio owned by Joan Gist. She thought it was amazing that I was so young and already had two years of experience, and she let me use her facility occasionally. I quit BREC and looked for a job at a big gym, which was one of my goals during that semester of my life. Shortly after attaining my personal training certification through NSCA, I applied for a job at Bally Total Fitness and I got the job. I received a promotion after eight months of working for the company, and I was promoted as one of the Fitness Directors. This job typically required a degree in Kinesiology, which I didn't have at the time. However, I did eventually graduate with honors and I received my degree in the fall of 2012. The position required me to train, teach, and conduct weekly meetings with other fitness trainers on how to grow their businesses. The people I was conducting meetings with were ten to twenty years older than than I was. Remember this: never be confined or defined by every rule, because sometimes, what naysayers think isn't possible, is more possible than what they might realize!

So now you have the story behind why I decided to choose an exercise-related field once I enrolled in college. I mentioned earlier in this chapter that I did not go to college immediately after finishing high school. I sat out what would have been my first semester of college. When it was time to enroll in school I decided to pursue something associated with health and fitness. My original plan was to pursue something with writing, but I figured I didn't need a degree in literature to write books. However, after two years of college, I decided to change my major to Therapeutic Recreation and Leisure Studies. I had accumulated so many Physical Education courses that I decided to minor in that as well. I majored in Recreational Therapy and I minored in Physical Education at Southern University Agricultural & Mechanical College in Baton Rouge, LA.

I postponed my writing dreams because I started to think that I needed something that would bring immediate and consistent income. I developed that philosophy primarily based on the fears of others, and because I knew I needed to have a way to support myself until my writing dreams were manifested. My fears were conditioned by other people who didn't know what they were talking about. How could someone give me advice about writing if they had never pursued a career in writing? People do this all the time, so don't listen to the naysayers. Always seek advice from people who have done what you desire to do. As you begin to chase your dreams, you need to expect adversity from your inner circles, and haters from your outer circles. Your inner circles are your close friends and relatives who may be cursed with a limited vision for life's possibilities, and your outer circles are your acquaintances and the things you watch and listen too.

Ironically, some of your naysayers, not all of them, will start to encourage you to pursue your dreams. Why? Because your inner genius will give birth to a new light that the world can fully see. You are a beast! Now it's time for you to do what real beasts do! Just like a lion you must hunt, and you must hunt until you get the job done! It's been over twelve years and I have maintained a stable income from my personal training career. In fact, some of the people who doubted me have asked me for money, and they're dependent on me to provide for them.

You Will Always Be Your Own Worst Enemy

"You are your own frenemy." Frenemy means a person or group that is friendly toward one another because the relationship brings benefits; however, feelings of resentment or rivalry are imminent as well. So keep your negative feelings close in sight and combat any type of procrastination with passion and action. Do not become your own worst enemy.

Retrospection

After I saw all of my years of relentless dedication to my goals start paying off, I knew at that moment I was called to be a public figure. Determination produced a new pair of eyes in me that enabled me to see that life can be easy, and life's algorithm to success is innate. It was at this moment I realized I had a destiny to embrace, and it was my job to bring my destiny into fruition. The same applies to you! As a kid, I wanted to be one of the greatest trainers, poets, motivational speakers, songwriters, and authors of all time. On my journey, I have started the process of fulfilling all of these goals, and I will fulfill them all!

Being self-employed and thus fulfilling one of my many dreams has afforded me the funds to have three cars that are paid for, a new house I had built, paid off student loans, and full control of how much money I make. I take off when I want to because I had the courage to decline five job offers that I received after college. For six years I battled with the dilemma of trying to get out of personal training to pursue a career in my academic major. My Mom used to call me on a weekly basis to remind me that it was time to get on someone's payroll, so that I could have some financial security. Unfortunately, during my six years of fear, I allowed fear to compel me to go on interview after interview, and I was offered jobs by five employers, but something within me just wouldn't let me accept the jobs. I had to train my mind to refuse the urge to negate my true destiny, and I eventually stood up for myself and said: "This is who I am: I'm Isaac, The Fitness Trainer, I'm Isaac, The Motivational Speaker, and I'm Isaac, The Author." I have accepted who I truly am and I will work for myself for the rest of my life!

If I had made the mistake of surrendering and quitting the freedom of self-employment, I would be miserable. I allowed my conditioned fears to create doubts because my family and friends were still telling me I needed to leave personal training alone, although I had proven to myself that I could provide for myself and a family. I still battled with doubt, which is why I applied for jobs just to see what would happen. Working for myself has allowed me to reignite my flame and pursue my career in writing, poetry, and motivational speaking. I wouldn't have had this freedom if I was tied down with a nine-to-five job. I discovered that everything is connected, and whatever I did to better myself was worth it!

For example, working out at a young age, writing, preaching, reading, selling, conducting meetings, hiring people, seeking to attain certifications, going to college, and working in a field that gave me the home court advantage to use my gifts was a brilliant decision! I didn't know what I was doing, but I just knew that if I pursued my passions and developed my gifts, that something special was bound to come from it. I knew where I was going and I saw it before it unfolded. *"Everything*

I've relentlessly pursued I've eventually attained." I remember when I finally decided to get the sports car that I had wanted for five years, but when I tried to get one in 2008, I wasn't quite ready for the big car pricetag, or the high car insurance; however, I was able to get the car five years later, and it was a brand new car with only fourteen miles on it. Once I signed the papers, I cried in the car and my Mom, who dropped me off at the dealership, just looked at me crying, and patted me on the back saying, "You earned it!" Finally, some positive feedback! I surprised myself with the car note because I was able to pay off my brand new sports car in eleven months. I love Camaros, so I purchased a brand new 2014 Camaro.

I'm looking forward to all of my many dreams continuing to be manifested. I currently learn one to three new words every day. I read two books a week, I write my goals down every day, and I review them at night and in the morning, I listen to motivational speeches every single day, and I aim to meet at least one new person every day. I aim to give back via money, time, and resources to those who need it. I pray and read my Bible every day, and I have a regular share in the ministry. I do more than what I'm paid for; I smile, and have a good time. I'm obsessed with greatness!

Here is something I do that symbolizes that I'm getting better every day. I add an exponent or a power to a saying that I'm known for. If you ask me how I'm doing I'll say, "I'm phenomenal times whatever number I'm on." I'm currently on phenomenal times 202, and by the time you read this book I'll probably be phenomenal times 1,000. I'm getting better every day, and if you truly desire to live your dreams then you must do the same!

I became something from what appeared to be nothing, and so can you! When you have everything to lose and a lot to gain, there is a power that begins to surface. This is a power that *ALL HUMANS HAVE!* When this power erupts, we become super humans. The human will is very powerful, so don't underestimate it. However, it can only be unleashed if it's used for survival. Your dream's survival depends on you unleashing your will, and it will be obvious when you're manifesting your inner genius because you won't be able to stop. And it will be during that moment and only during that state that the impossible will seem absolutely possible.

"What this power is I cannot say; all I Know
is that it exists and it becomes available only
when a man is in that state of mind in which
he knows exactly what he wants and is fully
determined not to quit until he finds it."

—Alexander Graham Bell

Throughout my discovery process I began to realize that failures are successes. I've lost count of all of my failures and I eventually developed this motto: If I only give an endeavor I'm passionate about fifty attempts, then I'm not trying hard enough. I'm willing to fail 1,000 times if I have to. I don't care about my failures; all I care about is winning, and I know that I will win if I only give myself two options: Do or Die! I discovered that you can fail fifty times in ten years or fifty times in one day, and my experiences in life have taught me this important treasure: The quicker the failures are out of the way, the sooner you can learn from them. By relentlessly suffering I learned to focus on intensifying my efforts to fail, so that I could learn and capture my dreams as quickly as possible. I learned that one of the main reasons I was able to enthusiastically face rejection again and again, was because I only pursued the things I loved.

I learned not to abuse myself, that is, I stopped fighting for things I didn't really want. My life's channel revealed to me that failing doesn't make someone a failure. You can only be a failure if you stop moving forward. I didn't believe in tries; I just kept going until poverty surrendered. I love failing because it allows me to get better. I discovered that when I didn't feel sorry for myself I was able to make things happen. Furthermore, I have come to appreciate that all humans have the capacity to force life to surrender the things that we deeply desire. So remember this along your journey: *"If you truly want change, you must be prepared for the closest people to you to possibly treat you like you're estranged." "Greatness is uncommon, and adversity is necessary before you have your dream's love story, with all of its glory."*

I have seen firsthand what dedication, faith, self-belief, and determination can do. I mean this with all sincerity: You are smarter than what you may currently think, and better stated, you are a genius! You're more capable than what you're currently displaying in your life! Your mind controls everything and this is important for you to grasp! You must have the proper mental programming to display your unstoppable drive: the next chapter will help you to develop this. It's time for you to fully tune in to your own channel, so thanks for tuning in to mine! However, before you move on, please focus on the gems and the quotes you've learned from Chapters 1-3. Your journey has officially shifted into another gear!

CHAPTER 4

THE PURSUIT IS ON: REMODEL YOUR MIND

Are You Traveling In The Right Direction With Your Life?

Imagine it's eleven p.m. and you're on a road trip with your family and friends. You're the driver and you're having a blast chatting with the people who mean the most to you, and all of a sudden, you see flashing lights from a police car. The officer pulls you over and proceeds to tell you why. The officer informs you that you were doing seventy-five miles an hour, and the speed limit is fifty. However, you didn't realize the speed limit changed from seventy-five to fifty on this highway because the speed limit sign was obscure. So, the officer asks you, "Why are you speeding?" And you tell him, "I didn't realize the speed limit had changed." Then, the officer asks you, "Why are you in a rush?" And you tell the officer that you're trying to make your destination before eight a.m. Subsequently the officer asks you, "Where are you headed?" And after answering the officer's question, you begin to realize you've passed your destination, and you've driven six hours too far in the wrong direction. Subsequently, the officer gives you a speeding ticket and now you have to reroute as well. How would you feel? Probably frustrated and annoyed! Compare this analogy to your life and ask yourself this question: What if you've been traveling in the wrong direction with your life?

Are you extremely satisfied with where you are in your life right now? Are you working at your dream job? Have you started the business that you've been contemplating? Have you taken the first steps toward any of your heart's endeavors? A dream job is a job that isn't viewed as work, but is viewed as fun. Of course, even a dream job can be stressful at times, but if it's truly your dream job I can assure you that it's never the job. On the contrary, the culprit may be your circumstances, your environment, or the people associated with your job.

You may be wondering, "How do I know if I have been traveling in the wrong direction with my life?" If you want the answer to that question, take a moment to think. Think about your gifts, skills, and dreams, and think about the careers you would pursue if all jobs paid the same, and if every job offered you the same benefits. What would that dream job be for you? Be honest and answer from your heart!

Change Your Perspective Whenever Life Pulls You Over

Sometimes we fall prey to the mistake of feeling like our lives are cursed because we experienced a catastrophe along our journeys in life. Only a few people would view the opening illustration in this way: maybe it was a good thing that the police officer pulled you over. You could view it this way: the officer helped you to realize you were going too fast, and that you were headed in the wrong direction. So, adversities in life aren't all bad! What if the officer didn't pull you over and you continued to go in the wrong direction, only to realize it twelve hours later? What if you continued to drive too fast and it resulted in a deadly car wreck? If you crashed, it could have possibly ended your life, and the lives of your passengers. Life is serious business and you should always approach your future with seriousness. We all have people who look up to us and they're among our friends, relatives, spouses, children, and even strangers from our communities. So we all have the capacity to inspire a lot of people.

Would you want someone you love to follow your example in life? If you don't feel like your life is worthy of being imitated as an example that can lead to success, then life has pulled you over, and your life is giving you clues that you're traveling in the wrong direction! You have a moral obligation to drive your life in the right direction because you never know who is watching. Life will continue to give you signals if you're headed in the wrong direction. It's never too late to turn around and travel toward your true destiny! However, you must display the full potential of your inner genius in order to travel in the right direction with your life. Do you truly know that you're a real genius?

Definitions of a Genius

When you think of a genius, what comes to your mind? Most people would probably think of someone who is extremely smart. Here are a few definitions for the word genius: 1. Genius—an exceptional natural capacity of intellect, especially as shown in creative and original work in science, art, music, etc. 2. Genius—natural ability or capacity; strong inclination: a special genius for leadership. A few synonyms for genius are gift, talent, aptitude, faculty, endowment, and predilection. Interesting definitions! I'm certain it's apparent that all humans are geniuses in our own unique ways. It was Albert Einstein who said, "If you teach a fish to climb a tree, the fish will go its whole life thinking it's dumb." A fish can't climb a tree because fish weren't designed to climb trees; they were designed to be in water. If you pursue your gifts and work in harmony with your talents, you will do unbelievable things! I can promise you that this is true because I discovered this personally, along with plenty of others who decided to take life head-on. Some of these brave souls will be mentioned in Chapter 10, entitled *Mind Frame of a Genius.*

Always Live Your Dreams

To live and never fulfill your dreams isn't living, that's called existing! Maybe you have attained your main goals in life or maybe you haven't, but it's okay because you're a genius, and you must know and believe this. Geniuses are born every day all around the world. The issue is that we are conditioned to think of Albert Einstein and so many others as the only geniuses. You are a genius! You just have to discover what you're in love with. *The problem is that we become victims of being like others rather than being inspired by them.* By deciding to manifest your inner genius, you're making a full commitment to discover who you truly are. If you don't know your gifts or how to discover them, then the remaining chapters will help you to discover your gifts!

You Must Become Your Own Self-Determining Agent

What are the aptitudes and the existential faculties of who you truly are? What does this mean? Aptitude and faculties refer to your skills, abilities, education, and any licenses you have attained. Any skills that you have will create opportunities for you to leave your personal mark on the universe. You have something to offer, and if you're already giving the world your best, then there is still a little more inside of you that the world needs to see. Existentialism is a philosophical attitude that opposes rationalism and empiricism. It stresses the individual's unique position as a self-determining agent responsible for the authenticity of his or her own choices. *"I've discovered that in order to create change, you cannot be overly rational, and you cannot be trapped inside your past negative experiences. Simply put, don't become the marketing agent for your negative experiences. You will always have the opportunity to promote your positive or your negative experiences in life, and the one you talk about the most is the one you're promoting."* If you aren't talking about either one, then the one you're working for will be demonstrated in your actions. Remember, "Actions speak louder than words!"

"Your life will only give you facts, and what you decide to plant in your life's field will grow into whatever you've planted." If you plant negative seeds in your mind, then you're feeding your negative experiences! Throughout your journey, you will notice a few biblical verses that are profound and incontrovertible such as Galatians 6:7, which states, "God is not one to be mocked; whatever a man is sowing, is what he will reap." That's a universal law that is true. You cannot plant apple seeds and reap oranges. What type of seeds does your life show you're planting?

The Holistic Approach

You must master the art of implementing *The Holistic Approach* in order to discover your treasures. I discovered this philosophy is necessary for unleashing unstoppable self-belief. Remember this: if you don't believe in yourself, nothing else will matter. *The Holistic Approach* was a prominent philosophy that I studied under my major in college, and it refers to how we care for ourselves physically, mentally, emotionally, spiritually, and socially. If these five domains aren't adequately maintained, the symbolic horsepower of the human will will be compromised! I will go into more detail about the horsepower of the human will at the end of this chapter. The *spiritual* domain refers to our belief systems regarding religion, our philosophy on life, and our application of morality. The *mental* or cognitive domain refers to how we think and the things we choose to feed our minds. Ultimately, our cognitive domain will influence our spiritual domain and vice versa. All of the domains are intertwined! The *physical* domain refers to our health, quality of living, and our physical fitness. The *emotional* domain refers to being at peace with how we handle new and old situations. A good way to sum up how to assess the emotional domain is to ask yourself, "Am I happy?" The *social* domain refers to the relationships and friendships that we have or desire to have. Examples of some of these types of relationships are romantic relationships, relatives, friends, business relationships, co-workers, etc. When all five of these important domains are combined and effectively nurtured we are applying *The Holistic Approach.*

The proper implementation of *The Holistic Approach* will lead to *holistic discoveries. Holistic discoveries* are lifelines that will help to protect your dreams. For example, suppose Bill feels like he loves his job on Monday, but after he gets off from work he has a nasty argument with his wife, and then on Tuesday all of a sudden he begins to feel like he hates his job. Bill doesn't hate his job, but his mood is off because of his argument with his wife, so now Bill doesn't feel like going to work, and he begins to view all of his job tasks as burdens. Bill continues to have nasty arguments with his wife and he eventually feels convinced that he hates his job. Also, Bill starts to distance himself from healthy association because he doesn't want anyone to ask him about the obvious change in his mood.

Furthermore, Bill isn't able to exercise like he wants to because his wife isn't helping him to pick up their kids from school anymore, so he has to use his workout time to pick them up. On top of this, Bill isn't reading for thirty minutes a day like he normally does. Bill's mood is so distraught he doesn't feel like doing anything, and he begins to complain about life.

Bill must resolve the issues with his wife, otherwise, his ability to stay focused on capturing his dreams won't happen. Avoiding conflict is nearly impossible, but you have to protect all of your domains under *The Holistic Approach* if you truly want to win in life. So, always quickly address any negative tones that you're detecting in your mood. Most importantly, a lack of motivation can come from just one off-balance domain, or several of the domains. To further illustrate: if you have negative friends who are a source of discouragement for you, and if you're listening to negative information, it will affect your emotional and mental domains. However, it's important to thoroughly recognize the true source of Bill's problems mentioned in the illustration. The true source of his problems actually springs from the *social* domain, which eventually affected his emotional and mental domains.

Holistic Discoveries

A *holistic discovery* means that you're able to understand how a situation can affect your ability to successfully complete a task. A *holistic discovery* is unearthed whenever you've learned something that's worth applying. However, the application of a newly learned construct must help you to make progress in one, or all, of the domains under *The Holistic Approach* in order to be a *holistic discovery*. For example, Bill doesn't have a good workout because he forgot to eat and he didn't prepare his mind. If Bill doesn't investigate the true roots of why he had a bad workout, it could potentially result in him breaking the potency of his usual workout rituals. Over time, Bill's workouts would slowly decrease in intensity, and either he would quit, settle for average fitness conditioning, or regress in his physical appearance, health, and conditioning. So in the example, if Bill's feelings of discouragement aren't properly addressed, it will lead to Bill losing his drive.

Don't ever think that you're too strong to lose your motivation to be great. Instead, be humble and safeguard your *holistic discoveries*, which are similar to lifelines. Lifelines are normally used to protect someone, or rescue them from a dangerous situation. However, think of *holistic discoveries* as gems to help you sort through what's really bothering you. An example of one of these bothers could be someone who is trying to figure out why they aren't feeling excited about pursuing their goals. Also, think of lifelines as a system to help you to come up with the solution to why you're stuck in a slum. *Holistic discoveries* help you to return to your heart's default settings, which will always bring you back to your heart's true passions. You will discover that *holistic discoveries* are essential and beneficial. Finally, you must train yourself to focus on how every decision that you make will affect each domain under *The Holistic Approach*.

For example, Bill's social defect with his wife affected him mentally, emotionally, spiritually, and physically. If just one of your domains under *The Holistic Approach* becomes negatively tainted, it will have a correlational effect on the other domains. So you must aim to maintain balance in all aspects of *The Holistic Approach*. You can accomplish this necessary balance by protecting each domain, so that the disruption of one domain doesn't have the domino effect on your other domains. So always look at each aspect of *The Holistic Approach* whenever you're feeling down and beat up. Remember this: sometimes feeling discouraged doesn't have anything to do with the difficulties you're facing. It could simply be not having the energy to be relentless because your physical domain is off, and maybe you aren't getting enough exercise, or maybe you don't have a good support system from your family and friends.

Only Pursue Things You're Passionate About

To manifest your inner genius, you must learn to only pursue your passions. Your true passions are in alignment with your gifts. For example, if someone has an ingenious gift to display critical thinking skills, then they should pursue passions that are in harmony with their critical thinking skills. To illustrate the importance of passions and gifts being in alignment, simply think of a car that is out of alignment.

When a car needs an alignment it won't drive as well, which will force you to focus and hold on to the steering wheel more forcibly. However, if the car had proper alignment, you wouldn't need to grab the steering wheel so hard. I can guarantee you that you wouldn't enjoy driving your car as much if you need an alignment. Furthermore, if you don't correct the alignment it will get worse, and if you hit bumps in the road it will only make a bad alignment worse.

So, ask yourself this question: Is your life out of alignment and are you trying to experience a smooth ride to your dreams with a bad alignment? You must align your life's vehicle by adjusting your gifts to symmetrically flow with your passions. Your life's vehicle is you and all of your faculties. Also, remember this: A true genius is obsessed with knowledge and self-development.

Most importantly, before you fully embark upon your exciting journey of self-discovery, it's essential for you to accept the responsibility that you're the driver of your life. Also, you must have relaxed faith accompanied by self-assurance. Faith is required before you can do anything, and Hebrews 11:1 defines it best to me. It says, "Faith is the assured expectation of what is hoped for, the evident demonstration of realities that aren't yet beheld." *"You must have faith and patience as you begin to dig up your true genius that may be buried alive inside of you."*

Step one to manifesting your genius is to realize that you can *Just Get Up* in the same way I decided to; with relentless effort, self-belief, and relaxed faith. Relaxed faith is devoid of anxiety! If you're confident about your goals and dreams being fulfilled, then there is no need to panic. When you think about faith, self-belief, and relaxation I want you to think of them as essential attributes for a successful person. So accept the truth that you are a genius!

Abandon Your Shadow

Focus on yourself and not your shadow! Your shadow represents your past and you can't move forward in life if you're stuck in the past. *"Leave your shadow's reflections where it belongs, in the past and behind you."* If you strengthen who you truly are, you won't notice your shadow unless you're concentrating on it. Think about a time from your past when you walked on a sidewalk on a bright sunny day. Did you notice your shadow if you were focused on your destination? You may have seen your shadow, and acknowledged that it's there, but you didn't stop walking toward your destination to focus on your shadow. The only way you would have time to focus on your shadow would be if you didn't have a sense of urgency. Are you walking through life without a sense of urgency?

Focus on your goals and have a mission in life. Your shadow can't compete with you without your approval and consent. It's time for you to start a new journey along life's sidewalks. Do you know how to use your passions to unlock your dream's treasures? Your treasures, once they're discovered, will create wealth for you along with a complete state of happiness, and I'm not referring to money. If you're already rich and you discover your dream's treasures, you'll begin to experience a life full of true riches.

Excavate Your Emotional Whys

It's important for you to recondition your mind by allowing a new form of thinking to permeate your current belief systems. This is important for you to do regularly, so that you can ignite or reignite the unstoppable drive that you most certainly have within. Remodeling your mind is necessary for the maintenance and the ongoing fulfillment of your goals. *"Do not look back at your shadow. Your past is your past, so let it go."* Go after your dreams and do not stop until they are in your hands. It's imperative that you make it your mission in life to keep digging until you excavate your life's treasures.

"If you see it in your mind you will hold it in your hand."

—Bob Proctor

My own experiences fueled my heart with sensations I didn't understand as a young person, but I understand them now! A part of my desire to be someone and make a difference in the world came from wanting to make my father proud. I decided to dig deep within myself as I was writing this book, and discovered that I was seeking my father's approval. I often felt like I must have done something wrong because I couldn't comprehend why my father would desert his only son! Knowing my emotional "whys" guided me, and helped me to unleash the power that erupts inside any individual who has a fully determined mindset.

Your emotional whys, if positively controlled, will give you powers! You think you have seen all that you can do? Trust me, my friend: you haven't! My father has no idea of the man I have become today and he probably never will. However, despite his mistakes, I believe that he is capable of revolutionizing his own life—anything is possible!

Develop a Personal Code

It's important for you to know who you truly are and what you stand for. If you do not have a personal code, you will be poor. I'm referring to being poor as far as not knowing your heart's boundaries. You must have integrity to maintain your genius and to feel good about your mission in life. You must develop a personal code! Your personal code will be a part of one of your many *holistic discoveries*. So think about your personal code like a password. We have passwords for our alarm systems, cell phones, and computers, but what about a code or password for our heart's mind? *"Your heart's mind is the most sensitive aspect of your willpower and it must be protected! It is the one thing that you know that can steal your joy. If your heart's mind is hacked, you will constantly battle with feelings of doubt. Doubt is normal, but wrestling with any temptation all day and every day is taxing on the heart and on the mind."*

Aim To Become a Person Of Value

"Aim to be a person of value by being a load lifter and not a load giver." Change your own woes in life; don't weigh others down with your seemingly unalterable realities. If you can recall, I made it my mission in life to defeat my impoverished surroundings. So, likewise it's your moment in time to be the genius that you were born

to be, so never run from life's challenges: always step up and fight back. Remember this: if you continue to run away by mishandling your seemingly doomed paths, you will miss the magnificent opportunities to create and redefine your life's story. So step up and accept the responsibility to change your circumstances, or else your negative emotions will keep you impoverished holistically. You will never discover your true genius if you allow your five domains, under *The Holistic Approach,* to become undernourished. Remember this quote, and this quote is one of my original and personal quotes:

"When your value goes up, your demand goes up; when your value goes down, your demand goes down. So, always seek to become a person of value."

It was the standards I chose that allowed me to believe in myself. Once I believed and was fully committed, I knew I was capable of more. During my pursuit to greatness, I became successful without fully understanding how! My process of becoming successful happened as a child, I know how it happened now, in retrospect. My experiences have equipped me with the ability to understand both perspectives, that is, not knowing what to do vs. knowing what to do. This also means not knowing how to start vs. knowing how to start. Along my personal journey of self-discovery I eventually experienced this revelation: you don't have to know everything to start the process of capturing your dreams, but you do have to *Just Get Up* to get started, and eventually find your purpose in life. *"If you fail by trying and if you fail by not trying you still lose. Not attempting to manifest your geniuses over and over again are still losses for you."* So start saying this to yourself every day: "I will figure it out eventually because what I have already figured out I'm not happy with." If you're not happy with your current state you must know within your heart's mind that there is something better. Actually, the simple fact that you can differentiate between your life being legendary and manifesting your passions vs. living a life of mediocrity is really all the proof that you need. If your brain didn't give you feedback saying, "this isn't fulfilling and you can do more," then you wouldn't know if you were happy or not. The fact that you're able to differentiate is proof that something in your life isn't quite the way it should be.

I know that you know there is a brighter genius within you than the one you're displaying. It's true, my friend, there is something better, and all you have to do is take the first step, and *Just Get Up*. If you can recall from Chapters 1 and 2, I was angry and I had no desire to remain in poverty forever. I knew I had no one to depend on, only Jehovah God, so I told myself *one day I'm going to be somebody, and I'm going to work hard to achieve my goals*. Don't let anyone stop you from manifesting your inner genius that's waiting to be unleashed!

"You have to think of yourself as a gift to the world, and believe that you have too many gifts to keep hidden." You need to feel as though you're caging a beast that the world needs to see. It should feel like you're doing the world a disservice by not chasing your dreams. This mental disposition will allow you to accept the reality that you do have gifts and that you're capable of fulfilling your dreams. If you know you have the gifts and the skill-set for an endeavor, then forget about everyone else and go after your dreams. You can do it!

Be Obsessed With Improvement

"Becoming obsessed with greatness is so powerful that no matter what you do, you'll stand out." I was able to figure out that it's okay to take a detour in life because if you develop the habit of working hard toward whatever you're doing, even if it's not your passion, it will lead to something that's great. You won't see it right away, but trust me: it's never a waste. It's called being in love with the process, and once you fully understand it's the process that makes you great, then the type of person you need to become from the process will be manifested. *"I learned there is always a road to travel to fulfill any dream, and each dream mandates a love for the process."*

Dominate Your Dreams

You must remodel your mind to develop an insatiable desire to fix any errors in your life. I used this mindset as a child and I said to myself, "Okay poverty, I'm taking you down. Okay Dad, I'm going to do this thing without you!" I beat poverty into the ground so badly, figuratively speaking, until it ran away from me. Poverty couldn't keep up with my determination to conquer. *"Make your goals submit to your will!"*

I had no clue that one day, the past decades of my life's reality nightmares would one day become my lifeline to protect me as my present shadow. My shadow's past serves as my reminder that my adversities were a necessity for me to walk into my future of success. I trained my unwanted past to walk with me into my future as my friend, rather than as my nemesis!

The Power of The Human Brain's Potential

The following illustration will help you to grasp the importance of how to gradually unleash your brain's horsepower. The horsepower in this example represents your brain's potential. How we unleash our brain's figurative horsepower is based on each individual. We all have unlimited subconscious mind storage space within our subconscious minds. This is the part of our minds that stores all of the information that's consciously and unconsciously received through our five senses. We can either let our minds govern us, or we can choose to rule our minds. If you put a car in cruise control and never pressed on the gas or the brakes, it would result in a catastrophe. Similarly, you still have to consciously control your unconscious and conscious mind, so that your brain's full positive potential can be released. If you don't control your mind, your subconscious mind's cruise control will control you. Your subconscious mind will continue to travel in the direction where you're unconsciously cruising, unless you figuratively turn off your brain's cruise control. Furthermore, unconsciously your mind can take you on a disastrous path, similar to trusting a car to take you on a faraway destination on cruise control while you're asleep. The *subconscious, unconscious,* and *conscious mind* will be thoroughly developed in Chapter 13 entitled *The Octagon Way.*

Consider this example: two 2017 GT Mustangs are stocked with 435 horsepower each. A Mustang GT has a V-8 engine, which means it will only take premium gas, so if you put regular unleaded or super unleaded gas in the car, it won't run as efficiently and will eventually malfunction. Sometimes we think it's the engine that's the problem, but it's the fuel we are putting into our brain's engines. What type of fuel are you putting into your brain's engine? To manifest your genius, you have to give your subconscious mind great and positive things. Your brain can only operate off of what you feed it. Our brains aren't the issue! Instead, it's what we're feeding our minds. Humans are unstoppable! Just imagine if everyone used the proper fuel and tapped into their brains the way we are truly capable of. Research shows that the average person is only using five to ten percent of their brains. So know that you have the power to let go and let your brain's engine roar on life's highway.

Let's suppose one of the 2017 GT Mustangs is blue and it's owned by Jim, and the other one is black, and it's owned by Scott. Suppose Scott changes his oil on a regular basis, keeps up with all of the recommended maintenance for the car, and puts premium gas in his car. Jim doesn't change his oil regularly, doesn't put the proper fuel in his car, and doesn't do any of the required upkeep on his car. Whose car do you think will function more efficiently and unleash the most horsepower? You answered correctly! Scott's car! Although the car's engine is the same, the horsepower will vary based on how the owner takes care of his car. If you put regular unleaded or super unleaded gas in a V-8 engine or supercharged engine, it won't run as efficiently. Eventually the car will malfunction and compromise the engine's potential. Our brains are the same way. We choose the amount of potential our brains are able to unleash, and this is accomplished through how we take care of our minds.

Our brains aren't the issue; it's what we're feeding our minds. Regardless of who you are, we all can do more in life by searching for a variety of ways to use one percent more of our brain's horsepower. We all have an unlimited amount of storage capacity for information in our subconscious minds, and we all have about the same quantity of neurons and neural synapses. Our brains have unlimited potential, and this is proof that we all are more capable than what we might realize! If you aren't feeding your brain with positive and challenging information, it will be hard to unleash the genius that is roaring inside of you!

Chapter 5 will introduce the *Limelight Spot Effect*. This theory will help you to become unstoppable!

CHAPTER 5

THE LIMELIGHT SPOT EFFECT

CHAPTER OBJECTIVES: THIS CHAPTER WILL present an important theory that can be used to maintain your inner drive. *The Limelight Spot Effect* was designed to strengthen your self-assurance.

Your self-assurance is your belief system about yourself. Do you truly believe in yourself? Your level of belief in yourself will always be manifested in your actions. *"The more you believe in what you're doing, the more you will do to keep it going."* The more you believe in your dreams, the more you will fight for your dreams. When your belief in yourself becomes unstoppable, you won't be able to stop until you're living your dreams. In Chapter 4 we discussed the importance of remodeling your mind, but if you don't believe in yourself, then none of that will matter. I recommend that you refer back to the concepts from this chapter at least once a month. It's important to have the proper belief system about yourself if you're going to fulfill your dreams. The theory's concepts are necessary to defeat the greatest threat to your success. The greatest threat to your success will always be you! This chapter will present an example of one of my adversities, and how I applied *The Limelight Spot Effect*. This chapter will show you how to use the theory in your personal life.

Adversity: As I pursued becoming a personal trainer and a writer, my Mom and trusted friends told me that I was wasting my time. This created doubt in me because I allowed myself to be consumed with what people thought of me. I was told I wouldn't be able to provide for a family or for myself. This was engraved into my skull as I continued to pursue a career in writing and personal training. I was constantly reminded that personal training wasn't a real career.

Application of The Limelight Spot Effect: I decided to focus on me and what I wanted. I remember telling my Mom, "How can you doubt my dreams when you haven't pursued what I'm pursuing?" I realized that all of the people who doubted me were projecting their personal insecurities. I focused on learning as much as I could about my dreams. I stopped focusing on what people were saying, and I focused on me, myself, and I! If you're willing to put the work in, who has the right to tell you what you can or cannot do? Use *The Limelight Spot Effect* to help train you to focus on your self-belief as one of the main weapons to help you secure your dreams.

The Limelight Spot Effect will help you to develop the proper perspective for fulfilling your dreams. However, there is another theory that contrasts with *The Limelight Spot Effect,* and it's imperative that you understand the opposing theory's origin along with its meaning before we discuss *The Limelight Spot Effect.* So, let's take a moment to discuss the opposing theory along with its correlations to *The Limelight Spot Effect.* The opposing theory is *The Spotlight Effect.* *The Spotlight Effect* is based on your perception of what others think of you. The only thought process that should matter is yours, which is why *The Limelight Spot Effect* needs to be employed.

It will be very hard to *Just Get Up* if you consciously or unconsciously use your life to fulfill someone else's dreams. You must take control of your life by using *The Limelight Spot Effect.* *"Train yourself to love you and block out everyone else."* You know what you feel in your heart's mind and that's all that matters. Moving forward, you must view yourself as someone who has brilliant ideas. You possess the skills to make the world need your dreams!

The Spotlight Effect

History: The term "Spotlight Effect" was coined by Thomas Gilovich and Kenneth Savitsky. The phenomenon made its first appearance in the world of psychology in the journal *Current Directions in Psychological Science* in 1999. *The Spotlight Effect* is the phenomenon in which people tend to believe they are being noticed more than they really are. One is constantly in the center of one's own world, but a truly accurate evaluation of how much one is noticed by others has shown to be rare.

It's easy to fall prey to the mistaken ideology that people are consumed with our failures and where we are in life. The reality is that people really aren't judging us and they really don't care as much as we think. Being overly concerned about people's thoughts of you can create a fear of man, which will result in you losing your courage to keep on keeping on.

It is healthy to abandon the misguided thinking that other people are consumed with our personal accolades and failures. They aren't! But *The Spotlight Effect* theory is false in this way: someone is concerned with what you're doing, and it's you! I can promise you that people will talk about you whether you're doing good things or bad things. The most important thing for you to remember is that you're the main person who will constantly recall any failures you've experienced.

The Limelight Spot Effect means that you're the main person who notices and you're the only one who deserves to be concerned with what happens in your life. When you apply *The Limelight Spot Effect* theory, it helps you to realize that you're in the *limelight* of your own world. Also, it establishes that only you know how many times you have failed and how many times you have succeeded. *The Spotlight Effect* should be used to help you appreciate that people do not pay attention to you the way that you think they do, and neither do people keep a record of your failures. No one else cares as much as you do! It's like being in a classroom and just because someone is present and able to pass a few tests without studying and attentively listening to the teacher, it doesn't mean that they were attentive in class or that they study all day. Some people are good at getting by, and doubters can be good at inattentively discouraging others.

You will encounter people along your journey who have made it their mission in life to forewarn you with their mistaken views about life's possibilities. In their sincere attempts to keep you from harming yourself, they will unknowingly discourage a real dreamer from being happy. And there will be people that you know who will purposely try to make you unhappy. Fortunately, the majority of your doubters will be people who mean you well, and who are figuratively in your life's classrooms and inattentively watching you until you are able to prove yourself with results. *Life's classrooms* represent each individual segment or step of your dream that you have to learn before your dreams can fully be manifested.

A Winner's Belief System

You don't need anyone's approval! The fact that you believe it's possible that you can pass your dreams tests by working, learning, and studying hard is all the proof that spectators need, so don't give them any power over you. Don't worry about people possibly saying things like, "Well, I never had to study that hard, and the people who are doing what you want to do had experience, and they have been doing it since they were kids."

It's all in your head that naysayers are consumed with your life's journey. The reality is that only you are, so don't allow inattentive doubters to decrease your faith and belief in yourself. Their experiences in life are valuable, but their experiences aren't valuable if it takes you away from your true destiny. Most importantly, be wise and smart about discerning when good advice is being given as a precautionary measure. There are some things you should be cautious about, but good advice will only make the pursuit of your journey a calculated risk by giving you good reasons why you shouldn't stop your journey of self-discovery.

Life's GPS

If you tried to follow three GPSs all at the same time to get to three different locations, you would never get there. It's not the GPS's job to tell you where to go first, even if your destination requires multiple adventures. It's your job to tell the GPS which journey you would like to embark upon first. When a GPS is working properly, it will guide you the right way, but remember, you're still the ultimate map! You must know how to read your heart's map. If your life is headed in a bad direction, it's because of the wrong directions that you have put into your life's GPS. If this ever happens to you, please know that it's okay to stop using your life's GPS and instead follow your heart's map until your life's GPS is working properly again. Your life's GPS represents the execution of your plan or the plan you're using for execution. Sometimes we end up in the wrong places during our lives because of a poorly executed good strategy, or a poor strategy that we are executing well.

Your life's GPS can easily lose its signal if it's in a bad environment. It's similar to how a literal GPS starts to malfunction if it loses its satellite's signal. So your environment must be positive and in harmony with your dreams. Your environment consists of family, friends, relationships, work, music, health, spiritual matters, TV, and reading. Remember if your environment is negative, then your life's GPS will malfunction and lead you in a bad direction. Please follow your heart's map if this ever happens, and whenever your life's GPS regains its signal, then you can trust it again. If a GPS loses its signal, it is no good, so at some point you will have to use a map or another source for directions.

How do you know if your life's GPS has malfunctioned? Start by asking yourself, "If I'm making a lot of money or a little amount, does my career path give me the freedom I want, and do I feel like I'm tuned-in to my life's channel?" Is your life exciting because of your job or is it boring? Are there ways for you to grow at your job? If your job makes you look every day for ways to retire, then you may have arrived at the wrong destination. There is nothing wrong with making plans to retire, as far as making sure you have some income. But the desire to retire should never be because you hate your job. Here is another perspective you can use to reflect on your current career path: it should feel like if you stopped working that you're letting someone borrow something that is precious to you. And although you're letting someone borrow this precious thing of yours, you can't help but check in weekly or daily to make sure they're taking proper care of it. If you retired today, would you be itching to check-in with your job just to see what's going on? Or would you pass by your job, and not even have the urge to walk in and get a piece of the action? *"Your heart's map will always take you to your true love!"*

Your life's GPS is capable of doing this as well, but only if it has the proper coordinates while maintaining a strong signal whenever it's being used. Think of your life's GPS as a plan of action. But, plans aren't always guided by your heart's true desires. Sometimes our life's plans are manifested through conditioned thoughts of others, and our own fear of the unknown. Sometimes our dream careers are risky; at least that's what we have been mistakenly instructed to believe. If you strengthen your belief in yourself, I can promise you that you will become unstoppable! When you truly grasp how important your belief system is, you'll be successful at whatever you do!

You Must Know How to Read Your Heart's Map

Always remember that it's okay to stop using your life's GPS and instead follow your heart's map, if your life's GPS starts to malfunction. But you must know how to read your heart's map, so how can you achieve this? Sometimes when we are traveling and using a GPS, and if it's taking longer than anticipated to reach our destination, we usually start to get the intuition that the GPS is starting to malfunction. Consider this illustration: Suppose that your GPS indicated a trip would take four hours, but now you have been driving for five hours, and the GPS indicates that you have arrived at your destination! When you stop at the destination indicated on the GPS, you notice that it's not where you wanted to go. So you try to reroute, and let's say it still doesn't work. What do you do now? You probably would stop using it and try to figure it out yourself. That's how you need to be with *The Limelight Spot Effect*. Other people can help guide you along the way, but once they start to malfunction with displays of lack of faith, misguidance, negative projections, and lack of knowledge, it's time for you to turn them off, or take them out of your *life's mirror,* because their role has run its course!

Your dreams should be absolute and you need to know the right coordinates for your dreams. If you ever get stuck along your journey, always view it as misreading your heart's map rather than feeling like it wasn't meant for you. You know what you were called to do: now, do it! Stop figuratively going west if east is on your life's map. Stop trying to sing if you sound like a tractor: maybe you should learn another aspect about the music industry that you can pursue. Sometimes we spend too much time getting to know other people as opposed to fully getting to know ourselves. Sometimes we pursue a dream just because it's popular. Instead, only pursue things that involve your strengths and passions. Your strengths will overshadow your weaknesses.

Once you know your strengths, your weaknesses will be revealed. However, there is no need to focus on your weaknesses in the same way that you focus on your strengths. If you focus more on your weaknesses, it will take away from improving your strengths. There are things that you will always have trouble with. Your strengths should never be sacrificed at the expense of your innate abilities, which are the things that are the easiest for you to do. For example, if you're better at jobs involving yourself, wouldn't you agree that you're more likely to have success and enjoy pursuing jobs that fit your personality? It will be an easier process to simply pursue the things that are the easiest for you to do, so always put the right directions into your life's GPS. And just for clarity, the things that I'm referring to aren't easy in the sense that you don't have to work really hard, but easy because it's your true passion, and because it's your true passion you won't mind putting in the work. Compare it to working on a relationship with someone that you don't love vs. with someone that you do love. When you truly love someone, if the relationship ever gets in a rough spot, it'll be easier for you to work through your issues if you're in love with them, and if they love you, too. Finally, when you're using your life's GPS properly, it will take you to the destinations that are already on your heart's map.

You can't successfully achieve goals that aren't on your heart's map. The achievement of a goal is only successful if you're achieving the goal intentionally with the continuous realization that it's intentional. Your heart's true goals will never produce feelings of contrition. If the manifestations of your goals are aligned with your heart's map, you will always feel fulfilled and happy. You should never aim to achieve goals that are defined by what other people want or how they think. Your dreams are like being in love, and just because someone possesses beauty, money, and great qualities doesn't mean that you will fall in love with them. Again, we become victims to *The Spotlight Effect* theory by concerning ourselves with what other people think. Being overly concerned with what other people think usually leads to unhappiness. Remember this: no matter how great something may seem or appear to be, if your heart isn't into it, it won't last! Eventually, you will lose your desire to remain loyal to a goal that you aren't truly in love with.

Life's Mirror

If you truly desire to restructure your life's channel to display an Oscar-Award-winning movie, you'll need your *life's mirror* to reflect what you need to see, and not the things that you may currently see. What does this mean? And what are the things you need to see? If someone told you that you had something on your face, and you were not aware of that, what would you do next? I'm certain that you would begin a process of trying to remove whatever is on your face. I'm sure you've had this experience before, so let's say you decide not to look at it yourself. Instead you decide to use the vantage point of the person who informed you that you have something on your face. So subsequently, after you attempt to correct the situation, the person tells you, "Hey, you got most of it, but there is still a little more there." What would you do next? I'm sure you would continue to try and remove the rest of it. But for some reason you just can't remove it all. So the person who informed you attempts to remove it for you, and they're able to make a little progress, but they're still unsuccessful. Finally, you begin to feel where the spot is located, and you make another attempt to remove it by using the person you're with as your pair of eyes. However, after this attempt you probably would ask your companion if it's finally gone. But they reply and say, "It's still there, you didn't remove all of it."

What would be your next move? You are right! You would probably try again yourself, and then you would attempt to find a mirror so that you can take a look for yourself. Suppose that you finally go to the restroom, and look in the mirror, and it's clear to you where the spot is located on your face. Now you see exactly where you should start to progressively remove the stain that's on your face, and in a matter of seconds you begin to acknowledge what you may need to use for further assistance to remove the stain.

Also, suppose while you're looking in the mirror there are others things such as a hand dryer, trashcan, and paper towels being reflected in the mirror as well. You may notice those things, but do you actually think that you would be consumed with the things being reflected in the mirror? Of course not! You may notice the other things in the mirror, and yet, you wouldn't really notice them. Your focus would be centered on working to remove your stain. Furthermore, if you did allow yourself to focus on the other things being reflected, it would distract you from the task at hand. Being distracted could result in your inability to fully remove the stain, or more time to remove the stain.

When you decide to *live your dreams*, your *life's mirror* will be the same way. If your reflection is distracted with things other than the main problem, it will delay the progression of your goals. As you continue to develop your self-assurance, *The Limelight Spot Effect* will train you to reflect yourself in your *life's mirror* whenever you're experiencing adversities or a stain on your dreams. Sometimes we make the mistake of being consumed with what other people think, and we allow them to get into our heads. Yes, other people can assist you in fixing a problem, but trust me: no one knows how to fix it better than you do! If you lack experience in any area regarding your dreams, then someone with more experience can help you by giving you guidance.

At times, you may need to use some of the other things your *life's mirror* is reflecting, but only if you determine it is necessary. So feel free to use that trashcan you see reflected, or ask someone to help you. But remember: it's your reflection, so don't become overly consumed with other people or with distractions that take you away from progressively focusing your *life's mirror* to reflect your dreams. Sometimes you will have to remove the trashcan, hand dryer, and the paper towels so that you aren't aware of those potentially unnecessary additions in your life's reflection. But you still have to be the one to do the work. *"No one can do it the way that you can do it."* No one cares the way that you do. Most importantly, no one can pursue your passions and dreams the way that you can!

You know that you won't let you down, so why put someone else in the middle of your life's battle? You're the best player and the most knowledgeable about your goals. You know what truly makes you happy! Besides God, who can truly love and know you better than you do? Once you eliminate unnecessary distractions from your mirror's reflecting light, it will help you to identify the location of your problems. However, remember that you're the one who will always have to fix any problems that you have, and you're the one who's most qualified to do that.

Believe In Yourself

Notice in the illustration that if you decided to use another person's pair of eyes, you could only go so far when trying to resolve a problem. No one can see your dreams the way you do, and no one will care the way that you do. Your life is your personal mirror and no one can reflect your life's journey the way that you can. One of the secrets in the illustration I'm developing is that at the beginning of the process to remove the stain, and unbeknownst to you, you always had an advantage over the person who was trying to help you. If you had used your own eyes from the beginning, you would have clearly seen the stain right away. To sum it up, it's okay to seek help, but you must know when it's time to trust in your own abilities.

It's reasonable to conclude that we all have been guilty of trying to attain a goal while using someone else's mirror. If you use someone else's mirror it will force you to see things the way that they do. For example, if someone is pursuing their dreams, and they're unconsciously using someone else's mirror of belief instead of their own mirror, it will reflect how others see them, whether it's positive or negative reviews. Some of these negative reflections can be things like my Mom and Dad told me, that "I wasn't good enough to do this particular job and "You didn't achieve your goals, so maybe it wasn't meant to be."

"When you look into your life's mirror, you have to use your own eyes and see your own problem along with the solution." Along your journey you may see figurative paper towels, hand dryers, and trashcans reflecting in your *life's mirror*. However, you don't have

to focus on those things. In your *life's mirror* you will always see yourself and your mirror will always reflect everything that's a part of your life. However, you don't have to focus on the stains of your life through someone else's mirror. People will always doubt you and those people will always consists of strangers, family, and friends.

It's important to remember that your *life's mirror* will only reflect the things that are in your environment. In the illustration, I used the restroom mirror and the things that are typically accessible in a restroom. However, you could have used any mirror to help you to locate the stain that was on your face. Here's the point: if you ever experience a stain on your dreams and if you need help removing your stains, the people that you associate with will be your immediate assistance and will be reflected in your *life's mirror*. So your environment is reflecting the things that you will initially try to use to help remove any stains or doubts placed on your dreams. If your environment currently reflects the wrong tools for assistance, you will unconsciously make your stain worse, or nothing will happen at all. Does your current environment reflect a positive support system that you can use to help fulfill your dreams? Can you use your current support system to uplift you and remove any stains that will come from the pains of potential adversities?

Sometimes, the people who you think doubt you actually do believe in you. So it's necessary to maintain humility, because it's so easy to become consumed with impressing others or desiring their approval. This is a distraction as well! You have to be consumed with your problems, and if you determine you can't solve the problem by yourself then feel free to ask for help by using the figurative paper towels. However, after using any assistance you might need, you must appropriately place the assistance out of focus from your mirror's reflection. Using someone else's assistance for too long will cripple your self-assurance, thus making it harder for you to overcome your adversities.

The Limelight Spot Effect theory will help you reflect only you, the problem, and how you can fix any negative reflections that you don't need in your life's mirror. Negative and positive influences will always be reflected in your *life's mirror*. However, you need to be conscious about keeping your environment as positive as you can. Unfortunately, the world we live in is so negative it's almost impossible to escape all negativity. So I advise you not to focus on any negative reflections. Also, I advise you not to focus on the positive reflections for too long, either. You will always have to clean your *life's mirror* to manifest a clearer view of your genius, so never get too comfortable! It's similar to any mirror or window you have cleaned from your past: just because you cleaned it and it began to sparkle, doesn't mean that you will never have to clean it again.

If the things reflecting in your *life's mirror* aren't contributing to your successes, then you must remove them! For example, one could say, "Okay, friend," "Okay, drugs," "Okay, food," "Okay, job," and "Okay, all negative influences: you're out of my life." Whatever is holding or whatever could potentially hold you back from manifesting your inner genius must be obliterated. You must inform all of your negative distractions that you're on a mission and that they're interfering with your limelight's reflection. If you properly implement *The Limelight Spot Effect,* it will train you to do this! Once you train yourself to focus on your mirror, reflecting your opinion as the final opinion, then you're using *The Limelight Spot Effect.*

Sometimes it's easy to mistakenly assume that people are overly concerned with what's going on in your life. People don't pay you as much attention as you might think. The people who you think are observing you and who you think are concerned about any setbacks you may experience really aren't! Once you achieve your goals, that's all people will focus on! They won't consume themselves with the ninety-nine times you did not achieve your goals. No one is keeping count, so don't worry about what others think. If you tried to win the lottery 2,000 times, but failed each time, would the failures really matter if you finally won after one more attempt? Of course not! All you would be focused on is the money and the new life that you are about to start.

Only focus on your *limelight* and not the *spotlight* of the way others see you. If you continue to focus on the spotlight of people's opinions, it will blow your inner motivation's fuse. This fuse is similar to a light bulb: once the fuse is blown, no light will be seen. So protect your inner *limelight* or your *belief system* by allowing *The Limelight Spot Effect* to train you to focus on your opinion and yours only. Your limelight's fuse can easily be blown if you're extending yourself beyond the watts you possess inside.

Take a moment and ask yourself: do you focus on the sun for

hours at a time? *The sun is the ultimate source of light, spotlight, and limelight!* The sun is magnificent and we notice it, but we do not spend all day focusing on it. However, its greatness is appreciated. Your light is a little more tangible than the sun because you have a personality and the sun does not. The sun doesn't need us to validate its worth and brightness. You don't need others to validate your light, either. Just because people can't see your light because it's not bright enough from where they stand doesn't mean that your *limelight* isn't connected. Sometimes you will figuratively have to change your bulb, tighten your bulb, and check the wiring.

The Limelight Spot Effect teaches you that you're the sun and you're glowing! The sun seems large from a distance, but it's more than just large, it's gigantic. When you stop focusing on *The Spotlight Effect* you will be able to see *The Limelight Spot Effect*. Your personal *limelight* is bigger than the world. Your belief in yourself needs to be gigantic and unstoppable. The sun is bigger than the earth, so which one actually needs the other? Does the sun need the earth or does the earth need the sun? Stop looking for other people to be your light when you're the sun! The sun isn't consumed with what the earth needs! The earth feeds off of the sun and that's how you need to be. The world is feeding off of you! Who cares about what people think? Certainly not you! You're your own light and you exist separately. All you need is to be consumed with YOU! *Let your inner sun radiate throughout the world and set us on fire with your self-assurance that will be manifested as your limelight.*

You must work on your belief in yourself and always use your imagination by keeping your dreams constantly in front of you. You can achieve this by displaying your dreams on your life's channel every day. This is a concept necessary to eventually attain any goal. "Things change when you change the way you look at things."

"You have to make your life's mirror reflect the circumstances you need to see." Instead of you becoming a victim of *The Spotlight Effect*, all of your doubters will become victimized by you as you use *The Limelight Spot Effect*. The only reflection that matters is yours and how you see your adversities. *"You want to be your own boss, but your life is being used to work for someone else's dreams."* What does this mean? All inactive people have a dream of not accomplishing anything! I know that seems harsh, but it's the truth!

You can accept the responsibility to keep your conditions as they are, or you can take on the responsibility to change them. Someone with negative energy works hard at getting others to doubt themselves, even if they genuinely love you. An individual like this can be referred to as an obscurant. In fact, we all may be guilty of doing this at times when we project our personal fears onto others. A part of me just getting up came from supporting other people's beliefs in their dreams. When I was trying to escape poverty, I encouraged my peers to pursue their dreams, but also to have several alternate routes to success. I wanted them to develop an eclectic mindset toward making a living. When you start supporting other people's dreams, it inspires you to fulfill your own dreams. *"Spirits are transferable, so sometimes you have to be the person that you want the people around you to be."* If people truly believe in you and see the genius in you, it's safe to say that they will support you!

If you fall a few times along your journey, don't be shocked. We all fall down at different times during our lives. But that doesn't mean you have to stay down. You can gradually get up or you can lie on your back, side, or stomach. Also, you can sit on your butt. The point of that analogy is someone who puts constant effort into staying down actually feeds their negative energies and unconsciously turns off their limelight or self-belief. In reality, our desire to win isn't strong enough at times. You have to know that if you keep moving forward you will eventually reach your destination. For example, if you got lost twenty times, possibly more trying to find a particular destination, do you think you will ever reach your destination if you decide to stop trying?

If you experience any setbacks along your journey to find your life's exciting episodes, this must be your resolve: "If I'm not progressing, I just need to figure out why and then I can see how to win!" Never quit your passion by lying to yourself and saying this isn't for me! Remember this and this quote is one my my original quotes: *"Never doubt your ability; only question your strategy and your inner desire to truly live in your greatness."* You will always have two options: you can put all of your energy into being proactive, or accept inactivity toward your dreams. It's easy as an imperfect person not to realize that we're working hard no matter if we are proactive or inactive. *"Either you're working hard to achieve your goals with action, or you're working hard not to achieve them with constant inaction."* Even if you're inactive you're still working hard, so since you'll be working hard either way, whether you're proactive or inactive, you might as well go with the route that leads to the rewards that agrees with your heart's map. Either you will have a fulfilling life or you won't, and you must accept that you will have purposely traveled to either place. You will be working hard either way. What type of person does it take to allow a passionate ambition to poke at them every day of their lives, and choose to ignore it? It takes energy to turn off the things that we truly want to do! Since fulfilling and unfulfilling actions both require energy I recommend you use your energy in a productive way.

If you don't feel this way about your dreams, then it's not a dream, it's just something that sounds good. Stop pursuing endeavors that you aren't passionate about, since you will be working hard either way! On the contrary, work hard to *Just Get Up* and make things happen! Don't work hard to make an anticipated mistake to fall and remain on your back, side, or stomach. Don't work hard to be able to tell people, "I gave it my all, but it didn't happen." Work hard to get up and make it happen! *"Some people want success, until it's time to do the work that successful people do."* I chose not to stay down. I chose to fight by recognizing that my dream's fulfillment depended solely on me. I had to train myself not to think of what others thought. It's very hard to keep fighting when it appears that you are defeated and when people are telling you that it's okay to surrender. Use *The Limelight Spot Effect* and focus on your thoughts because opinions do matter. Still, the opinions that matter most are yours.

Always Reflect The Right People In Your Life's Mirror

Sincere successful people will see your genuine attempts and will show appreciation for your boldness. The inner light that exists inside of you is *The Limelight Spot Effect* that I'm referring too. So take out the word *lime* and *light* from my theory and you'll just have the *spot effect*. This is what happens when your figurative fuse blows. There isn't any *limelight* so you're in a *spot* with no *limelight* that creates an effect of feeling lost and blind. However, learn from The Spotlight Effect that people aren't consumed with you being lost. It's only you that views it this way. Remember this: if you're off track and then get back on track and achieve your goals, no one will focus on the past. People may remember it for a split second, but you're the one that will torture yourself worrying about something that no longer matters. Only you are attentively focused in your *life's classroom.* So enjoy each step and learn all the necessary things you will need from every step associated with reaching your destination. Forget about all the failed attempts and turn on your inner light, so that the *spot* you're currently in will have *light* that produces you as the *limelight!*

If you're experiencing inconsistencies regarding your personal belief in yourself, then *The Limelight Spot Effect* theory can help you to create a clear path to properly medicate such a poisonous spirit. A lack of belief in yourself will lead to a lack of faith, so remember this: *"You own your world and you own how you feel."* Your dream is your *spot* in the world and your necessary *limelight,* so make the world see and feel what you do. *The Limelight Spot Effect* comes from *you,* and it involves *only you,* and *how you allow yourself to feel.* The *limelight is always inside of you. "You need to be your own fan and you need to treat yourself like you're the star of the century."* Only your opinion matters and how you feel about yourself is what really counts. It's *your limelight!* When your mind is clean and filled with unstoppable belief in yourself, your *life's mirror* will properly reflect you, along with any assistance you will need, and you'll have a clearer path to manifesting your greatness. You must learn to focus on you and how you're going to win! *The Limelight Spot Effect* teaches you to focus on your destination regardless of any distractions you may experience along your journey.

Just because people don't mention your efforts in a grandiose way doesn't mean they don't feel the presence of your inner limelight. So keep shining as you continue to unveil your gifts to the world with *The Limelight Spot Effect.* One theory promotes that people aren't concerned, and my theory promotes that you're the only one that needs to be concerned. You must feel and see your inner limelight!

You must condition your brain to know; when it comes to your heart's road map you're the only person that knows how to read it. You must train your brain to focus on you, and when this is accurately done it will unleash your unstoppable self-belief. It's important for you to know just how tricky life can be. It's not good enough just to desire to win in life. You must know how to play life's game of chess as well. You must believe in yourself and believe that you can do whatever you have a true passion for. As your journey throughout *Just Get Up* continues, it's important for you to understand how life really works. It's necessary for you to know how to develop a winning strategy, so that you can achieve your goals. Chapter 6, *Life is like a Game of Chess*, will help you to develop a winner's strategy.

Here are some exercises to help you avoid *The Spotlight Effect*. These exercises will also help you to implement *The Limelight Spot Effect*.

Limelight Spot Effect Exercises:

1. What are my gifts?
2. What are some of the things I enjoy doing?
3. What are my strengths regarding my perception of others?
4. What are my weaknesses regarding people's perception of me?
5. What are my strengths mentally, spiritually, socially, emotionally, physically, and financially? (If you're lacking any necessary strengths in one of these domains, then set some goals to develop the strengths you will need in your weaker domains.)
6. What are your weaknesses in the six domains listed above? What positive things do you do every day to work on yourself?
7. Who do you know personally who is striving to be balanced in some or all of the six domains? (Search for individuals who are succeeding in one or all of the six domains and befriend them.)
8. Say this to yourself every day: *"Someone's perception of me is their opinion, but how I see myself is the only fact."* (Research someone who has accomplished what you desire to do, and learn from them. Also, start attending seminars and hire a motivational and personal development coach. Listen to my podcast show on my Youtube channel on Fridays at 1:30 p.m. central time zone and feel free to contact me for coaching by going to my website www. isaacsmiller.com)

CHAPTER 6

LIFE IS LIKE A GAME OF CHESS

BEFORE YOU BEGIN READING THIS chapter, you should take five or ten minutes to complete the exercises below. But first, I want you to imagine that all jobs pay exactly the same and all careers offer the same benefits. Also, imagine the benefits cover everything an employer or employee could hope for. Benefits can be things such as health insurance, paid time off, flexible schedule, commute compensation, etc. (it's your world, so write down all of the benefits your heart desires).

1. On a piece of paper, write down the jobs or careers you want to pursue. The jobs that you choose as careers should be jobs you're absolutely in love with.
2. Write down why you would love to have the jobs or careers you've chosen.
3. Write down the adversities that you think will come with the jobs or careers you chose.
4. Write down all of the resources you think you will need to help you become successful at the careers you've chosen. (Resources can be money, people, time, skills, abilities, support, motivation, responsibilities, health, etc. After you identify the resources you will need, write down the resources you currently have, and the resources you don't have.)

Just Get Up's Mantra

Get Up! Wake Up! *You don't have any more* of your time to waste! Wake Up! Get Up! You don't have any more *of your time* to waste! You don't have any more of your time *to waste.* Wake up! Get Up! *Just Get Up*!

It's reasonable to conclude that the world's greatest chess players had to first learn how to play before they mastered their craft. All of the greats had to take the first step to becoming a grand master. What was the first step? The first step was simply learning about the game of chess. They all had to put forth the effort and learn. Of course, some may have learned more rapidly than others. However, regardless of the pace of each individual learner, the point remains clear: they all had to learn how to play, and your life is the same way. You may currently be in a bad situation and you may feel like you don't know how to win life's game of chess. However, this chapter will encourage you to learn about life, and discover how you can create any necessary changes in your life. You must examine your current skills, and you should aim to refine your abilities, so that your life can reflect the conditions your heart truly desires. You must realize and believe that you're capable of taking control of your life by making the right moves.

I'm sure you've heard the saying that knowledge is power. Being knowledgeable about the things you want to do is arguably one of the first steps to success. For example, do you know all the rules to the game of chess? If you don't know all the rules, mistakes will take place simply out of ignorance. Once you have committed several hours to taking in knowledge about an aspiration that you want to master, it will eventually turn into understanding. However, true understanding can only be produced after you've learned the various complexities pertaining to your goals.

It's a necessity for you keep progressing in life and to become a master of life's game of chess. Whenever you learn anything that's beneficial, you should aim to start applying it. It will lead to a positive understanding if you consistently apply any new skills you attain. Eventually, your understanding on the subject will grow and produce wisdom as one of its fruits. Once wisdom is apparent regarding an endeavor, you will always make the right moves.

Looking back, think about when you first learned how to cross a street. The process of learning how to properly cross a street started when you took in knowledge regarding how and why to cross a street with caution. The knowledge you took in eventually produced the understanding that if you don't look both ways, you could get hit by a car. The wisdom is displayed once you fully comprehend how the meaning of safely crossing a street correlates to your existence. Your newly acquired comprehension then forced you to look both ways whenever you attempted to cross a street. However, true wisdom can only be demonstrated by actually crossing the street when it's truly clear that you'll be safe. Although there's always an inherent risk when crossing a street, it becomes a calculated risk that lowers the chances of something going wrong.

This analogy illustrates how life unfolds. Some things are absolute, which means some things will happen in a certain way if we do certain things. This is called a *law* in the field of science. A science law will produce the same results even if the experiment is conducted by someone else. Some things are relative and there's a degree of uncertainty when something is relative. You can't directly control an outcome when something is relative. On the contrary, if you were crossing a street, and it's obvious that it's safe for you to cross, that is an example of something that's absolute!

However, relativity is intangibly intertwined because you can't control whether someone falls asleep at the wheel, even after you have safely crossed a street. For example, suppose you have safely crossed a busy street, and after crossing the street you begin to pleasantly stroll along the sidewalk. You're unaware that a driver has fallen asleep behind the wheel, and all of a sudden the driver pummels into you at full speed. This is an example of how things are relative. In relation to life, the things that are absolute are situations we can directly control.

Unfortunately, we can't control what other people do, which makes life's possibilities relative, and to a degree arbitrary by nature. A literal game of chess is somewhat arbitrary, but if you acquire knowledge and understanding, eventually your wisdom will compel your decisions to be selective and calculated, rather than too risky. In other words, your experiences will enable you to rapidly compare and contrast your possible outcomes. Once you're able to intellectually compare and contrast life's possible outcomes with wisdom, it will consistently help you to make the best possible decisions.

It's important for you to recognize that your life is similar to a game of chess, and sometimes you will enter life not knowing how to play. That was true in my situation because I was born into poverty and I didn't have the proper guidance. Children can't control the environments they're born into, so we all should dig deep into our upbringings to rectify some of our sullied roots. We all have sullied roots and imperfections that have been passed on to us unconsciously. When babies are born they don't know anything, so most of our roots, as far as our foundation for learning and believing, are in our environment and the things we were conditioned to learn. So life has the offensive and the defensive advantage at the beginning of all our lives because babies don't pick or choose their parents.

When you were a baby, you were unable to strike a winning blow until you started the process of learning how to win. When a baby is born, a baby's mind is empty and a baby literally doesn't know anything. Babies have to learn how to do everything! So regardless of who you are, all of us start off not knowing how to win in life. And some of us have better starts than others, but this fact remains: we all have to learn and that's the perspective that you must maintain! However, you must believe in yourself, remain fully committed to your dreams, and stay focused on learning how to achieve your goals just like anyone who has achieved anything in life. Notice, I mentioned until you started a process of learning how to win, and not once you were older, and learned how to win. The human body is genetically designed to mature over time, and although our bodies eventually mature, unfortunately some people allow their minds to remain underdeveloped. You can't win life's game of chess if you're thirty-five years old with the mindset of an infant. So accept the moves that life has already made on you and adapt this as your motto: Failure is only a teaching experience to allow you to understand what you need to do differently so you can be successful. The more adversities you experience, the better off you will be only if you daily commit to changing your circumstances by constantly developing your mind.

You Must Become a Student of Life

If you don't know how to play chess, then you should not expect to start off beating some of the best players in the world. Instead, you should become one of their students. You should apply this principle to any new endeavors along your life's journey of self-discovery. If you become a student of life, here is what you can expect—and I'll stick with chess as the analogy. After you've gained knowledge, understanding, and wisdom about chess, you will be able to anticipate your opponent's move, and you'll have a counter move for their future moves. The same concept applies during life's game of chess. Remember this: *"It's appropriate to expect to be defeated several times before you master any game."* This is why you should start learning about the complexities associated with your dreams, so that you can progress faster by developing wisdom as soon as possible.

It's easy to lose your motivation if you don't understand a game and your opponents, and if you don't know the right moves to make during a game. When you're able to recognize the key elements of being successful, that's when you'll start to be successful. These elements are knowledge, understanding, and wisdom. Once you're applying these three elements you will increase your guarantee of being successful! Remember: the person who makes the most right moves during a game of chess always wins. This same concept is true during your life. How your life's game of chess begins to unravel depends on how you decide to let it unravel. *"An important step to take while you're chasing your dreams is to recognize that each day is a new day and you have to invest into your future before your current episode runs its course. In other words, before your current episode or day ends, you must have the next one planned. Every day that you're working from behind makes it harder to catch up."* If you're currently not winning your life's game of chess, you must change your life's strategy or a dichotomy will surface. A dichotomy will result in a division between your mind and your actions. If you allow this to happen you will fall prey to allowing procrastination to become a personality trait. If you don't learn how to win, along with understanding how to improve your odds of winning, you will assume that you're losing because life gave you all the wrong moves.

Know Your Opponents and Know Your
Personality Traits vs. Your Emotions

Think of your personality traits as attributes that you have individually nurtured throughout your entire lifespan. Personality traits help to differentiate your personality from anyone else's. You are truly unlike any other human being on this planet. I'm sure your family and friends admire some good qualities about you. I'm also certain that you have some attributes that you appreciate about yourself. However, have you ever sat down and reflected on the quality of your attributes as an evolving mechanism? To illustrate an example of an evolving mechanism, let's suppose you're adamant about demonstrating various forms of giving, but what have you done lately to grow in this area? Are you a good listener? How do you know? How do you know if you're becoming an even better listener? Or perhaps maybe your listening skills have started to diminish? Whatever personality traits you're exceptional in, whether they're negative or positive traits, they should constantly be worked on. For example, having a bad temper as a personality trait could easily dictate how you use your emotions. There will be different situations during your life when you could rightfully be upset, but if you naturally have a temper problem; it could lead to you misconstruing the bigger picture. Any negative personality traits that you may have must be corrected, and any positive personality traits that you have must be improved.

Suppose that you were a hothead, and you allowed your anger to compel you to attack someone because they said something inappropriate to you. In the long run, would this be the best decision? The decisions that give you constant room for growth, and that help you to discern how every decision you make will affect your ability to make progress, should always be your default decisions. Improving your positive personality traits will help to alter how you use your emotions when you're under stress. Start reflecting on your personality traits and ask yourself this question: Do I have any personality traits that could produce negative emotions that will affect my possibilities to progress in life? Personality traits can also be things that seem innocuous, such as being very kind. Think about how many people are unhappy from allowing people to walk over them because they don't have the courage to stand up for themselves.

It's noble to be very generous; but no one should be overly kind if it's lowering their self-worth. Lowering one's self-worth would be a clear indication of the misapplication of the quintessence of personal integrity. Your personality traits and emotions must positively be coherent to weather the storms of life's unpredictability. You should always aim to improve your good attributes along with improving attributes that aren't the easiest for you to apply. Some people have a hard time displaying patience and they are quick to be presumptuous. Always improve your great qualities, while also aiming to improve any qualities that could be a liability as you play to win life's game of chess.

You may be wondering who your opponents are. Your opponents are your emotions. Your opponents during your life's game of chess will be the various personality traits you're capable of employing. The personality traits you embody will always be manifested and displayed through your emotions. Your personality will dictate how you use your emotions whenever it's time for you to make a move during life's game of chess. Your emotions can help you to win, or they can help you to lose. Let's reiterate one of the concepts I mentioned earlier in this chapter. Suppose you decided to burn someone's house down because you were upset with them, which would be an example of allowing yourself to be controlled by your anger as opposed to controlling your anger. The misapplication of your emotions in this analogy could result in a potential loss in your life.

The interesting thing about chess is that you truly are your own opponent and your own teammate. Think about all the sixteen pieces that are on the board for an actual game of chess. A game of chess requires one king, one queen, two rooks, two bishops, two knights, and eight pawns. These pieces can be your friends or they can be your enemies, and it all depends on how you decide to use them. How you decide to use your pieces during a game of chess will dictate how your opponent responds to your every move. If you make too many wrong moves, you won't get a chance to make all of your possible moves. If you continue to make too many wrong moves, all you will hear is "checkmate!" If you're going to *manifest your genius,* you must be the one saying "checkmate!" *"The emotions you embody into your life's moves for your dreams will help you or hurt you."* For example, being overly anxious could lead to you making a move that could cost you several pieces during a game of chess.

We all are capable of opposing ourselves, and we do this unconsciously whenever we block our dreams paths. So, identifying all of your positive and negative personality traits will allow you to scrutinize all of the emotions you're capable of embodying. You must recognize all of the emotions that can potentially derail your train's progress. There's nothing wrong with displaying different emotions and personality traits as you journey through life's game of chess. But the personality traits and emotions you consistently display should be the right ones for your dream's strategy.

In your attempt to win life's game of chess, you must understand that it will be normal for you to display several different emotions. One minute you may feel afraid, the next minute you may feel happy, and sometimes you may feel doubtful. Another common emotion is that you may feel anxious, and your emotions represent all of the pieces to life's game of chess. If you make a good move for your life, then you're directing your positive emotions to make the right moves for your life, and if you make a wrong move during your life, then you're directing your negative emotions to make the wrong moves for your life.

Being cognizant of your personality traits along with your emotional compulsions should always be applied to all of your real-life situations. You must know yourself and honestly self-examine how you respond to positive and negative situations. So examine your personality, and look for ways to improve your good qualities as well as working on your not-so-good qualities. You must carefully consider how everything that you do can, and will, affect your possible moves throughout your life's game of chess. So, how well do you manage your emotions? Do you handle criticism well? Do you burn bridges with friendships that you may need later on during your life? If you can't control your emotions, you won't be able to control your life.

"Not being able to control your emotions can literally mean that you have lost control over your mind." If you lose control over your emotions it will affect you *holistically*. Chapter 4 discussed *The Holistic Approach,* along with the theory's five domains. For emphasis, these domains are spiritual, social, emotional, physical, and cognitive domains. *"To effectively execute any winning strategy you must embody yourself holistically. Either you control your emotions or your emotions will control you. You can't think as clearly when you're drowning in misery, overly confident, and holding grudges."*

Everything is *holistically* connected, and if you lack self-control in any one of the domains under *The Holistic Approach*, you're more than likely aborting your maximum potential. You absolutely have to take full control of your life, along with each decision that you will consciously, or unconsciously, decide to make!

Do You Know How to Win Life's Game of Chess?

You must have a strategy to continue to successfully win at anything. Your strategy is simply your eclectic plan for being flexible. The strategies you implement should always be based on the circumstances of your problems. So, if you're winning you must have a strategy to keep it that way, and if you're losing you must have a strategy to reverse any unwanted fates. Your strategy will allow you to center your focus while implementing your winning philosophy. For the rest of your life you will always have to coach your life's strategy. *"Your strategy to fulfill your goals will naturally begin to go astray unless you continuously coach your own life through its many quarters of adversities."* In order for you to successfully capture your dreams, you must learn how to develop a winner's strategy!

Just for a moment, I want you to take a few minutes and reflect on any individual sport. As you're reflecting I want you to think of a great athlete who became successful at an individual sport such as Serena Williams, Muhammad Ali, Jesse Owens, and many others. Their gifts only took them so far. Their gifts had to be directed and perpetually nurtured. Talent isn't enough and it will never replace hard work. As you begin to develop your strategy to capture your dreams you must develop an insane work ethic as well. You will know when you have developed the proper work ethic. How will you know? When people start to make comments such as, "Woman, you don't ever stop? or man, you don't ever stop?" You will know when your passion has the proper intensity because people will begin to encourage you to slow down by saying, "Stop working so hard." People may start to tell you that you're possessed and obsessed. When you arrive at this point, then that's when you have developed an insane work ethic.

However, keep in mind that there is such a thing as going overboard with pursuing your dreams. Do not neglect your other major responsibilities such as caring for, and spending time with, your family and friends. To keep it simple, have the wisdom to know when you're being balanced and when you're not. Do not allow someone else to dictate what's defined as being balanced for you: only you can adequately assess your passion. If your heart ascertains that you need to spend more time working on your dreams, then do so. However, if you determine that you need to relax and go party, then you should go party. You should develop the habit of analyzing your life's telescope of divisions from an objective view. *Life's objective telescope* only focuses on results. To illustrate: suppose you set some goals to achieve before the end of the day. The question that should be asked is: Did you accomplish the goals you set for the day by the end of day? If you set a goal to read fifty pages of information and you only read five pages, then you haven't earned the right to go party. You must implement your plan of action by coaching yourself through the many moments where there are divisions. Your *life's telescope* of divisions will always consist of urges to do something else, instead of doing what you know you need to do! So use this illustration as one of your barometers to determine if you're being balanced toward pursuing your dreams, and go party after you've accomplished the goals you've set for the day.

Life's Telescope Of Divisions

To identify your *life's telescope of divisions* will require you to do a little soul-searching to unearth what's really affecting you. If you find yourself procrastinating, then it's time for you to use your figurative telescope, and analyze the divisions of your heart and mind. If you ever start to feel like you don't know what to do, I can promise you that you're experiencing a dichotomy. To successfully correct a dichotomy, I recommend you start by analyzing the true feelings of your heart. Always be honest with yourself whenever you're excavating your feelings. Once you have brought your true emotions to your heart's surface, then you should use your brain to guide your feelings to a clear path of action. If you ever feel like you don't know what to do, you should remember that it's probably because you may feel like you're lacking certain resources. Refer back to the exercise for resources at the beginning of this chapter if you ever experience a dichotomy. Finally, discuss your strategy with another winner who has demonstrated by their lifestyle that they're manifesting their genius.

Understanding Probability vs. The Human Will

There are times you can be equally or unequally matched against a worthy opponent and your adversary isn't always as talented as you are. And, for some seemingly unexplained reason, the less talented opponent finds a way to win! So clearly, there is no substitute for hard work! If you allow your life to display mediocrity, then that's what you will see, and if you allow your life to display greatness, then that's what you will see as well. Remember this: life will always outwork you if you allow your life to become a victim of being on autopilot. You can never stop looking for ways to grow if you truly desire to be phenomenal. Time doesn't slow down for anyone, so you must recognize that time isn't on your side. Remember this: *"Always aim to stay ahead, and never get behind because it's hindsight that's cripples a broken spirit."*

Recap to Readjust

So far, along your journey of self-discovery, you have remodeled your mind which helped you to create a new system for learning. Most importantly, you have reactivated, and strengthened your belief in your abilities. Your journey has established why you're a phenomenal talent and that you're a genius. However, even experts can lose in life if they don't have a great strategy. You must have more than an excellent strategy. You also need to know how to defeat the oppositions that you will encounter along your journey. A good coach will help a good athlete to become better, and it's the philosophy of a coach's strategy that a good coach teaches his players to implement. An athlete can't control every move the opponent makes, but he can control his countermoves by accurately applying a good coach's strategy. The implementation of a good coaching strategy can help a determined athlete to win. Have you ever heard an athlete mention that they don't like their coach's coaching style? Or maybe you've heard this phrase, "The player isn't coachable." In order for you to win life's game of chess, you have to train your emotions to be coachable with an urgent readiness to adapt at any given moment. Your emotions will cause you to lose in life if you don't continuously coach them. There is a philosophy known as a *Player Coach* and that's what you must be. You're the player and the coach, and you must create your own winning strategies, and implement them as well. *"You must know how and when to change your life's strategies whenever life gives you a new challenger."*

Putting Your Strategy into Action

If you don't commit yourself to fully learning how to play life's game of chess, you will make the wrong moves unknowingly and lose. Whatever games or segments in life you aren't familiar with, you must master them. Not knowing how to play or how to control your emotions is an excuse that may cost you your dreams.

The beauty of being your own opponent is that you will always make mistakes. However, because they are your mistakes, you can reason on why they were made better than anyone. The goal isn't to avoid mistakes; the goal is to recognize that mistakes will always be made, and to have a system in place to change how you view your mistakes. Doing so will allow you to figure out how to win. You're in control of your life and you decide how to deal with your life.

You can't always control how your life unravels or how a game of chess unfolds. For instance, your opponent may make the first move and then you have to respond to it. Your life may be like my situation: I couldn't control the fact that I grew up in poverty because kids can't control their environment. But at some point when we are adults, regardless of our upbringing, we all are responsible for our actions. So if you have children, I recommend that you start helping them to understand at an early age that no matter what hand you're dealt, you can get out of any situation. Teach them that they don't have to be a statistic or a perpetual failure. Help them to appreciate that mistakes will be made, but as long as they understand life, and how to win, they will be successful. It won't be easy, but the better you understand life's intricate parts and all the paths available, the more likely you will avoid unnecessary pitfalls. Remember this: Ignorance is never an excuse for inaction! So, you should be obsessed with growing and getting better every day.

You Can Make a Comeback

Regardless of your level of experience, you must acknowledge that sometimes the moves you think you have remaining will appear doomed and irrevocable. However, this is only true during an actual game of chess. During life's game of chess you can always enter the game at a disadvantaged state. Simply put all the pieces back on the board and then decide how to correct your figurative *zugzwang*. Are you familiar with the word "zugzwang?" It means a situation during a game of chess where a player is limited to moves that cost pieces and it will result in a damaging position. It originates in German and means "compulsion move". *Compulsion* means that we are compelled, or internally coerced, to make irrational moves. And I think it can be argued that all compulsions during a game of chess involve a degree of impulsions, especially if you're trapped in a state of zugzwang, which could force you to make a move that you wouldn't normally make. Furthermore, compare this concept to life: the only way you can set yourself up for *zugzwang* during life's game of chess would be if you allowed yourself to constantly stay in a disadvantaged state. Life is like a game of chess, and if you make too many wrong moves, it'll become extremely hard to come back and win the game. So never allow your dreams to experience a damaging positional effect by taking or making too may wrong moves.

Resources, Resources and Resources

It's very important for you to know all of the resources you don't have and all of the resources you will need for your strategy to work. The exercises you completed at the beginning of this chapter were designed to help you understand the significance of understanding your dreams' connections to life's resources. This may seem redundant, but that's how significant it is for you to understand the concept of resources. Take a moment to reflect on the resources you believe you have, and the resources you lack. Focus on the resources you have and set small, manageable goals. Always acknowledge the resources you will need, but don't overly concern yourself with what you do not have! When you start to implement your strategy with the resources you do have, the resources you lack will begin their manifestation through different ideas. Subsequently, more ideas will begin to enter your mind. Whenever you're experiencing this process, I encourage you to start writing down your ideas for thirty minutes, every day, until you discover an idea that resonates with your heart. You will know when you have unearthed the right idea! After you discover this idea, I can promise you it will feel ironic: it will be something that was already within your reach.

Always Know When to Blame Yourself

It's so convenient to blame others, but when we do this, we often avoid addressing the real problem. For example, if someone is on parole and they continue to commit crimes after the judge has given them multiple chances to change, eventually they will be forced to serve their time. This example illustrates how someone can run out of moves that can help to control their outcomes. Sometimes, you can simply run out of chances during life's game of chess as well. Wrong decisions can even lead to death. However, it's healthy to develop the mindset that, regardless of where you may be in your life, as long as you're breathing change is always possible! Suppose someone's moves throughout their life don't lead to death, but their decisions culminate in being incarcerated for life. Although imprisoned, they could still look for ways to better themselves: they could help others to learn from their mistakes, and though it wouldn't change the reality of being in prison for life, however, it could help them to better manage their own situation. "*In reality, the only real definite move during life's game of chess is death.*" If someone is serving a life sentence, they can still *manifest their genius* by accepting responsibility for their errors and looking for ways to help others.

"*A winner is always scheming on how to win even if they're losing. If their inner realm has collapsed, they feel convinced that there is always a way to reverse their circumstances because winning is a trait that is earned, and it cannot be rewarded.*" Winning starts long before it's manifested to the public eye, and that's why it's earned! When winning becomes a personality trait for you, you will accept winning as the only option. When winning hasn't been developed and perceived as the only option, you will often hear people say things like, "I know we didn't make it to the Super Bowl, which was the goal, but that's OKAY because we still had a good season, we can always try again next year." This is noble if you truly gave it your all, but it's still a loss. Never excuse a loss by trying to make yourself feel better about how you lost. Simply accept the loss and get better and execute differently. An individual who continues to find a reward in a failed endeavor by pursuing comfort in a loss will never unleash their winning personality traits.

There is a difference in learning from failures vs. viewing failures as success. *"Failure is never success. You need to keep failing until you achieve success, but you should never celebrate trying as though you have arrived. Failure shouldn't be feared; it should be embraced and expected, but never continuously tolerated."* When winning becomes a personality trait as opposed to a rewarded achievement, you will begin to only see ways that you can win. Winning as a personality trait will never communicate expressions such as "there is always next year" and "this was my only year."

For instance, let's suppose you're sleepy, and you're thirty minutes away from a job interview, and you need this job to take care of your family. You only have three weeks until the rent is due, and if you get the job it will allow you to pay your rent on time. But remember, you're sleepy! Do you think you would pull over and take a nap, knowing you only have thirty minutes to make it on time? Probably not! You wouldn't risk not getting the job or giving it less than your best. That opportunity could be your only option and your only chance to get a job before the rent is due. So despite how sleepy you might be, you still would recognize the significance of being on time because that job might be your only way to succeed. Most importantly, I can guarantee you that you would most likely override your mind's attempts to be weak and you would show up on time, despite being extremely sleepy.

When humans are in a "do or die" state of mind, we automatically develop winning as a personality trait because we recognize what's at stake, and that there is no tomorrow. Whenever we're in this state of mind, our mindset produces *right now* as the only option! This state of mind makes winning a personality trait, and when it becomes a trait, you will always figure out a way to win. But on the contrary, winning as a rewarded state of mind looks for next year, and it says maybe the job wasn't meant for you anyway. Sometimes this is a coverup to hide our feelings about our failed attempts. In order to develop winning as a personality trait that defines you, you must identify why you need to win. A major step to winning life's game of chess is to know exactly why you're playing the game in the first place. So, always have a purpose when you want to be successful. Life is referred to as a game, but it's really not. Life isn't a joke, and the more you identify your purpose for doing something, the more you'll put the proper emotions into your endeavors. *"The main difference between winners and losers is that the winners keep doing and going until they win. They keep Just Getting Up!"*

Now Is the Time for You to Win

The best thing to remember during any type of adversity is that as long as you can breathe, you can still succeed. No matter where you are and no matter what you have done, there is still time for you to win. Simply change your perspective on what winning means for you, based on your circumstances. *"Don't quit good things, only give them up, and don't give up on bad things, always quit them."* I'm saying if you quit something good it will always be trapped in your memory of regrets. You should never quit a good thing; you should only physically let it go. However, you should always hold on to all of the good things within your mind by daily keeping them on your brain. *"As long as your dreams are constantly flowing through your mind's river, you can always throw a life vest at your dreams and bring them onto reality's surface."*

If you make the mistake of abandoning the good ideas you have within your heart, you will be reminded that you shouldn't have let those good ideas go. To quit something means to stop pursuing it holistically. This means that your life will demonstrate you aren't doing anything toward your goals mentally, physically, spiritually, emotionally, or socially. You won't talk about it, you won't feel for it, you won't act on the idea, you won't pray about it, and most importantly you won't even think about it! *"To quit a good achievable goal can lead to developing a quitter's mentality for other things. You should only quit things that are bad for you, and you should never quit anything that is good for you. Never quit a good thing: maybe let it go for a while, but always revisit it."*

The Secrets to A Winning Strategy

Suppose someone started college and dropped out with only one year remaining, and they find a job that pays more than the degree they were pursuing. The individual in this example chose not to finish their degree program because they started to feel like the degree wasn't worth it. I'll humbly acknowledge that in some situations this may be true. However, life is full of serendipity; so, your life's strategy should never follow this notion. I would say, finish the degree program because it's not a bad thing, so why quit? Never quitting a good thing is an essential personality trait that you should aim to possess. You can't rent this trait; you must buy it, and never sell your integrity by taking the easy way out. Remember, it's okay to physically let a good thing go for awhile, if that's necessary, but always revisit your good ideas. If you never quit, you won't have any quits on your mental résumé. This will help to build your character, and it teaches you that no matter how difficult an obstacle may be, you can conquer it with persistence.

Quitting a good thing indicates a lack of persistence, and you need persistence to *Just Get Up*. Someone could pose the question, "What if they dropped out of school because they couldn't afford it, and they were about to lose their house trying to pay for school? The degree wasn't a necessity because they have a job that pays them more than a degreed position." In this argument, they're suggesting it is a good thing to get a degree, but finishing the program doesn't actually impact the person's life. My response to that would be: "When you're developing a winner's mentality, you have to recognize that life's game of chess is a deeply rooted and nurturing process that you aren't always aware of." With that being said, always prepare for the unexpected. *"The expected is the true unsure thing and the unexpected is the only sure thing."*

I'll explain why the person who decides to drop out of school with only a year remaining would be better off finishing; despite the fact if he or she already has a higher paying job. For example, let's say you didn't see a need to fill up five gas containers with five gallons of gas as a safety preparation against an imminent storm. Let's suppose you were warned to evacuate as well before the storm arrives, and suppose you only live 30 feet from the gas station. So your thoughts might be, "If I have to evacuate, I'll be the first person to get to the gas station!" And it would be logical to think that way, because you know everyone will need gas. So, you acknowledge the possibility that the gas is likely to run out. However, you still say to yourself, "If I didn't live by the gas station, I would fill up in advance before the evacuation notice is given." The expected here is a sure thing; at least it appears to be. But here is a different possible outcome: tons of people could possibly show up at the gas station with or without a sudden change regarding the severity of the storm. The decision to relax in your sense of urgency could possibly result in you not getting gas from the gas station that's only 30 feet away from you.

Suppose you decided to get gas, but the gas station ran out and you realize you still have two days before you have to evacuate, so you delay in going to another gas station. The clerk at the gas station informs you that a gas truck is coming the following day to refill the gas tanks. So you decide to wait until the next day, and to fill up once the truck arrives. The clerk is aware of this, so the clerk informs all of the customers via a sign on the store's door. The sign indicates that the companies responsible for refilling their gas tanks have been instructed not to send their employees out into a possibly deadly storm. However, the sign indicates that, as of now, someone is on schedule to come the next day with gas. So now, all potential customers are aware of this as well. Now, suppose you still don't feel a need to take action, and at least go to another gas station because you're under the impression that someone is coming the next day. Also keep in mind, an evacuation warning has been given, however the storm is two days away, and it isn't expected to strike before the anticipated date.

So you relax and all of a sudden it happens: the weather prediction was wrong, and the natural disaster starts to happen. So you rush to the store, but they're out of gas. They were going to run out of gas whether you filled up in advance or not. You knew the store only had about thirty gallons of gas remaining for the day, but you decided to wait and surrender your fate to the hands of serendipity. Now you can't get gas from the store near your home, so you rush to another store. Unfortunately, you're stuck in traffic and all of the gas is gone from the nearby stores as well. The moral of this story is: there is no such thing as being too prepared. *"First-hand preparation stops all last-minute desperation."* Your mentality should always be to be prepared for the only sure thing, which is the unexpected. The unexpected is the adversary that you can never fully be prepared for; however, you can be ready for the unexpected. You should always aim to have a certain degree of mental readiness that allows you to be resourceful under unexpected circumstances. This approach will make the inevitable and difficult processes easier to cope with, while you're excogitating another strategy for success. Finally, never make any presumptuous decisions driven solely by your emotions and the possible fears of your future's possibilities.

This analogy teaches you that it would have been better for someone to finish a degree program that he or she was truly passionate about, even if it takes ten years. However, this only applies if your dream requires you to seek higher education. In this analogy, the individual could have taken one class a year, using the good money from their high-paying job to support it. On a college degree it doesn't say how long it took to earn it, it only says that you have it. If it took some people four years to get a bachelors' and it takes other people eight years, so what? The point is, they got it. Another wise thing the person in this illustration could have done from the beginning would have been to determine their passions, and determine how attaining a degree would help improve their evolving mechanisms throughout life. Remember, *evolving mechanisms* are the things that you naturally do effortlessly, and they're congruent with your personality traits. Remember this as well: It doesn't matter how much money you're making, if it's not your true passion, you will begin to feel empty.

So the real question to ask the person in this analogy would be: How could pursuing a particular degree program help you to better display your *evolving mechanisms*? If one of your *evolving mechanisms* involves giving, then you should pursue an education that will help you to learn how to better serve others. If you love giving, then pursue an eclectic educational program that involves giving. But this applies only if you desire to seek higher education.

What if the person in this analogy loses their good-paying job? If this happened and they had a degree in a field they loved, then they would have a solid backup. A solid backup could be having another ambition that didn't require a degree, or maybe an ambition that only required experience or a type of certification. Suppose the person in my analogy one day is recommended for a promotion, several years after they decided not to finish their degree. For example, let's say their current job progressed to the point where it required a degree after ten years of working. Unfortunately, the person in this analogy most likely would be denied the promotion because they don't have the necessary education required for the promotion. Furthermore, what if they got laid off because it required a degree? This could potentially happen if a new owner takes over the company. Here is the point: Are you developing a strategy for your life that will prepare you for something similar to this?

Select A Strategy That Can Evolve with Your Life

By never quitting, even if it takes you ten years to get an academic degree, you could potentially be in a ready and a prepared state. You will see further why this is a good thing, once you arrive to Chapter 12: *Numbers Don't Lie*. Furthermore, I'm not saying everyone has to go to school. But I am saying, whatever you start that's a good thing; just make sure you finish it! You should always aim not to have any quits on your mental résumé, and whenever you do have to let a good thing go or postpone it, you can always revisit it, and whenever you're pursuing the endeavor again, you will always be a step ahead of where you were when you stopped. So, it's okay to stop something temporarily, but never let it go permanently: always hold on to the dreams that are within your heart's mind. This cannot be achieved if you quit something good.

Always Be Ready and Prepared

"A quitter's mentality is out of shape and it's not conditioned to think in a winning way. You can let something go and still work toward fulfilling it. When you quit something it doesn't involve any action." An example of someone letting a good thing go without quitting would be, if someone sits out a semester to save money for school, so that

they can pay for the next semester. To further illustrate: Their goal might be to pay for school, while not having to be worried with paying back a loan. Although they aren't taking any classes, they're still making decisions that will eventually bring into fruition the things they seemingly let go. *"We can physically let go of our dreams at times, but always mentally hold on to them."* When you master how to do this, you won't have any quits in your life's column of quits. You will know that you can and that you must do whatever it takes to succeed.

So always take in knowledge, so that you can gain understanding that will eventually lead to wisdom. Life's game of chess is a mentality that you must learn and master if you truly want to learn how to play and win! Most importantly, not knowing how to win is an excuse that can no longer be tolerated! Once you commit to the important decision to never quit something worthwhile, it will eventually convert your newly acquired winning trait into a standard. What are your standards? The next chapter will discuss this.

CHAPTER 7

VALUES, RITUALS, CORE VALUES, AND STANDARDS

Complete the exercises below, before you begin reading this chapter.

1. In one sentence, write down what values mean to you.

2. In five words, describe what rituals mean to you. (*Hint: the correct answer contains five words and it starts with these two words*: The things.)

3. What do you think is the difference between values and core values?

4. Solve for x, x = standards. Values (rituals + core values) = x

5. Develop your personal philosophy on life. Sum up your philosophy in 3-4 sentences. When creating your philosophy,

encompass the holistic mindset by focusing on your spiritual, emotional, cognitive, physical, and social domains of life. Refer back to Chapter 4 to refresh your memory on *The Holistic Approach,* if necessary. After you develop your philosophy, read it every morning before you start your day. Also, before you develop your philosophy, I recommend that you read at least one chapter from Proverbs, Ecclesiastes, and Psalms. Read the entire chapter of Matthew, Chapter 7. Finally, I recommend making it a goal to read a chapter of God's word every day, and meditate on it.

Here is an example of my personal philosophy on life: "*To constantly strive to evolve spiritually, emotionally, socially, mentally, and physically. My aim is to live my life in a way that creates value for others. I believe it's important to acquire wisdom by surrendering my life to God. In the end, I'm defined by the positive elements I leave behind.*"

I know you're progressing well throughout your journey, and you've reached a defining moment in your journey. The previous chapter demonstrated how tricky life can be. Life can be hard, like a game of chess. This chapter is important for your integrity. This chapter will teach you how to win with a sense of pride. As you begin to digest the nutrients from this chapter, it will help you to appreciate why having a personal philosophy is important. Your philosophy dictates the story you tell yourself and how you view your life. If your philosophy is bad, you will develop the wrong standards to put into action. This chapter will help you to develop the proper code of ethics for yourself. You will need that personal code of ethics to complete your journey and arrive at your dream's destination!

Always Have the Proper Takeoff

Would you board a plane that could only guarantee you a proper takeoff and not a safe flight? To arrive safely at a destination via an airplane requires more than just a proper takeoff. However, without a proper takeoff, the plane will never take flight. How will your flight's takeoff begin when you take flight? If you have poor values, the offspring of your values will be standards that can't maintain flight. To illustrate: Suppose a pilot's flight repertoire consists of traveling to six different destinations every day for an airline. Do you think the pilot could repeatedly arrive at his or her destinations without the proper maintenance of the plane? Do you think a plane can fly to several destinations throughout the day without continuing to refuel with the proper gasoline? If a pilot attempted to take a plane to several destinations every day without respecting the importance of maintaining the plane, I can guarantee you the plane would eventually crash.

Without the appropriate maintenance of an airplane, a proper takeoff will be compromised, which will lead to a crash. Do you think that a plane can continue to have a safe takeoff without constant maintenance? Would you chance getting on a plane that you knew wasn't working properly? Would you leave your life in the hands of serendipity? Of course not! Why would anyone knowingly fly their lives to a path that's unproductive? Your life is at stake! You want the plane that you're traveling on to work properly, just like you want your life to work properly. However, if you don't properly maintain your mind, it will result in a crash! Do you think a plane can take flight and soar for hours without enough fuel? Do you think you can continue, or begin to soar in life, without daily or perhaps hourly refills of determination?

If you nurture the proper values, you won't waste your time pursuing pointless goals. When you develop standards from a good value system, it will enable you to make wise decisions. In the flight analogy, the proper take-off represents your values, and the actual air flight represents your standards. Your standards are similar: if your values aren't constantly maintained with regular and daily refills, your standards will run out of gas, and your motivation will crash.

You must aim to never have a bad takeoff! So don't allow your motivation to crash because you decided not to prepare properly! Never allow your dreams to become a figment of your imagination! Your dreams are real and they're awaiting their fulfillment through you! Have you ever felt like you've been moved to do something, but nothing happened? *"If you go through life with "I should have" and "I could have" too long, guess what? You will become the opposite of what you should and could have become. Which is? Nothing at all! It's so easy to feel, and then press the button to turn off your emotions as if your feelings aren't attached to your emotions".* What does this mean? To illustrate, let's say you're in a relationship, and your significant other made a mistake: they forgot to say, "I love you" one night. After that incident you ended the relationship. Do you think this is a legitimate reason to end a relationship? Let's go a step further. Suppose the person said: "I love you" every night. But for some reason they forgot to say it one night or maybe several nights. Would you actually end a relationship over someone's minor imperfections? I can assure you, if you truly love someone, you won't end the relationship because they forgot to say, "I love you." The normal thing to do would be to talk about it, and express how important it is to say, "I love you" to one another each night. Or, you could simply overlook the matter, and just attribute it to human nature. The reality of the matter is if someone ended a relationship over something minor, then maybe they wanted out of it anyway.

We can easily become guilty of searching for anything to complain about so that we can more easily end something we might unconsciously or consciously want to get out of anyway. Someone who cares for you wouldn't turn off their emotions over something petty. In fact, it's possible for a romantic love to be so strong that, even if someone committed the ultimate betrayal, they could still be forgiven. The ultimate betrayal is cheating on your spouse, of course. However, forgiveness would only be possible if the innocent mate is willing to overlook the iniquity. If people can remain in love after infidelity, then people should be able to continue to love one another, and overlook any minor flaws. When you truly love something or someone, you can't just turn off how you feel, because true love controls your feelings, and it's not the other way around.

If you ever get to a point where you're able to continuously turn off your heart and mind from acting upon your goals, then this simply means that something is causing you not to have an intense desire to accomplish your goals. You must keep your flame going and keep dating your dreams. Temptations will always arise and tempt you to cheat on your dreams. One of these temptations can be caused by taking on unnecessary responsibilities that may cause your relationship with your dreams to die. *"The grass isn't greener on the other side unless it's with the dreams you love."* This is why you need standards: without standards you're like a GPS that doesn't have internet or satellite. A GPS can't work properly without its connections. Your goals are the GPS, and your standards represent the satellite and internet connections. It's important to know that goals inherently have directions because goals are meant to evolve! *"Any goal without action to bring it to life is as empty as 'I love you' without action."* Can a GPS work without internet and satellite connections? The answer is no! Can your goals be met without values, rituals, core values, and standards? The answer is yes! But it won't be the goals you want. Your rituals are *"The Things You Do Every Day."* A GPS is good, but if it doesn't work, it's useless. Goals are good, but if they don't work they're useless, and a waste of direction. If you use a GPS that doesn't work properly, it will guide you in the wrong direction. So never develop the wrong standards, because they will mislead you!

Self-Analysis

You have to reevaluate your values because they will dictate your rituals. Your rituals will develop into your core values, which will eventually become your standards. Values and standards force you to adhere to the things that are necessary to accomplish your goals. In the previous chapter we discussed taking in knowledge, understanding, and wisdom. For emphasis: you must master how to successfully implement this three-step process, which is *knowledge, understanding, and wisdom,* before you can adequately develop your standards.

Your standards are derived from your values, and any area in your life that you desire to be great in will require goals. After your goals are set, you must have directions for how to attain them. Once you have done this, take in knowledge about your goals. Subsequently, commit to understanding the knowledge you have attained that pertains to your goals. Most importantly, fully commit to understanding the process of how to reach your goals.

Sometimes, knowing exactly how to attain a goal doesn't always lead to action. For example, someone may know how and what they need to do to lose weight, but the knowledge alone doesn't lead to action. Knowledge and understanding doesn't always result in someone taking action. You need to have values attached to your knowledge and understanding, which is wisdom. When you develop your values, it will progress into standards. How motivated you are depends on the foundation of your values. If you develop poor values from the knowledge, understanding, and wisdom you accumulate, then your values will be poor as well.

For instance, if someone's value is to cheat on tests, and manipulate other people to get what they want, then their values lack integrity. An individual similar to the one I'm describing would eventually become someone who cheats their way through life. However, if they're able to have the proper intervention, then this negative value can be reversed before it progresses. If anyone nurtures the value of cheating, it will become a core value. If something becomes a core value for anyone, it will be demonstrated in other aspects of their lives. So it's always best to address any bad values before they become core values. If a developing value fully develops into a core value without an early intervention, then the developing core value will most certainly become a standard.

Once a core value becomes a standard it will dictate your actions and how you think. If anyone develops bad standards, they will have a bad philosophy on life. Some people never capture their dreams because they have bad standards. *Having bad standards doesn't make someone a bad person; it just means that their standards may be bad for the person they're trying to become.* Your values dictate how you see yourself through the world's eyes. You shouldn't care if people believe in you or if they doubt you, but you should care about how others view your values and standards. Values are the kiddie version of your standards, and standards are the adult version that your values grow into. Remember this: values are easily reversible and standards are not!

The Developmental Philosophy of Standards

The development of any mental construct, whether it's abstract or concrete, will eventually give birth to your standards. Once a mental ideology is nurtured into a standard, it will become very hard to change. The mental construct I'm referring to can only be developed from exposure to various elements of life. These elements will ultimately shape or reshape how you think. These elements can be good things or bad things. To illustrate: Think about the process of growing a plant. A plant will grow based on how the seeds are sown and fertilized and. The seeds won't grow if you plant bad seeds with poor fertilization, a lack of water, and too little sunlight.

However, if you plant the right seeds along with the proper fertilization, sunlight, and water, then the plant will grow. A mental construct is the same: whatever you surround yourself with will dictate the type of seeds you're fertilizing for growth. However, a mental construct differs from a plant in this way: a plant will only grow if you nurture it properly, but a mental construct will grow regardless of what you do to it. So the question that must be asked is this: "Are you growing and producing the results you're looking for in your life?" Always pay attention to your environment, and always control your environment, so that you can grow the proper seeds for motivation.

The Development Process of Standards

Your values are like a single cell and they simply start the process for cell growth. However, eventually a cell turns into billions of other cells for the same purpose. As your values are nurtured by adding more figurative cells to them, eventually your values will become a standard that's almost irreversible. Wouldn't you agree that it's easier to reverse 500 cells compared to 5,000, 50,000, 500,000, or 5,000,000? Once a cell evolves massively it's almost impossible to reverse the cell's preponderance. However, it will always be possible to reverse the cell, even if the percentage is less than one percent. Sometimes, all you need is a small percentage of hope and you can still get the job done.

The process is similar to any cancer that spreads. Once the cancer progresses to a certain stage it is irreversible. However, there are several cases where a doctor informs a patient that they only have a certain time to live but their analysis is grossly wrong. So, if someone is ever in a seemingly doomed state, why not just hope for the best, since technically the individual doesn't have anything to lose anyway? There have been a plethora of cases where the person who gave up mentally, spiritually, emotionally, and physically died sooner than expected, compared to the person who believed that they could conquer their morbidities. So, long story short, no one really knows life's possibilities, so always be positive when under duress.

To further illustrate the development of standards, let's compare the development of values to your DNA. Once a cell containing DNA gives birth to other cells, the cells will continue to develop based on the genetic code that was programmed during the fertilization process. Remember your DNA strands consist of forty-six chromosomes that come from your parents. And you receive twenty-three from your mom and twenty-three from your dad. This preset genetic code will dictate all of your features and your structure. You can only enhance the genes you were given and you can't reverse them. This is why some people naturally have certain genetic structures that are desirable. For example, some guys naturally have broad shoulders and when they lift weights for their shoulders, their shoulders will develop quicker than someone who doesn't have the same genes. However, that doesn't mean that someone with narrow shoulders can't develop their shoulders, it just means that they will have to work harder.

Let's compare your chromosomes to your values. If you never have an intervention to fix any bad values that you have formed, then they will become harder to reverse as the years progress. The process is similar to old age; the guy who has bad genes for his shoulders will have to work even harder as he gets older, especially if he wants to enhance his shoulders, despite the fact that he is predisposed to genetically not have wide bones in his shoulders and back. For emphasis, these bones are the acromion process, carotid process, and the scapula bones. To continue with this analogy, it's only fitting to compare this scenario to someone who has shaped bad values for twenty-five years, and to contrast them with someone who has only shaped bad values for five years. Who do you think will have to work harder to reshape their values? That's why it's critical for you to start your intervention process right away, so that you can reverse any bad values that you may have unconsciously formed throughout your life. This is why it's so important for you to have a proper takeoff, from the start to the finish of your decision to bring your dreams into fruition! You must give your figurative genetic cells, or values, the proper knowledge, understanding, and wisdom during their rudimentary stages.

If you currently don't have great values, then they must be reshaped before they become your core values. *"Bad values are living mental organisms that must be reshaped!"* Do not allow your mental DNA to keep adding thousands, millions, or even billions of figurative bad cells or values because, if you aren't vigilant, the process may become irreversible. It's exactly like fat cells; the amount of fat cells you develop as kid dictates how many you will have as an adult. When people lose weight, their actual number of fat cells doesn't decrease, it's just the size of their fat cells that decreases. Someone who has one billion fat cells will always have one billion fat cells; only the diameter and circumference of fat cells can change. Someone who has one billion fat cells will always have a higher proclivity to gain weight than the person with one million fat cells. People with more fat cells will have more of a struggle throughout their life to maintain their body composition. The same is true, figuratively speaking, in relation to the values you formed during your upbringing. If you allow your values to evolve over the years unproductively, your figurative mental DNA will produce unproductive standards/paradigms. These standards will become a part of your living mental organisms and they will infiltrate your ability to develop productive standards. Your living mental organisms, or the thoughts that are formed from your experiences, represent your cells. Most importantly, these cells are synonymous with your values.

However, just like losing weight decreases the size of your fat cells, you can do the same with your values. It's important to remember that you can't decrease the number of values that you have formed in your mind, just like you can't decrease the number of fat cells that you have formed. What you can do is decrease the effectiveness of any bad values by lowering their ability to affect your life. You can achieve this by exercising your mind, and by eliminating all of the things that cause your negative values to outweigh the positive ones. If eating fatty foods expands your fat cells, then you must stay away from fatty foods. If your environment nurtures negatives values, such as looking for the easy way out, then you must surround yourself with people who are hard workers. If you implement this it will suppress any negative values, and your negatives values will become so small in size that they will be forced to become inactive.

Any bad values that you may have formed from your past experiences will always be in your subconscious mind. However, they will never be awakened again unless you dwell on them. Just like fat cells remain small through eating properly and exercising, the same will be true for any nefarious values that you may have formed in your life. If you continue to exercise your mind, eventually you will begin to suppress any and all of your unproductive values. So, continue to take action and always look for ways to grow your mind! "*You should never feel like you don't have to keep working and fighting to be great. When you decide to Just Get Up, you must to do it forever, or you will eventually return to being the person you worked so hard to defeat.*"

Your values and how they're applied will affect your goals. For example, if you want to get into shape, then you should go to the gym! However, your values will determine if you don't have time or if you will make time! If someone wanted a new promotion that requires an academic degree, then they should stop wishing they had stayed in school. Instead, they should go back to school! Do you see how damaging it can be if someone's values are based on regrets? It can lead to acceptance and passivity and years of inaction, which will be accompanied by years of remorse, that will break anyone's spirit. In Chapter 6, you learned that the term "zugzwang" is a position during a game of chess where you're forced to make a disadvantaged move. So, don't ever allow your lack of vision to force you to make or take disadvantaged moves.

How To Develop The Proper Values

One of the secrets to elevating your values, and changing how you see yourself, is to talk about your goals every day, and thus speak into existence the things that you want to have. (*Read Hebrews 11;1 and verse 6 every day*) You can have a conversation every day with yourself, silently, because no one has to know that you're reviewing your goals every day. Reviewing your goals every day will also help to strengthen your belief in your ability to attain your goals. Remember this: How will others begin to believe, if you don't believe it first? It's life's job to doubt you, however, it's your job to eliminate the doubt! Life will always test you to see if you truly desire to do the things that you're declaring. And most importantly, you must aim to develop the habit of never blaming other people for anything that may or may not come your way!

So always ask yourself, "What have I done lately to help make my dreams a reality?" Most importantly, ask yourself, "What have I not done lately that's essential for achieving my goals?" The first step to altering your standards is to accept your current standards. If you can't see that you have a problem, then you won't be able to change the problem.

Changing How You Think Is Challenging

The human mind is very hard to change; in fact, some would argue that it is the hardest thing in the world to change. For example, although exercising is primarily a physical adaptation, the mental aspect is the most important thing associated with exercising, because if you quit mentally, then the physical will most certainly follow the path of your mind. It's proven that before changes are noticed in the physical domain, the spiritual and mental domains must first desire change. With that being said, you must train yourself to know your emotional whys and you must exhaust all of the unexplored help that's available to you. The most important role for shaping and reshaping your standards is to constantly evaluate and reevaluate your rituals. Remember, rituals are *The Things You Do Every Day*!

Do your actions show that your values are attached to your goals? That might seem arbitrary, but once you fully comprehend that you're your own worst opponent, it will make sense. Your actions hold the key to your status in life, and your actions influence how you pursue your greatness. Actions start off as feelings and they eventually become living mental organisms. Your thoughts and feelings can only manifest actions that are congruent with your thoughts. For example, if you think you're a loser, you will begin to act like one. If you grew up around go-getters, guess what? You're more likely to have that emotional resolve as well.

During the development process of our lives, we shape our core values based on the things we are exposed to. As an example, if you grew up in a household where your father and mother worked hard to stress education, you will more than likely feel that way as well, once you're an adult. However, there are exceptions. I'm sure you can think of plenty of children who have chosen a wayward course for their lives. Many people ask, "How could a child be brought up in a great household, and yet they still pursued a wayward course? What happened?" The answer is that a child will be exposed to things other than home life that can shape their thoughts, too. Often these other things are negative and immoral. Remember, children are born not knowing anything. Ivan Pavlov established the classical conditioning theory, proving that people can be conditioned. The child may have seen the opposite of what their parents were trying to instill in them from other children, teachers, television, radio, internet, books, and other family members. Unfortunately, negative experiences have a higher likelihood to corrupt the good experiences. If this happens, your mind will be negatively conditioned. However, the good news is that you can use counter and operant conditioning to undo and change negative mindsets. Most importantly, I recommend that you research Ivan Pavlov and explore his scientific and fact-based discoveries regarding counter and operant conditioning.

You Must Devalue Your Fears To
Successfully Reshape Your Values

The formation of values can be compared to a fetus that grows to become a newborn baby. All values will continue to develop throughout your lifespan, and it doesn't matter if they're productive or unproductive values. For example, a child who starts to display feelings of apathy toward a particular experience may become apathetic as an adult, unless the mental construct is interrupted. For example, if a child is apathetic toward homeless people, then more than likely the child will feel that way as an adult. Now, I'm not saying we can't change our feelings. I'm saying it's very hard to change our values toward something after our feelings have grown from a figurative fetus, and into a newborn.

Are you set in your ways? Do you tell yourself "I have always been like this"? If you tell yourself negative things like that, and then say "I'm just a realist," unfortunately your reality will remain the same. Start being the person that you want to be and not the shadow of who you are. You're unlikely to change if you tell yourself that you can't. In fact, I can guarantee you that you won't change unless you change the story you're telling yourself. Change is always possible! Do not allow yourself to be stuck in your ways! That's a victim mentality. What are you doing every day to work on your goals? Do you have a schedule?

For centuries, mankind assumed the earth was flat, and this belief became a part of their values. This was considered "truth," until the belief that the world was flat was challenged. And, it was later proven that the earth is definitely a ball. So what happened here? Why did people change their strongly entrenched beliefs on a matter they thought was true? I'll tell you what happened: science proved that the belief was false, and that's how the irrevocable changed. However, some people still didn't accept the facts of science during the Christopher Columbus era, and that's true even today: using all of the facts, you can expose truth to someone and they still may not accept it. But please don't be or become this type of person because if you do, I can promise you that you will never achieve your goals!

Always Be Humble

Humility is a key attribute to have when you're developing your standards. Anything that helps you to get better you should view as a gem. Reshaping your thinking is essential for developing new standards, but just because you have standards, it doesn't mean they're the standards you will need for success. So always be humble and never think you know everything.

Examining Your Rituals Is Important

The values that we nurture are achieved through our daily rituals and they subconsciously evolve into our morals and standards. If you don't constantly examine your rituals, you will become a victim of portraying the norms of society. Most of the things we do are governed by laws and principles. If you don't think so, I would love to see you drive by a police officer pushing 100 miles an hour. Laws and principles are quintessentially one and the same; however, they aren't exactly the same. Allow me to explain! God's word has tons of laws and principles that are completely accurate when we follow them. You can't go wrong by using God's word to help you shape your standards. An example of this is The Golden Rule, which is a principle mentioned at Matthew 7:12 and it states, "All things, therefore, that you want men to do to you, you also must do to them." Before a married person cheats, other things will happen first, such as flirting. Fornication is the law that is broken if someone cheats, but the principle of treating others the way that you would want to be treated would have to be broken first, before the law of committing fornication is broken. So, if the cheater had implemented Matthew 7:12, they would have reasoned that it's not okay to flirt because they wouldn't want their mate flirting. Most people who are in a relationship view flirting with someone who isn't their partner as disrespectful. And flirting can lead to other things.

Galatians 6:7 however, is another law and this verse states, "You reap what you sow" so if you plant orange seeds you will reap oranges. Please live according to this law, because the work you put in is what you will get out. Do not convince yourself that, if it didn't work out, then it wasn't meant for you. Maybe you didn't accurately sow the proper seeds? Chapter 12, *Numbers Don't Lie,* will provide more details to help you see if you're sowing the proper seeds.

Do or Die Should Be Your Strongest Standard

"Stop dating your dreams and go certify your true love by marrying your dreams." You can have exactly what you want in life, and it all starts with your standards. For example, if someone's standard is to

eat unhealthy foods and never develop a health plan, then they should expect to be unhealthy. The goal of getting in shape as an example isn't good enough. If you have misguided standards on health and fitness, such as eating unhealthy things, and not exercising at the proper intensity, you won't get any results. You may have the goal of getting in shape; but if your standard toward a goal is built on a poor foundation, you won't achieve the goal. When someone is truly trying to get into shape, and they fully understand that their previous methods won't work, they will abandon their old form of thinking and adopt the correct form of thinking. They will stop trying to make something work that clearly doesn't work, and if they don't stop, no results will be achieved. This is why you must have a good philosophy: because it's the foundation to your success. It's not about what's the right or wrong way; it's about the science and what actually works. You can have excuses or you can have results, but you can't have both. Standards always get met, but goals don't. You have to change your values and rituals by taking in new information, along with being humble enough to accept any clear signs that change is necessary.

For example, all professional sports teams have the goal of winning each game, but their standards dictate the validity of this goal. More than likely, a team will not win every single game, so the goal isn't always attained. However, suppose a team's standard is hard work, which can be achieved in a win or a loss. So the standard of working hard can always be achieved, regardless of whether or not you achieve the ultimate goal of winning.

So, what are your standards? Notice these examples to further illustrate the application of standards in real life situations. Suppose someone is in a bad relationship and they choose not to change it; then, that's their standard. If someone isn't in shape and they choose to do nothing to change it, then that's their standard. You may be wondering how to determine what your standards should be. The first thing you should ask yourself is, "Why do I need standards?" After considering this information the answer is simple. You need standards to identify who you truly are, and what you truly stand for. Without this identity, your actions will become weak, ultimately allowing you to lower your expectations, and your accountability. If you're struggling with motivation, and you don't have the proper standards, then your motivation will be empty. Finally, just do the simple and positive things every day that will help you to accomplish your goals! For something to become a standard you need to work on it continuously. It's important for you to focus on your standards so that you can capture your dreams.

How To Change Your Standards

Implement the Strategy Below to Form the Proper Values, Rituals, Core Values, and Standards

Change your values by increasing and altering your knowledge about yourself, your association, your work ethic, and your morals. Read, write, listen, and visualize positive things every day that are in harmony with your dreams. Start the first thirty minutes of your day with something positive. For example, you can read the Bible, pray, and visualize yourself achieving your goals. Seek to do something nice for someone every day, and it doesn't have to involve money. Do massive amounts of work and schedule time for relaxation and fun. Start off small and focus on the first steps that you can take tomorrow, rather than the steps that might be a year away.

This is an established saying, but I'm adding my own twist to it. *"The future belongs to those who do the work today for it; it doesn't belong to those who worry about it and doubt it."* Worrying won't change anything or add a day to your life. If you don't have a schedule, make one and stick to it by all means. Do not think about your goals and work when you're enjoying your recreational time. Keep these things separate! Before bedtime, take three minutes to review your goals for the next day and pray about them. Do weekly, monthly, and quarterly checkups to track your progression, and if you're stagnant, then make the necessary adjustments. The next chapter will help you to learn about the four main types of goals and why they are important.

CHAPTER 8

RELATIVE/ABSOLUTE VS. ABSOLUTE/ RELATIVE GOALS

WHAT TYPES OF GOALS ARE needed to fulfill your dreams? There are four main types of goals: *absolute, relative, relative/absolute,* and *absolute/relative goals.* It's imperative that you understand the differences between these goals. An example of an absolute goal would be to run a marathon in three hours or less. If someone had a goal to do this, then they would need to find out how much exercise is needed, what types of exercises are needed, how to eat, and the appropriate exercise intensities. If the proper method for attaining an absolute goal of running a marathon in less than three hours is properly implemented, I can guarantee that the person who sets this goal will achieve it. However, it's important to know that corollaries can unfold during the course of any goal, and they can possibly disrupt a goal's fulfillment. But if someone is fully determined to achieve an absolute goal, then they will! Finally, you must possess the proper faculties and aptitudes to bring certain goals into fruition. Remember, don't try and be a singer if you sound like a tractor.

An absolute goal is a goal that you have 100% direct control over, and only you can dictate the outcome. Some more examples of how absolute goals can be applied are: the person you choose to marry, your health/fitness lifestyle, your relationship with God, most jobs, your actions, and how you live your life. It's absolute because only you can control the outcome and how the goal is implemented. In relation to marriage, you probably can't control the outcome of the relationship, but you can control who you marry, unless you live in a culture where your marriage mate is picked for you. However, the individual who complies with this tradition still would have to make the decision to comply with the tradition. So the outcome is still within their control.

A relative goal, on the other hand, involves a reasonable degree of good fortune and it's primarily at the discretion of other people. For example, there are a lot of athletes who are talented enough to play a professional sport; however, everyone won't make it because of the arbitrary nature of the business. Only a few slots are open for athletes in any professional sport. As an example, the NBA only has room for about 500 players for each season, but all around the world, millions are chasing this dream each year, and out of the millions only a few thousand are actually given the opportunity to try out.

Do you think all of the hopefuls who aspire to play in the NBA will make it, if the league can only accommodate 500 players? Here are some of the possible corollaries that an athlete may experience: sometimes, athletes don't get the exposure they need, and sometimes athletes have bad performances when the scouts come to examine their skills. It's possible that an athlete can work very hard, and have the abilities necessary to play professionally, and somehow they're still overlooked. So, an athlete's fate is reasonably at the discretion of others. I phrased it as reasonably at the discretion of others because athletes can still contribute to their fates, and perhaps, even manhandle their outcomes.

In order for an athlete to have full control over their draft prospects, and whether or not they're traded, would require the athlete to be the one who has the final say-so. However, athletes can't directly control whether they're drafted or traded. And it's known that professional athletes work for the coaches and the owners of the teams. So it's important to understand that a goal can have some features that are absolute, and a goal can have some features that are relative. All goals have tangibles and intangibles that are embedded into the quintessence of goals. So it's imperative and helpful for you to know when a goal is eighty percent absolute and twenty percent relative. Also, you should know whether a goal is seventy-five percent relative and twenty-five percent absolute. If a goal's components has relative and absolute features, then its *absolute/relative* or *relative/absolute*. If a goal is mostly absolute with a few relative components, then it's an *absolute/relative goal*. If a goal is mostly relative with a few absolute components, then it's a *relative/absolute goal*. *Most importantly, a relative goal can never be 100% relative, but an absolute goal can be 100% absolute.*

A couple of examples of *absolute/relative goals* are all self-employment jobs, and all sales jobs. Examples of *relative/absolute goals* are all sports jobs, all entertainment jobs, and anything involving the sole discretion of others, which means you can't directly control the outcome. A goal that is mainly relative means you can do everything right, and still not achieve the desired outcome, and an example of a goal like this would be to be elected to a political office. Just because a political candidate didn't win their campaign doesn't mean they didn't run a great or perhaps a better campaign than their opponent. In sports, sometimes the best team doesn't always win. Sometimes it's all about timing, so anything that involves others will always be relative, to a degree. The only way something can be 100% absolute is if you and only you have 100% complete control of dictating the desired outcome. An example of a goal that's 100% absolute is getting in shape, and eating properly.

Know The Statistics and The Probability of Your Goals

It's imperative that you understand the concept of statistics and probability as you're setting your goals, especially if your goals have relative components. Understanding statistics/probability and their correlation to *The Holistic Approach* is necessary if you're going to use your standards to guide your goals. *Relative, absolute, relative/absolute,* and *absolute/relative goals* can be set in each domain of *The Holistic Approach*. To effectively achieve your goals you must know the statistics and the probability of a goal. For example, if someone wanted to be a professional football player, then they should research and study the position that they want to play. They should find out what scouts look for, and how to improve their game. They should gather all of the information that they possibly can, and then form a plan similar to what their successful predecessors followed. Most importantly, you should always be prepared to go the extra mile by doing more than your predecessors. If one of your predecessors became successful by practicing for two hours every day, then you should do two and a half. This would be a good format, but it's still a relative goal, so your mindset toward a relative goal should always be accompanied with an absolute goal. The implementation of this format will help you to have an alternative route for your life, being that a relative goal can be very risky, unless it has absolute components. *"Regardless of how risky a goal may seem, if it's in your heart to do it, then you must go for it!"*

My aim is to set you up for success by explaining the different types of goals, especially if your goals contain a large number of relative components. The format that will be discussed in Chapter 9 will help you to discover your true passions, even if a *relative/ absolute goal* such as becoming a professional athlete doesn't go as planned. The format discussed in Chapter 9 will help you to see that there is something else you probably were called to do that's associated in the same field that sparks your interest.

When you're pursuing a goal, you should always aim to know the statistics and probability. Also, you should research how you measure up to other people who have become successful doing what you want to do. However, just because someone doesn't measure up from a statistically and opinionated perspective, doesn't mean they can't revolutionize a relative goal. That's the beauty about relative goals! You can always defy whatever the statistics and probabilities are. *Remember this: it's a privilege and a huge accomplishment to be the first person ever to do something that has never been done before.*

Don't allow any systematic biases to sway you if you pursue a relative goal. If you know you're good enough despite what the stats show, if you're willing to do the work and sweat tears for your dreams, who has the right to tell you what you can or cannot do? It's your dream, so you have to make it happen! However, just always remember: if a goal isn't 100% absolute, then a part of your goal's achievement will be at someone else's discretion. For example, an athlete may not make it to the pros, but their hard work could earn them a job as a sports commentator, coach, gym owner, or related profession. If you properly invest in a relative goal, and accompany the relative goal with an absolute goal, it will lead to phenomenal things. However, you must be consistently patient to discover the truth of this ongoing process. Chapter 9 will introduce to you *The 27-Month Plan,* along with the ideology of its format, and how you should use the plan's format to successfully capture your dreams. *The 27-Month Plan* is the format I used to become successful, and to discover my path to greatness.

Your self-development process is about to take on an entirely different meaning, so keep reading, and prepare your heart's mind for Chapter 9 as you begin the process of learning how to develop your genius, so that you can give birth to your dreams!

CHAPTER 9

DEVELOP YOUR GENIUS TO GIVE BIRTH TO YOUR DREAMS

TAKE A MOMENT AND LOOK at the table below and examine it. You will see it again in the middle of this chapter. As you read through this chapter you will begin to understand what Table 2.2 represents, and how to use my *27-Month Plan* to help you to discover your true passions.

The 27-Month Plan

TABLE 2.2

Genders/ Babies (dreams/careers)	First Trimester (months 1-3) Focus:	Second Trimester (months 4-6) Focus:	Third Trimester (months 7-9) Focus:
(1) Basketball player (2) Basketball coach (3) Basketball scout	*Frequency and knowledge*	*Duration and understanding*	*Intensity and wisdom*

1.Basketball player	First month (Basketball player) Second month (Basketball coach) Third month (Basketball scout)	Fourth month (Basketball player) Fifth month (Basketball coach) Sixth month (Basketball scout)	Seventh month (Basketball player) Eighth month (Basketball coach) Ninth month (Basketball scout)
2. Basketball coach	First month (Basketball coach) Second month (Basketball player) Third month (Basketball scout)	Fourth month (Basketball coach) Fifth month (Basketball player) Sixth month (Basketball scout)	Seventh month (Basketball coach) Eighth month (Basketball player) Ninth month (Basketball scout)
3. Basketball scout	First month (Basketball scout) Second month (Basketball coach) Third month (Basketball player)	Fourth month (Basketball scout) Fifth month (Basketball coach) Sixth month (Basketball player)	Seventh month (Basketball scout) Eighth month (Basketball coach) Ninth month (Basketball player)

I want you to take five or ten minutes and write down everything you've quit from your past. Write down the good things and the bad things! For example, if you ended a relationship that was toxic, write that down. If you stopped an addictive habit such as smoking, write that down. If you lost weight from working out, and then you stopped working out, write that down. If you were eating healthy, and you stopped, write that down. After you've completed the above exercises, I want you to write down your potentials as well. The potentials are things that you may have desired to do in the past, but for some reason you just never pursued them. After you write down your potentials, you should write down your dreams on the same sheet of paper as well. Subsequently, I want you to write down three ways you plan to manifest your dreams. As an example, if you want to be a singer, you would write down three different ways you can be a singer. If you want to open a restaurant, you should write down three types of restaurants you want to open. If you want to get in shape, you should write down three ways you plan to start the process of getting into shape.

Your Dreams Are Headed Your Way

What I'm about to discuss is paramount to developing your genius. Whether you're a woman or a man, I want you to imagine that you're a soon to be parent. I want you to imagine you're expecting triplets, and the triplets you're pregnant with are your dreams and ideas. Your dreams and ideas represent your babies! But in order for you to manifest your true genius, you must first develop your genius, so that you can give birth to your dreams!

Research has proven that there is a timeline during pregnancy for labor and for the birth of a newborn. Doctors will normally give someone who is pregnant an expected delivery date for the birth of their baby. A doctor normally informs the parents when the pregnancy started and they usually indicate that it'll be about a nine-month process. The baby may be born sooner or later than the doctor's projection; however, the doctor, family, and the parents all have a responsibility to help give birth to the baby. The pregnancy process is comparable to how dreams are formed. Sometimes we don't realize we're pregnant with ideas until we sit down and reflect on the things we really want out of life. Whether you have been trying to give birth to your dreams, or you have already started the process and you haven't realized it yet no longer matters. All that matters is that you know how to develop your dreams!

Here is an interesting aspect about pregnancy: after the baby is born, you still have to do a lot of things to develop the baby. You might wonder how tall your babies will be and what type of personality your babies will have. However, you will never arrive at these stages without first raising your babies and taking care of these children. Your dreams are the same way, so nurture your dreams, and raise them in the same way that you would raise newborns. Just because parents don't know the genders of their babies during the early stages of pregnancy and just because they don't know the qualities their babies will have when they grow up, doesn't mean that they will never know. The only thing that's certain during pregnancy for soon-to-be parents is the pregnancy. So likewise, as you're developing your genius, all you need to know is that your dreams are certain, despite the fact that your dreams' true identities will take time before their true paths are fully identified.

You Don't Have To Know Everything To Start Developing Your Dreams

Let's suppose a guy named Sam wants to earn one million dollars by starting a restaurant business. However, Sam will never have the possibility to make one million dollars by owning a restaurant until he actually opens a restaurant, right? Furthermore, suppose Sam decides not to pursue his dream to open a restaurant because he is scared he won't be able to provide for his family if his business venture fails. If you truly desire to find your true passions, you must be fearless, and you must be willing to take all of the risks that may be necessary to give birth to your dreams. So rather than drown in the fear of the unknown, it would be healthier, and more beneficial, for Sam to have patience, similar to parents who are expecting a child, especially if he really wants to make one million dollars. Here is the point of this illustration: you must accept that whenever you start to manifest your greatness, and fight against life, not everything will go as planned. Patience is essential for nurturing a baby prior to a baby's birth, because that's a nine-month process. So, it would be natural to be concerned about certain things regarding the successful arrival of a baby. However, fear is unlikely to stop an excited parent from going through with the pregnancy process, and giving birth to their baby.

How to Begin to Nurture Your Dreams

No loving parent who really wants to have a child would give up on their child if they wanted a girl and ended up with a boy. Your dreams are the same way, so who really knows what's going to happen once your dreams are born? Maybe having a boy instead of a girl would actually be better. Most importantly, how could an expecting parent really know if it would be better to have a girl or a boy?

A soon-to-be parent may have a preference for a boy or a girl, but regardless of the outcome they would be happy either way because the main thing was to get pregnant and have a child. Likewise, when you're implementing *The 27-Month Plan*, the most important thing for you to do is to dream, and to pursue the three dreams you're passionate about. It doesn't matter which direction you take because either route will take you where you want to go, or into another direction within the same field. *The 27-Month Plan* only works if you truly know the things you desire, and if you have a clear vision of where you want to go. Remember: do not be afraid to speak into action the things you're truly passionate and compassionate about. Always be true to who you truly are, whenever you're developing your genius, so that you can give birth to the proper dreams.

Complementary Goals

Create a separate category for three goals you want to achieve. However, keep this is mind: your complementary goals aren't the same as your career paths or your dreams. An example of a complementary goal could be to hire a personal trainer, do cross-fit, and take a boot camp class. Complementary goals are pursuits that will help to improve your holistic prowess as you're chasing your dreams. Being in shape isn't necessary to become a writer, for example, but it most certainly will help if the person is healthy and in shape. Why? Because he or she will have more energy, work more efficiently, possess a healthier mind, and possibly live longer so that they can write even more. However, being in shape is necessary if you have the dream of becoming a professional athlete. So you must know how to differentiate whether your complementary goals are actually dreams, and if your dreams are actually complementary goals. The three complementary goals you select must be encompassed and guided in the same direction as your dreams. Your complementary goals are only appurtenant goals that can change sporadically. However, your dreams ideally should never be sporadically changed, although it's okay to change one or all three of your dreams, if you're thoroughly convinced that the three dreams you originally recorded aren't your true passions.

How To Implement The 27-Month Plan

The first dream that you wrote down represents the dream, or the specific career path, that you most desire to pursue. Your first dream must be a dream you're currently compassionate and passionate about. The remaining two dreams should be things within the same career path you're passionate about as well. To successfully implement my *27-Month Plan*, it's important to know that the figurative genders of your dreams represent your occupations or careers. Let's use nursing as an example. Nursing is the gender, so the career is the gender. Someone may want to be a nurse. However, that's broad so they must specify what type of nurse. As an example, let's suppose someone wants to be a registered nurse. Becoming a registered nurse is the dream; however, you must indicate three different ways that you plan on utilizing the dream as well. Here is an example of how to do that: write down three dreams that are involved within the same field. 1. Become a registered nurse that works in ICU. 2. Become a registered nurse that's works as a charge nurse. 3. Become a registered nurse with the ultimate goal of becoming a Nurse Practitioner.

You must give the three dreams you wrote down nine months to develop, and then rotate your three dreams. But only rotate your dreams every nine months if you're unsure about the dreams you want to pursue. The example from Table 2.2 demonstrates three dreams being properly rotated every trimester with the dreamer maintaining the original dreams. Furthermore, you should stick with the same three dreams, and give your dreaming process up to twenty-seven months to form a firm foundation for success. However, *The 27-Month Plan* does permit you to change your dreams during the twenty-seven-month process if you determine you have formed some new passions. However, I strongly recommend you give your dreams a full twenty-seven months to develop before you consider changing any of your dreams. If you constantly change the three dreams you're pursuing without strictly adhering to the twenty-seven-month development process, then you aren't giving your dreams enough time to develop. So be patient as you're discovering your true destiny! Finally, whether you're sure or unsure about your dreams doesn't really matter because *The 27-Month Plan* will help you to confirm which path is truly right for you.

Now that you have your three dreams, I want you to divide each individual dream into three categories of their own. When forming your twenty-seven-month plan for your three dreams, I want you to divide the twenty-seven-month process into three (3) nine-month segments consisting of three trimesters, and that will give you a total of nine trimesters. You will see why this is significant as you continue to read this chapter. You need to form three-month plans or three trimesters consisting of three months for each trimester. That's a total of nine months for each individual dream. During the first trimester, your focus should be the *frequency* and *knowledge* you will need to be able to bring one of the three dreams into fruition. Although you wrote down three dreams, you will work on them separately in order to ensure that the discovery process of your dreams is expedient.

For example, work on the first dream for one full month, and then the second dream for one full month, and then the third dream for one full month. That will equal three months, which will complete your first trimester. The objectives for the first trimester or month's one through three are *frequency* and *knowledge* for your three dreams. The objectives for the second trimester or months four through six are *duration* and *understanding* for your three dreams. The objectives for the third trimester or months seven through nine are *intensity* and *wisdom* for your three dreams. *Remember: the three dreams you wrote down should all be connected to the same field, ideally.* However, they don't absolutely have to be connected to the same field. You're welcome to write down whatever three dreams you're absolutely in love with, even if they are totally different and unconnected to the same field. *But most importantly, I do highly recommend that the three dreams are in the same field if you truly want my discovery process to work best for you.*

Figure 2.2 will give you an example of how the pregnancy process of your dreams will work. During the first trimester, the focuses are *frequency* and *knowledge* for each month of the three dreams you wrote down. The *frequency* focuses on: How many times a week are you working on your dreams during the first three months? How many times a week are you taking in knowledge for each individual dream during the first trimester process? For the second trimester, the focuses are *duration* and *understanding*. The *duration* focuses on: How long are you working on your dreams when you're working on them? For the third trimester, the focuses are *intensity* and *wisdom*. The *intensity* focuses on: Are you intensely challenging yourself? Are you doing massive amounts of work to get noticed and are you going the extra two miles for the dreams you want?

During the second set of three months or your second trimester, you would start over with the first dream and focus on the *understanding* and *duration* for that dream for fourth month, and for one full month as well. On the fifth month, you would go back to your second dream and focus on *understanding* and *duration* for the second dream for one full month as well. For month number six you would focus on *understanding* and *duration* for the third dream you wrote down. After you have completed two trimesters, you will have arrived at the seventh month to start your third trimester. During the third trimester you would start with the first dream you wrote down during the first trimester: the focuses for the third trimester are *intensity* and *wisdom.* The same format applies for the seventh month as well, so you would focus on intensity and wisdom for a full month. For the entire eighth month, you would focus on the second dream you wrote down. Finally, during the ninth month, you would focus on *intensity* and *wisdom* for the third dream you wrote down.

Subsequently, you would repeat this sequence every nine months until you have completed a total of twenty-seven months. And for emphasis, you're welcome to change your three dreams every nine months. However, I suggest you stick with the first three dreams you wrote down, but only if you're absolutely positive that those dreams you originally picked are the only things you want to do for the rest of your life.

After you have created your table for the first nine months or three trimesters of your dreams, you should also make a separate table for your complementary goals. A complementary goal could be to buy a house, get in shape (unless your dream is to be a professional athlete), pay off a student loan, get married, etc. However, keep in mind the differences between absolute and relative goals from Chapter 8. Also, you must know if your dreams path consists of mainly absolute or relative goals and vice versa. Your dreams should always be career paths, discovery journeys, or jobs that you're passionate about. Think of discovery journeys as adventures during your life that you feel strongly about. For example, traveling the world can be a complementary goal and a dream. However, if you're traveling the world to have businesses in different countries, then that's a dream. But if you're traveling the world simply for pleasure, then that's more of a complementary goal, which is also perfectly okay. However, just know the differences, and remember that dreams and complementary goals should always be connected for optimal self-discovery.

People have all types of complementary goals, including the amount of money they want to make, getting in shape, developing a better relationship with God. Your goal is to write down three complementary goals you want to achieve that are connected to your dreams. Remember, your complementary goals can keep changing, but make an earnest attempt to only select three goals that are very important to you, and focus on just those three complementary goals. Create a table for your dreams and a separate table your complementary goals. Do not follow the same format from table 2.2 for your complementary goals. Also, it's important to remember that your complementary goals should be maintained on a daily or weekly basis. For example, if you had a complementary goal to get in shape, then you would have to maintain this goal with proper nutrition on a weekly basis and a daily basis.

A complementary goal of being healthy is an essential goal to achieve any dream, because your health affects your mood and your energy level. If you don't feel good or look the way that you want, it may affect your pursuit toward your dreams. Another good complementary goal is to have a good reading schedule, along with listening to daily motivational and spiritual audio programs. Your objective is to select two complementary goals that can become good habits, and one that can become a reward. When selecting your three complementary goals, always select two things that can become habits, and then select one that involves a reward such as a new home, car, marriage, friendship, vacation, paying off debt, donating, developing a better relationship with God, being a better wife/husband. However, maintaining an improved relationship with God or a spouse as an example is a complementary goal that can be both a reward and a habit. However, it's only a habit if the relationship is maintained after improvements are made.

Closely Examine The 27-Month Plan For Dream Discoveries

At the beginning of the chapter, Table 2.2 was presented for you to familiarize yourself with. Look over the table again and read the format once more, so that you can fully understand how this plan works.

The 27-Month Plan

TABLE 2.2

Genders/ Babies (dreams/careers) (1) Basketball player (2) Basketball coach (3) Basketball scout	First Trimester (months 1-3) Focus: *Frequency and knowledge*	Second Trimester (months 4-6) Focus: *Duration and understanding*	Third Trimester (months 7-9) Focus: *Intensity and wisdom*
1.Basketball player	First month (Basketball player) Second month (Basketball coach) Third month (Basketball scout)	Fourth month (Basketball player) Fifth month (Basketball coach) Sixth month (Basketball scout)	Seventh month (Basketball player) Eighth month (Basketball coach) Ninth month (Basketball scout)
2. Basketball coach	First month (Basketball coach) Second month (Basketball player) Third month (Basketball scout)	Fourth month (Basketball coach) Fifth month (Basketball player) Sixth month (Basketball scout)	Seventh month (Basketball coach) Eighth month (Basketball player) Ninth month (Basketball scout)
3. Basketball scout	First month (Basketball scout) Second month (Basketball coach) Third month (Basketball player)	Fourth month (Basketball scout) Fifth month (Basketball coach) Sixth month (Basketball player)	Seventh month (Basketball scout) Eighth month (Basketball coach) Ninth month (Basketball player)

To effectively focus on *frequency* and *knowledge* during the first trimester or (months one through three), you should make sure you're feeding your dreams at least two times a day, preferably in the morning and at night. You should aim to learn something new every day about the dream you're working on for that month. Look over your dream in the morning and at night for however long you desire, and don't worry about the duration, that's for the second trimester. For example, if during the first trimester you spend a total of six minutes every day learning something new about your dreams, that's acceptable. However, just make sure you're adhering to the frequency goal you set. If your frequency goal is five times a week, make sure you're doing five times a week for six minutes a day, if that's what you decided. However, the duration needs to be established as well, but it should be in minutes, and not in hours for the first trimester. So, if you want to start off with forty minutes five times a week during the first trimester, then that's okay. However, I personally recommend you work on your dreams every single day. And if you want to take a few days off, don't go more than two days without working on your dreams. So you need a minimum of five times a week for your frequency during months one through three.

During the second trimester (months four through six), I want you to focus on the *duration* and *understanding* of your three dreams. I want you to spend up to three hours a day feeding your dreams, and if you want to, you can break up the hours. For example, you could break the hours up by doing an hour and a half earlier in the day and an hour and a half later in the day. However, if you decide to work on your dreams for three hours non-stop, there is nothing wrong with that. During your second trimester, the shortest duration that's acceptable is a minimum of thirty minutes a day. You can divide it into fifteen minutes in the morning and fifteen minutes at night if your schedule is jammed. However, you should aim to spend three hours a day working on your dreams during the third trimester, and there are no exceptions for this during the third trimester, months seven through nine! Remember, we all make time for the things that we really want, so if you really want your dreams, then you'll make time to give your dreams their proper attention for three months.

During the second trimester, you will implement the *knowledge* you're taking in by forming strategies on how to apply your *knowledge*.

Also, seek advice directly from people who are doing what you desire to do, or study people who have become successful doing what you desire to do. During this trimester you should focus on attending seminars/webinars, and events associated with your dreams, so that you can network. Take a moment and think about the people you will need to help you, people that you know personally. Take a moment and think about the types of people you will need. Let me warn you, the people who you think should help you may not always help you, so be relentless until you're able to attract kindred spirits. During your second trimester, for instance, if you want to be a singer I want you to start auditioning for singing jobs. If you need more education, I want you to consider enrolling in school if achieving your dreams requires that. If you need to hire a coach, I want you to do that as well. During the second trimester you should be growing in your *knowledge* via reading, watching, and listening to audio recordings and motivational videos. Most importantly, you must study your predecessors and adopt some of their rituals for success.

During your third trimester, or months seven through nine, you must focus on the *intensity* and *wisdom* of your dreams. The *intensity* during this trimester is achieved by strengthening your efforts. You will do this by doing massive amounts of work and going the extra two miles. You must focus on putting forth your best efforts. For example, if you desire to be the head salesperson and outsell everyone, then I want you to do something that's never been done before. For example, if the norm is to contact 100 people in a month for potential sales opportunities, I want you to double or triple that number and shoot for 200 or 300 people. Massive amounts of quality work should be your focus during the final three months of each of your third trimesters to complete months seven through nine. So if you're looking for a job that might fulfill your dreams and you're averaging one job interview a week, then increase your interviews to five or ten interviews until you land a job. Also, don't be afraid to relocate and broaden your horizon. Where there is a will there is a way, so don't worry about the things in the future, remember to just keep pursuing your dreams.

Wisdom must be demonstrated during the third trimester or months seven through nine, to effectively complete a nine-month rotation. *Wisdom* is shown regarding how you use your time, so don't accept every audition or interview. Don't waste your time with malnourished opportunities that you know you really don't want to try. There are some experiences that aren't needed for you to complete your journey, so don't feed your dreams with unnecessary nutrients. Don't waste your time with distractions that will lead you away from the opportunities that are crucial to fulfill your dreams!

Some of the other things to focus on during the third trimester include accelerating your work ethic and narrowing your focus on your dreams. Also, during this trimester you should focus on hard work and making a decision regarding the three dreams you selected for your *The 27-Month Plan*. Also, focus on deciding if it's time for you to choose which of the three dreams are best suited for you to wholeheartedly pursue. So intensify your efforts to seek help and, ideally, narrow your focus to one dream before you start the second nine-month cycle. To narrow your focus means you're looking to pick one of the three dreams you wanted to pursue after you've completed your first nine-month cycle. However, if you're still undecided after completing your first nine-month cycle, then stick with the same three dreams for the second nine-month cycle, or you can swap out and change your dreams. After you complete your second nine-month cycle, and if you're still undecided, then finish your third nine-month cycle with the same dreams, until you complete a full *27-Month Plan* process. If you're still undecided after twenty-seven months regarding which dream you want to solely focus on, then simply restart the twenty-seven-month process. But only use the same three original dreams if you're absolutely certain they are your true passions. During the trimesters where the focuses are *intensity* and *wisdom*, you should spend insane amounts of time networking, and meeting people who are interested in your dreams.

During the third trimester you must search for ways to elevate all of the resources you might be lacking. Remember, resources can be money, knowing the right people, courage, faith, self-belief, health, family, association, opportunities, knowing what to do, knowing what not to do, motivation, time, licenses, certifications, degrees, skills, and experience. You must make advancements in the necessary resources that you're lacking. If you follow this format, your dreams will have the foundation they need for perpetual growth. *The 27-Month Plan* will help you to become a happy "parent" as you're developing and giving birth to your dreams. Just like a child is always growing and learning, you should view your dreams the same way. *The 27-Month Plan* is a journey and you'll always have to make corrections along the way.

But remember this: don't stop getting pregnant with new dreams! Keep repeating this format with the same dreams or use different dreams for your nine trimesters (twenty-seven months). Furthermore, remember to use the same dreams over and over again only if you're absolutely certain they're the dreams you're truly passionate about. Most importantly, remember to ideally stay within the same field and swap out your dreams only if you determine that's necessary. You don't have to keep a dream in your rotation if you discover you truly don't like the dream. *The 27-Month Plan* is a discovery process, so please immediately remove any dreams from your plans that you lose interest in. You can always reenter the same dreams during another *27-Month Plan* if you have a change of heart later on along your journey of self-discovery.

The main key to success when using *The 27-Month Plan* is to remember to never waste time pursuing things you aren't willing to fully commit yourself too. If you aren't willing to sacrifice your time and resources for your dreams, then that could be a clear indication the dream you're pursuing isn't for you! Sometimes a dream could be perfect for you, but if you don't properly nurture the desire to attain it, then your dream will die, and your actions will show that you don't want your dream anymore. So continue to alter your *frequencies*, *durations*, and *intensities* based on the development of your dreams. Remember this: Do not keep trying to follow a nutrition plan that your dream isn't digesting. For example, if you wanted to lose weight and you were following a diet plan that obviously wasn't working, it could lead to you quitting and feeling unfulfilled. So do not stick to a dream that doesn't make you feel fulfilled. Always be true to what you feel because if it's your passion then you won't be able to turn it off, even if you try. It's okay to change your approach by feeding your dreams the nutrients they need in order to grow. If you do this over and over again, your inner genius will eventually be exposed!

Always Have The Proper Viewpoints Toward Your Dreams

Always remember this: dreams don't always come out fully formed. Sometimes you have to discover the dreams that you're truly in love with over time. You must always make sure you're pursuing the dreams you love, and not the dreams other people tell you to pursue. As you continue to develop your genius you will need to have passion and compassion for your dreams. You need to be enthralled with achieving your goals and you must enjoy what you desire to do. Never pursue a goal you aren't deeply passionate about or willing to sacrifice things for. The reason I say you need to be compassionate is because you need to be so connected to your dreams, until they are as palpable as people. If you have compassion toward your dreams, it will motivate you not just pursue your dreams in a half-hearted way. Why? You love your dreams too much! Compassion for your dreams forces you to feel guilty whenever you aren't pursuing them with full passion. Passion and compassion are two qualities that are essential for developing your inner genius.

Focus On The Process Of The Dream
Rather Than The Outcome

My *27-Month Plan* teaches you to focus on your dreams and their different processes rather than on their outcomes. As an example, someone may want to be a nurse working in the ICU, but God may want them to be a charge nurse. Always pay close attention to your life's paths, and you will see God's blessings, but only if you have given Him efforts that He can bless. God allows us to pick our paths and to pursue the dreams we're passionate about. *If you miss the purpose of the process, you won't appreciate the dreams. The lack of appreciation will cause you to abort your dreams if things don't go exactly the way you think they should.*

At any given moment, a young child could disappoint their parents. However, whose job is it to teach the child? Whose job is it to direct the dream? Dreams aren't designed to direct and control their own paths. No sane person would intentionally get pregnant and expect their baby to raise themselves. So likewise, you must intentionally develop the dreams that you want.

Always Be Flexible

I'll refer back to the nursing analogy mentioned earlier in this chapter. Suppose Erika becomes a nurse and she discovers that working in the ICU department at the hospital isn't her thing. Erika enjoys nursing, but she starts to realize she actually wants to be a nurse practitioner, and then eventually teach nursing. What should Erika do with this new dilemma? I would encourage Erika to follow her newly discovered passion, and to keep growing by never settling for something that isn't making her feel fulfilled. *"All things must grow and nothing should be set in stone if you want to become progressively great. Your dreams must be a journey that never ends. If your life doesn't make you feel like you're on an exciting journey, then you have stopped growing or searching for ways to grow."*

My sincere advice is this: after you've given birth to your first set of dreams, please get "pregnant" again with more dreams. *Always try to elevate your mind and your inner genius!* If you become settled by not trying to continuously grow, it will lead to boredom and feeling discontented. You have to keep dating your dreams, and getting to know your dreams in order for you to keep growing. You will never learn enough about your dreams, so always dream big, and stay full of *new ideas* because life's possibilities are truly unlimited. *Most importantly, if you develop the relentless mindset to repeatedly become pregnant with complementary goals and dreams, then I can guarantee you that one or more of your babies will eventually make everything worth your while.*

Always Pay Attention to Details

The order of the dreams in the nursing example, mentioned a few paragraphs earlier, is in the inceptive form. You can't become a nurse practitioner without being a registered nurse first. A registered nurse needs a two- or four-year degree and to pass the board exam.

However, to become a nurse practitioner requires a master's degree and a registered nursing license. If your dream requires licenses and degrees, then you should focus on one element at a time. *Master the art of focusing on one step at a time and not complete flights of stairs.* If you have several dreams or goals to fulfill that have sequential steps to take, then you will never get to the next step if you skip steps during the trimesters of your dream's development process. To be successful, always start with the foundation goal that you must achieve first. For example, how could someone desire to have a mate, if they never go out to meet or talk with anyone? There is a quote that says "You don't have to be great to get started, but you have to get started to become great." So, find the smallest thing you can do to start working on your dreams and just get started.

An important thing to remember about actually having triplets, to expand on the baby analogy I'm using, is that they don't all come out at the exact same time, so focus on the dream you're pregnant with first. Do you feel like a movie is complete and good just because the first five minutes are great? No! Maybe that's why people don't go through several trimesters of being pregnant with their dreams: they never follow through with the process. Some people abort their dreams every time they confirm they're pregnant with new ideas. Why? There are many reasons why, but the main two are because maybe they haven't done it before, and they're probably afraid. Fear is normal, so always embrace your fears. All successful people have felt fear in many different ways. *"Never allow fear to stop you from running toward your reward. If you're bold enough to dream it, then you must courageously fulfill it."*

Always Do Check-Ups with Your Heart
Whenever You're Pregnant with Ideas

How many of your dreams have you aborted? How many more will you continue to abort? How many of your dreams have you put up for adoptions by witnessing someone else fulfill the ideas that you had? How many unhealthy dreams have you given birth to because you didn't properly nourish your dreams? You may feel like you don't have the resources, but have you become resourceful by relentlessly trying to attain the necessary resources that you need? Are you willing to be resourceful and hunt down the resources you need, just like a lion?

Did you ever wonder why all babies look different? It's the same reason why people's dreams are unique, even if they are similar: your dreams are your dreams and no one else's. Your dreams are in your DNA, so no one else can dream exactly the same way that you dream. No one can bring your dreams into reality the same way that you can. If triplets stayed inside a pregnant mother after her three trimesters ended, the mother would die and so would the triplets. Don't let your dreams die! If you don't give birth to your true passions, I can promise you that your spirit to *Just Get Up* will die inside of you. Will you allow this atrocity to happen? Will you allow this monstrosity to overtake you? Let me be frank with you: you'd better not! You must develop your genius by giving it the nutrients it deserves. You must study, visualize, and read about your dreams every day.

Martin Luther King, Jr. once said: "If you can't fly, then run; if you can't walk, then crawl; but by all means keep moving forward." If you stay still and remain in the same spot because you aren't moving as fast as you would like, then you will never grow! If you do nothing at all, no change will happen. If you do a little every day, you will eventually give birth to your dreams. So make sure you're consistently moving forward. If you can only crawl as of now, that's fine because eventually you will be able to walk. It's important for you to know this: before you give birth to your babies or your dreams, you don't have to know if they're figurative boys or girls. Ideas and dreams don't come out fully formed. So, just like you have to nourish a growing fetus to find out if it will be a boy or a girl, you must do likewise with your dreams to find out the true identities of your ideas.

When a woman intentionally becomes pregnant, all she knows at first is that she is pregnant. She doesn't know the gender of her child. However, does this mean she doesn't need to start educating herself about how to develop a healthy baby? Of course not! If she doesn't take in the right nutrients, she will compromise her health and the baby's health. Your dreams and ideas are the same way. They don't have to come out fully formed when they first enter your mind. But in order for you to bring the dream into fruition you have to start working on it. As you develop your dreams, you will begin to see all the components that are needed to help make your dreams come true. If you keep developing your dreams like an expectant father and mother does during a pregnancy, then your dreams will eventually develop into symbolic fetuses. You will eventually know the genders of your dreams, but only after they have been fully formed.

The next chapter will discuss the mind frames of various successful men and women who are geniuses. You will notice they all had to overcome adversities and they have some of the same key attributes in common. At this point along your journey, you have discovered the four main types of goals, and now you have a discovery format for pursuing your dreams. *The 27-Month Plan* was designed to help you to do that. The next chapter will help to strengthen your faith in your plan of action. Chapter 10 will help you to see that all things are possible if you will simply chase your dreams like your life depends on it! Remember this:

"Nothing can resist a human will that will stake its existence on its stated purpose."

—Benjamin Disraeli

Remember this: If you aren't actively working on your dreams or thinking about them every day, then you have mentally and physically quit. Don't fall victim to procrastination's deadly plague. In order for you to keep your dreams active, you need actions. It's not good enough to say things like, "I'm thinking about starting soon to discover my purpose in life." You must start putting actions behind your words, even if it's something small. For example, suppose someone used to smoke a whole pack of cigarettes every day, but eventually they work on reducing their usage to smoking half a pack a day. That's an example of gradual improvement and although it still doesn't immediately achieve the long term goal, the baby steps will eventually lead to the goal's achievement. So remember this: *"Progress is growth whether it's good or bad, so you will make progress! However, just make sure it's in the right direction!"* Every day you need to show signs of improvement in order to develop your inner genius and eventually give birth to your dreams. The next chapter will help you to develop the mind frame of a genius by examining real geniuses who have walked down difficult paths to release their individual greatness.

CHAPTER 10

MIND FRAME
OF A GENIUS

THE FIRST THING YOU NEED to do to develop the mind frame of a genius is to stop saying *want, try,* and *if.* Stop saying *I want* and replace it with ***I NEED.*** Stop saying *I will try* and start saying ***I WILL DO!*** Stop saying *if I* or *if it* and reinvent this phrase with ***I WILL*** or ***IT WILL!*** This chapter will assist you and help you to protect your mind by learning from other geniuses who have gone through adversities. It's important that you start telling yourself positive affirmations every day and always speak in an affirmative manner. You have to believe beyond what the human eye can see in order to manifest your inner genius. There is no need for you to *try* to do something: either you're going to do it or you're not! When you say to yourself you're *going to try* something, that's your subconscious mind preparing you for failure. Your subconscious mind will prepare you to quit by seeking a way out whenever your pursuit becomes difficult. So be bold and say what you're going to do, and do it at all costs. That is one of the secrets to unlocking your genius, so pick your heart's true destination, and don't stop until you arrive there.

Notice the list of questions below and observe how there aren't any preemptive measures embedded in the terminology of the questions. Do you **NEED** to start a business? Well, why haven't you? Do you **NEED** a better relationship with God? Have you started working on your relationship with God? Is your bank account where you **NEED** it to be? Is your career where you **NEED** it to be? Do you have the relationships and friendships that you need? The relationships that you do have, are they empowering you? Or do they tether your life? Tethering relationships will restrict you to repeat starts that lead to unproductive restarts of the same unproductive things! I know you've heard the colloquialism that insanity is defined as doing the same thing over and over again, and expecting a different result. Please: do not become an insane person who expects a different result from the implementation of a sullied game plan.

I personally have asked myself all of those questions. During my past, whenever I experienced seemingly intractable adversities, sometimes I would become discouraged if I didn't receive immediate gratification from my hard work. There is a saying that goes like this: "The light gets brighter at the end of the tunnel." When you're going through something, sometimes colloquialisms don't always bring you comfort until you have the experience to validate the truthfulness attached to them. So I can promise you this: the light isn't brighter at the end of the tunnel. Why, because the light is already bright inside of you! Sometimes we blow our inner light's fuse and we run out of energy because we're unnecessarily expending our life's energy in the wrong direction. The misguidance that results from expending our energy in the wrong direction is normally achieved when we seek advice from the wrong people. So, be cautious about who you talk to about your hardships because until you're fully obsessed with self-development your mind will be timorously vulnerable. However, even if you have a strong will, you still should be careful about who you're talking to when you're going through hardships.

You Are Unstoppable So Never Hesitate
to Take Immediate Action

Take a moment and reflect on an actual light bulb's filament and what happens once a light bulb's filament blows. If a light bulb stopped working, would it be reasonable for someone to expect to have light? Just like a bulb, you have to replenish yourself in life, and sometimes this means changing the light bulb. This concept applies to how you look at things as well, so at different times during your life you will have to change your eye's lens to reflect the proper views on life. In your endeavors to conquer yourself and manifest your gifts, it's essential that you have 20/20 vision. The first step you must take if you truly desire to change your light bulb is to recognize that change is first possible. So if your vision is impaired and if you don't view adversities as a privilege, then you must correct your impaired vision by acknowledging that the way you view adversities is flawed.

Knowing and acknowledging impairments are two different things, but most of the time we only acknowledge, which simply indicates that we recognize something is wrong. However, just because you acknowledge change is necessary doesn't mean you will change what you have acknowledged! To become an unstoppable force, you must conduct a self-analysis of your viewpoints on a weekly basis. So always make room for the possibility that your thinking capacity on a matter may be flawed. *(Read Proverbs 16:2 once a week)* The true meaning of someone who has fought to become unstoppable simply means they haven't stopped growing in their thinking faculties, and they clearly recognize they can learn something new every day. A true genius is obsessed with knowledge and learning. Are you learning something new every day?

If you hesitate to take action toward your dreams, arbitration will easily creep in and create an inner resolve that produces hesitation as a default setting whenever you experience adversities. If you allow your inner resolve to be programmed by cowardice and feelings of fear, then it will delay the necessary actions that you need to take. Also, too much hesitation will ultimately produce a quandary within your heart. If you allow this to happen, you will have to wrestle with the feeling of whether to act now or later. Normally, hesitation comes from a new stimulus and your brain acknowledges the lack of experience associated with the new experience, which produces fear based on your perception of the complexity of the new experience, even if it hasn't happened or if it never happens. So this is why 20/20 vision is necessary to capture your dreams. When in doubt, always train yourself to believe that the improbable is possible, and you must go after the things you're afraid to pursue. If you go after your dreams even though you're afraid, it will strengthen your courage, and your fears will eventually become famished, and then your fears will begin to die.

"Do the thing you fear and the defeat of fear is certain."

—William James

It's a normal human emotion to be cautious when we don't have enough experience or wisdom to accurately decipher how we should respond to a particular matter. It's completely normal whenever we do this, and it should actually be expected. Anything you're unfamiliar with creates hesitation because you've never experienced it. However, please understand this: as you continue to *chase your dreams,* dubious feelings and hesitation will inevitably begin to surface. My challenge to you is: acknowledge this and then act immediately! Most of your new endeavors will produce fear and doubt. Fear is a good thing, but only if it's used properly. Fear allows you to pay more attention to detail, which forces you not to underestimate your opponent, and your opponent is you! So I'm encouraging you to act immediately whenever you acknowledge you have a problem. Do not hesitate to act!

To develop the mind frame of a genius, you must acknowledge change is always possible. Furthermore, I need you to believe and have faith that change is necessary, as well. Do you feel this way? I want you to take a brief moment again and allow all of your goals to reenter your brilliant mind. Remember this: every time you think about your dreams, your vision becomes clearer. You cannot escape your destiny. Your dreams are still alive! As long as your dreams can be imagined, then they can reenter the universe someday to be manifested as a reality.

Your goals that remain unfulfilled will often circumvent throughout your brain, as your actions and inactions run parallel to one another. The reason I say your actions and inactions toward your goals run parallel to one another is because you're constantly reminded of them. *"Every time you see someone else fulfilling their dreams, you're witnessing their actions and your inactions. It's literally like your actions and your inactions are walking in the same direction, but your inactions are on the opposite side of the street, so whether you pursue your deepest ambitions or not, as you walk through life's streets you will always measure where you are against where you truly desire to be."*

If you don't chase your dreams, one day you will wake up and look to your left and right only to remorsefully see others fulfilling their dreams and manifesting their true geniuses. Remember this: your dreams will never walk away from you; only you can get rid of your dreams! Your dreams will always walk in the same direction as you. All you have to do is simply walk over to your dreams by positioning yourself on the right side of life's streets. So look over at your dreams whether they're on your right or left, and cross life's streets. Start walking with your goals and attach them to your hips. Super-glue your dreams to your mind! Staple your dreams to your heart! Nail your dreams into your spirit! Eat your dreams like it's your favorite meal, and pig out! Don't just take a small bite, go back for seconds! The pursuit to attain your dreams should feel like you're having your favorite meal. Just having a tiny bite of your favorite entrée when you're starving will never satisfy your craving. This is how you need to feel about where you are in life, especially if you want to have the mind frame of a true genius. You must be obsessed with greatness and with fulfilling your destiny.

Walk with Your Dreams

I think it's safe to say that you're now officially walking in the same direction as your dreams, and your dreams are attached to your hips. Because this is true, it's time for you to fully develop the mind frame of a genius. However, the body can't follow a poisoned mind and if it does, the actions will be poisoned as well. So it's important for you to have the proper mind frame to fully capture your dreams. Let's take a moment to look at a few success stories of some renowned geniuses, inspirational public figures, and their contributions to the world. Let's look at their mindsets, ambitions, and influential movements. This is important because success leaves clues, *and it's important to understand that these people are just examples, and not exceptions!*

Before you begin reading about some of the world's most gifted geniuses, it's important for you to realize they all have some things in common. It's important for you to reframe any thinking that you don't have the tools you need to bring your dreams into fruition. Also, you must understand there are hundreds and thousands of other geniuses who have made contributions that you can research. The geniuses I'm going to discuss aren't listed in any particular order. I'm listing the geniuses randomly, so don't think that one is more important than the other. So let's discuss the first of the many geniuses that we will examine.

ISAAC NEWTON

Isaac Newton was an English mathematician, astronomer, theologian, author, and physicist. He was described in his own day as a natural philosopher. He is widely recognized as one of the most influential scientists of all time, and a key figure in the scientific revolution. His book *Philosophiae Naturalis Principia Mathematica* ("Mathematical Principles of Natural Philosophy") first published in 1687, laid the foundations of classical mechanics. Newton also made path-breaking contributions to optics, and he shares credit with Gottfried Wilhelm Leibniz for developing the infinitesimal calculus. Newton's *Principia* formulated the laws of motion and universal gravitation that dominated scientists' view of the physical universe for over three centuries. He derived Kepler's laws of planetary motion from his mathematical description of gravity while using the same principles to account for the trajectories of comets, tides, precession of the equinoxes, and other phenomena. Newton removed the last doubts about the validity of the heliocentric model of our solar system, and demonstrated that the motion of objects on earth and of celestial bodies could be explained by the same principles.

Newton's theoretical prediction that the earth is shaped as an oblate spheroid was later vindicated by the geodetic measurements of de Maupertuis, La Condamine, and others. Newton convinced most Continental European scientists of the superiority of Newtonian mechanics over the earlier system of Descartes. That was amazing because Descartes was another genius, but Isaac took it a step further. I know what you're thinking: I'm discussing Isaac Newton first because his name is Isaac. But although his name is the same as mine, I'm mentioning him mainly because he was a true genius!

Newton also built the first practical reflecting telescope and developed a sophisticated theory of color. It was based on the observation that a prism decomposes white light into the colors of the visible spectrum. Newton's work on light was collected in his highly influential book "Opticks," first published in 1704. He also formulated an empirical law of cooling. He made the first theoretical calculation of the speed of sound, and introduced the notion of Newtonian fluid. In addition to his work on calculus, as a mathematician Newton contributed to the study of power series. He generalized the binomial theorem to non-integer exponents. He also developed a method for approximating the roots of a function, and classified most of the cubic plane curves. Newton was modest about his achievements. In a letter to Robert Hooke in 1676 he once stated, "If I have seen further, it is by standing on the shoulders of Giants." He was a disciplined religious man, scholar, visionary, and a hard worker.

Develop The Mind frame of Isaac Newton

I'm not saying that you need to be exactly like Isaac Newton; however, you can learn some significant lessons from his example. Isaac Newton sacrificed love for the sake of his dreams. He was obsessed with making a contribution. How did he do this? He had to first believe that he could do whatever he wanted to. I'm sure you're familiar with Newton's three Laws of Motion. He made tons of contributions that we all are governed by today. I encourage you to research Isaac Newton and read more about his personal life and achievements.

So, what are your contributions going to be? You must believe that your dreams will come into fruition before anyone else believes it, and you must expect criticism from the naysayers. You must devote time weekly, or preferably every day, to work on your dreams, even if it's a few minutes. Use Chapters 5, 8, and 11 to help you deal with procrastination. Do you think Isaac Newton could have accomplished his brilliant achievements without working on them weekly or every day?

Another notable thing about Isaac Newton is that he was patient. I'm sure there were times when he doubted if he would live to see his dreams become a reality. He even debated and competed with other mathematicians of his time who also made notable contributions. Isaac Newton was humble and some of his predecessors looked up to him, so to learn from his example. Remember and imprint this into your mind: You cannot become great by yourself! Furthermore, whenever you're doing something great, you will begin to attract other great people, and these great people will help you to attain the various resources that you will need.

If Isaac Newton had lacked faith and passion, he wouldn't have been able to follow through with his dreams. Do you have faith and passion? Also, it's important to remember that I'm not encouraging you to be Isaac Newton! You are your own unique genius! However, you should aim to learn from Newton's tenacity by contributing your gifts to the world, along with manifesting the inner genius that's inside of you. I know you have ideas that are inside of that genius brain of yours, and all you have to do is just believe and dream big. The people during Isaac Newton's day thought he was crazy at first, but look at what became of his dreams. *What will become of your dreams?*

ALBERT EINSTEIN

He was born March 14, 1879 and died April 18, 1955. He was a German-born theoretical physicist who developed the theory of relativity, which became one of the two pillars of modern physics (alongside quantum mechanics). His work is also known for its influence on the philosophy of science. He is best known by the general public for his mass-to-energy equivalence formula $E = mc^2$ (which has been dubbed the world's most famous equation). He received the 1921 Nobel Prize in Physics for his services to theoretical physics, and especially for his discovery of the law of photoelectric effect, a pivotal step in the evolution of quantum theory. Near the beginning of his career, Einstein thought that Newtonian mechanics was no longer enough to reconcile the laws of classical mechanics with the laws of the electromagnetic field. This led him to develop his special theory of relativity during his time of employment at the Swiss Patent Office in Bern, Switzerland. In 1917, he applied the general theory of relativity to model the large-scale structure of the universe.

He settled in the United States becoming an American citizen in 1940. On the eve of World War II, he endorsed a letter to US President Franklin D. Roosevelt alerting him to the potential development of extremely powerful bombs of a new type, and recommended that the US begin similar research. Einstein published more than 300 scientific papers along with over 150 non-scientific works. His intellectual achievements and originality have made the word "Einstein" synonymous with "genius." Eugene Wigner wrote of Einstein that, in comparison to his contemporaries, Einstein's understanding was even deeper than Jansci von Neumann's. His mind was both more penetrating and more original than von Neumann's. And that is a very remarkable statement.

His father intended for him to pursue electrical engineering, but Einstein clashed with authorities and resented the school's regimen and teaching method. He later wrote that the spirit of learning and creative thought was lost in strict rote learning. Contrary to popular mythology, Einstein always excelled at math and physics from a young age, reaching mathematical levels years ahead of his peers. At twelve years old, Einstein taught himself algebra and Euclidean geometry over a single summer. Einstein also independently discovered his own original proof of the Pythagorean Theorem at age twelve. A family tutor, Max Talmud, said that "after a short time, Einstein had worked through the whole book." He thereupon devoted himself to higher mathematics. Max stated, "Soon the flight of his mathematical genius was so high I could not follow. His passion for geometry and algebra led the twelve-year-old to become convinced that nature could be understood as a mathematical structure." Einstein started teaching himself calculus at twelve, and as a fourteen-year-old he says he had "mastered integral and differential calculus." In 1895, at the age of sixteen, Einstein took the entrance examinations for the Swiss Federal Polythechnic in Zurich (later the Eidgenossische Technische Hochschule, ETH). He failed to reach the required standard in the general part of the examinations, but obtained exceptional grades in physics and mathematics.

In April 1933, Einstein discovered that the new German government had passed laws barring Jews from holding any official positions, including teaching at universities. Historian Gerald Holton describes how, with "virtually no audible protest being raised by their colleagues," thousands of Jewish scientists were suddenly forced to give up their university positions and their names were removed from the rolls of institutions where they were employed.

A month later, Einstein's works were among those targeted by the German Student Union in the Nazi book burnings; with Nazi propaganda minister Joseph Goebbels proclaiming, "Jewish intellectualism is dead." One German magazine included him in a list of enemies of the German regime with the phrase "not yet hanged," offering a $5,000 bounty on his head. In a subsequent letter to physicist and friend Max Born, who had already emigrated from Germany to England, Einstein wrote, "I must confess that the degree of their brutality and cowardice came as something of a surprise." Einstein was now without a permanent home, unsure where he would live and work, and equally worried about the fate of countless other scientists who were still in Germany. Einstein fought for the Jewish scientist with people such as Winston Churchill on his side. Einstein later contacted leaders of other nations, including Turkey's Prime Minister Ismet Inonu, to whom he wrote in September 1933 requesting placement of unemployed German-Jewish scientists. As a result of Einstein's letter, Jewish invitees to Turkey eventually totaled over 1,000 people who were saved.

Einstein was a passionate, committed antiracist and joined National Association for the Advancement of Colored People (NAACP) in Princeton, where he campaigned for the civil rights of African Americans. He considered racism America's "worst disease." Einstein viewed racism as something that was handed down from one generation to the next. As part of this involvement, he corresponded with civil rights activist W. E. B. Du Bois and was prepared to testify on his behalf during his trial in 1951. When Einstein offered to be a character witness for Du Bois, the judge decided to drop the case. In 1946 Einstein visited Lincoln University in Pennsylvania, a Historically Black College, where he was awarded an honorary degree. (Lincoln was the first university in the United States to grant College Degrees to African Americans; alumni include Langston Hughes and Thurgood Marshall). Einstein gave a speech about racism in America, adding, "I do not intend to be quiet about it." A resident of Princeton recalls that Einstein had once paid the college tuition for a black student.

Develop the Mind Frame of Einstein

If you carefully examine Einstein's life, you will notice that he experienced a lot of adversities, and yet he pushed through life head-on. Einstein once said: "If you teach a fish to climb a tree, the fish will go throughout its entire life thinking it's dumb." A fish wasn't meant to climb a tree, a fish was meant to be in the water. Einstein's example, once examined, helps you to appreciate he wasn't better or smarter than anyone else. Einstein simply pursued the things he was most passionate about. He stated that his love for the things he pursued, accompanied with hard work, is what gave birth to his accomplishments. Furthermore, I think it's notable that Einstein didn't always pass some of the necessary academic tests he was required to take. Einstein had family problems, cultural problems, peer pressure issues, and life-threatening issues. However, he maintained his courage by fighting for his right to give his gifts to the world. Einstein took the initiative to teach himself, and he mastered the things he was passionate about. So learn from Einstein, and take the initiative to learn, and to teach yourself the things you're passionate about. *You're more capable than you might think, so follow Einstein's advice, and don't be the fish who is trying to climb a tree. You must follow your heart's mind and fulfill your God-given destiny!*

ALEXANDER GRAHAM BELL

Alexander Graham Bell was a Scottish-born scientist, inventor, engineer, and innovator who is credited with patenting the first practical telephone, and founding the American Telephone and Telegraph Company (AT&T) in 1885. His research on hearing and speech further led him to experiment with hearing devices, which eventually culminated in Bell being awarded the first US patent for the telephone in 1876.

As a child, young Bell displayed a natural curiosity about his world, resulting in gathering botanical specimens as well as experimenting, even at an early age. His best friend was Ben Herdman, a neighbor whose family operated a flour mill. So young Bell eventually asked what needed to be done at the mill. He was told wheat had to be dehusked through a laborious process, so at the age of twelve, Bell built a homemade device that combined rotating paddles with sets of nail brushes. This dehusking machine was his first creation, and it was steadily used for a number of years. In return for his first invention, Ben's father John Herdman gave both boys the responsibility to run a small workshop, so that they could come up with more inventions.

From his early years, Bell showed a sensitive nature and a talent for art, poetry, and music that was encouraged by his mother. With no formal training, he mastered the piano and became the family's pianist. Despite being normally quiet and introspective, he reveled in mimicry and "voice tricks" akin to ventriloquism that continually entertained family guests during occasional visits. Bell was also deeply affected by his mother's gradual deafness; it motivated him to learn a manual finger language. The language enabled him to sit at his mother's side, and tap out silently the conversations swirling around the family parlor. He also developed a technique of speaking in clear, modulated tones directly into his mother's forehead wherein she would hear him with reasonable clarity. Bell's preoccupation with his mother's deafness led him to study acoustics. In January 1915, Bell made the first ceremonial transcontinental telephone call. He called the AT&T head office at 15 Dey Street in New York City; Bell was heard by Thomas Watson at 333 Grand Avenue in San Francisco. Alexander Graham Bell most certainly accomplished a lot of great things.

Develop the Mind Frame of Alexander Graham Bell

You can thank Alexander Graham Bell for enabling us all to be able to talk on the telephone. Are you willing to fail over and over again until you capture your dreams? To have the mind frame of a genius, you must love failure, and you must view failure as an opportunity to simply learn how to do things better. One thing that must be noted about Bell was his drive and his relentlessness at an early age. Alexander Graham Bell teaches us the beauty of being intrinsically and emotionally motivated. He found a purpose by trying to invent something that would help his mother. A key to developing the mind frame of a genius is to have an emotional purpose for pursuing your dreams. Ask yourself these questions: Why is it a must for me to capture my dreams? Who is depending on me? How can my gifts make a difference in the communities around me?

Bell understood the concept of vibrating at an uncommon frequency so that he could attract the resources that he needed. A key attribute to developing the mind frame of a genius is to be willing to take on different challenges, especially the ones you don't know how to do. Always recognize the importance of attracting help and kindred spirits; you cannot manifest your true genius by yourself. What good is a gift if its only usage is solely for your benefit? So try your best to never become selfish and always think of how you can use your gifts for the benefit of others. Never seek glory; instead, you must seek to become a role model for discipline and relentlessness. Are you a disciplined and relentless person?

THE WRIGHT BROTHERS

Orville and Wilbur Wright were two American aviators, engineers, inventors, and aviation pioneers who are generally credited with inventing, building, and flying the world's first successful airplane. In 1904-05 the brothers perfected their flying machine into the first practical fixed-wing aircraft. Although not the first to build experimental aircraft, the Wright brothers were the first to invent aircraft controls that made fixed-wing powered flight possible. From the beginning of their aeronautical work, the Wright brothers focused on developing a reliable method of pilot control as the key to solving "the flying problem." This approach differed significantly from other experimenters of the time, who put more emphasis on developing powerful engines.

The Wrights gained the mechanical skills essential for their success by working for years in their shop with printing presses, bicycles, motors, and other machinery. Their work with bicycles in particular influenced their belief that an unstable vehicle like a flying machine could be controlled and balanced, with practice. From 1900 until their first powered flights in late 1903, they conducted extensive glider tests, which incidentally helped to develop their skills as pilots. Their bicycle shop employee, Charlie Taylor, became an important part of the team, building their first airplane engine in close collaboration with the brothers. Both brothers attended high school, but did not receive diplomas. The family's abrupt move in 1884 from Richmond, Indiana back to Dayton, Ohio, where the family had lived during the 1870s, prevented Wilbur from receiving his diploma, even after finishing four years of high school. The diploma was awarded posthumously to Wilbur on April 16, 1994, which would have been his 127th birthday.

In December 1892, the brothers opened a repair and sales shop (the Wright Cycle Exchange, later the Wright Cycle Company) and in 1896 began manufacturing their own brand. They used this endeavor to fund their growing interest in flight. In the early or mid-1890s they saw newspaper or magazine articles, and probably photographs, of the dramatic gliders by Otto Lilienthal in Germany. Three important aeronautical events happened in 1896. In May, Smithsonian Institution secretary Samuel Langley successfully flew an unmanned steam-powered fixed-wing model aircraft. In mid-year, Chicago engineer and aviation authority Octave Chanute brought together several men who tested various types of gliders over the sand dunes along the shore of Lake Michigan. In August, Lilienthal was killed in the plunge of his glider. These events lodged in the minds of the brothers, especially Lilienthal's death. The Wright brothers later cited his death as the point when their serious interest in flight research began. Wilbur said, "Lilienthal was without question the greatest of the precursors, and the world owes to him a great debt."

Despite Lilienthal's fate, the brothers favored his strategy: to practice gliding in order to master the art of control, before attempting motor-driven flight. The death of British aeronaut Percy Pilcher in another hang-gliding crash in October 1899 only reinforced their opinion that a reliable method of pilot control was the key to a successful and safe flight. At the outset of their experiments they regarded control as the unsolved third part of "the flying problem." Although agreeing with Lilienthal's idea of practice, the Wrights saw that his method of balance and control by shifting his body weight was inadequate, and this sparked an insatiable determination to resolve "the flying problem."

On the basis of observation, Wilbur concluded that birds changed the angle of the ends of their wings to make their airborne bodies roll right or left. The brothers decided this would also be a good way for a flying machine to turn — to "bank" or "lean" into the turn — just like a bird and just like a person riding a bicycle, an experience with which they were thoroughly familiar. They hoped this method would enable recovery when the wind tilted the flying machine to one side. They puzzled over how to achieve the same effect with manmade wings, and eventually discovered wing-warping when Wilbur idly twisted a long inner-tube box at the bicycle shop. After this, they experimented with over 700 gliders to discover more problems that needed to be addressed to ensure a safe flight. Eventually, they added power to their flights. However, years of progression and failed attempts followed. Several military personnel lost their lives flying their planes because of the experimental quality of their theories, and more work was needed. Lawsuits ensued as well, because of litigation and other people working on similar ideas who wanted to take credit for the work of the Wrights. The brothers were truly pioneers and they are one of the reasons why we fly today. Modern technology has corrected a lot of the concerns involved with flying, but they started the process with no degrees or even high school diplomas.

Fight for Your Dream's Rights

The Wright brothers were truly geniuses and their examples can definitely be used to help you to alter your mindset. I find it interesting that neither brother had an advanced degree. However, the Wright brothers suffered through shame and pain from the deaths of friends and military personnel because of the flaws in their planes. However, they didn't allow the regrets to get in the way of their dreams. Actually, it motivated them to get better and to keep going until they mastered their craft. The brothers opened a shop to help fund their dreams and they involved the community. The Wright brothers were notorious for being humble and involving the world as a whole. Their imaginations seemed crazy at first to naysayers, but after years of hard work they were able to capture their dreams. The Wright brothers experienced failure after failure, but their contributions have become invaluable. Use the Wright brothers' example to help you to develop the mind frame of a genius.

MARTIN LUTHER KING, JR.

Martin Luther King, Jr. was born on January 25, 1929 and died April 4, 1968. He was an American Baptist minister and activist who became the most visible spokesperson for the civil rights movement. He is best known for advancing civil rights through nonviolence and civil disobedience. His tactics were inspired by his Christians beliefs and the nonviolent activism of Mahatma Gandhi. Dr. King led the 1955 Montgomery, Alabama bus boycott, and in 1957 became the first president of the Southern Christian Leadership Conference (SCLC). With the SCLC, he led an unsuccessful 1962 struggle against segregation in Albany, Georgia, and helped organize the nonviolent 1963 protests in Birmingham, Alabama. He also helped organize the 1963 March on Washington, where he delivered his famous "I Have a Dream" speech. On October 14, 1964, King won the Nobel Peace Prize for combating racial inequality through nonviolent resistance.

In his final years he expanded this focus to include opposition towards poverty and the Vietnam War. He alienated many of his liberal allies with a 1967 speech entitled "Beyond Vietnam." J. Edgar Hoover considered him a radical and made him an object of the FBI's COINTELPRO in 1963. Subsequently, FBI agents investigated him for possible communist ties, recorded his extramarital liaisons and reported on them to government officials, and on one occasion mailed King a threatening anonymous letter.

King suffered from depression throughout most of his life. In his adolescent years, he initially felt resentment against white people due to the "racial humiliation" that he, his family, and his neighbors often had to endure in the segregated South. At the age of twelve, shortly after his maternal grandmother died, King blamed himself and jumped out of a second-story window, but survived. Growing up in Atlanta, King attended Booker T. Washington High School. He became known for his public speaking ability, and was part of the school's debate team. When King was thirteen in 1942, he became the youngest assistant manager of a newspaper delivery station for the Atlanta *Journal*. During his junior year in high school, he won first prize in an oratorical contest sponsored by the Negro Elks Club in Dublin, Georgia. On the ride home to Atlanta by bus, he and his teacher were ordered by the driver to stand so that white passengers could sit down. King initially refused, but complied after his teacher told him that he would be breaking the law if he did not submit. During this incident, King said that he was the "the angriest I have ever been in my life." An outstanding student, he skipped both the ninth and the twelfth grades of high school.

The summer before his last year at Morehouse College, in 1947, the eighteen-year old King chose to enter the ministry. He had concluded that the church offered the most assuring way to answer "an inner urge to serve humanity." In 1948, King graduated at age nineteen from Morehouse with a B.A. in sociology. He then enrolled in Crozer Theological Seminary in Chester, Pennsylvania, where he graduated with a B.Div. Degree in 1951. King's father had fully supported his decision to continue his education. On June 5, 1955, King received his PhD from Boston University, and the bus boycott of 1955 in Montgomery, Alabama was Dr. King's coming-out party. However, the bus boycott was sparked by a fifteen-year-old teenager and Rosa Parks, both of whom refused to give up their seats to white passengers. King became a national figure because of his leadership of the boycott's organization.

King believed that organized nonviolent protests against the system of southern segregation known as "Jim Crow" laws would lead to extensive media coverage of the struggle for black equality and voting rights. Journalistic accounts and televised footage of the daily deprivation and indignities suffered by Southern blacks, and of segregationist violence, and harassment of civil rights workers and marchers, produced a wave of sympathetic public opinion that convinced the majority of Americans that the Civil Rights movement was the most important issue in American politics in the early 1960s. King organized and led marches for black people's right to vote, and for desegregation, labor rights and other basic civil rights. Most of these rights were successfully enacted into US law with the passage of the Civil Rights Acts of 1964 and the 1965 Voting Rights Act.

King and the SCLC put into practice many of the principles of the Christian Left, and applied the tactics of the nonviolent protest with great success by strategically choosing the method of protest, and the places in which protests were carried out. There were often dramatic stand-offs with segregationist authorities, who sometimes turned violent. King was criticized by many groups during the course of his participation in the Civil Rights movement. This included opposition by more militant blacks such as Nation of Islam member Malcolm X, and Stokely Carmichael, both separatists who disagreed with King's methods.

Develop the Mind Frame of Dr. Martin Luther King, Jr.

King went to prison and chose prison over bail to stand up for his rights. He is noted for the Albany movement, Birmingham Campaign, St. Augustine, Florida movement, Selma, Alabama movement, New York City movement, March on Washington, and so many more. King was a visionary and his efforts led to desegregation. Martin Luther's King's dream eventually was fulfilled: his passion had moved him to follow his heart. Dr. King's legacy proves that gifts are nurtured throughout our lives and that our life's journey can always change. So always be flexible enough to know when your life has been elevated for a higher calling. Dr. King's vision pushed him to risk his life and to believe in something that seemed impossible at the time. He faced oppositions that we can't even begin to imagine, but he still chased his dreams. Be a visionary and use your imagination, and be willing to fight for your dreams. You must have a backbone like Dr. King to stand up for what you believe in, even when no one else believes in you. Dr. Martin Luther King, Jr. was a true genius who understood his purpose, and his visions were eventually manifested. His example also shows that when you're determined to do something you know is right, eventually the right people will begin to notice you, and they will help you throughout your journey of self-discovery.

LES BROWN

Leslie Calvin Brown, better known as Les Brown, was born February 17, 1945. He is an American motivational speaker, author, radio disc jockey, former television host and former politician. As a politician, he was a member of the Ohio House of Representatives. As a motivational speaker, he uses the catchphrase "it's possible," and he teaches people to follow their dreams, just as he learned to do.

Les Brown was born with his twin brother, Wesley, in an abandoned building in Liberty City, a low-income section of Miami, Florida. He was subsequently adopted by Mamie Brown, a thirty-eight-year old single woman who worked as a cafeteria attendant and domestic assistant. He was declared "educable mentally retarded" while in grade school. But despite the self-esteem and confidence loss issues this created, he learned how to reach his full potential with the encouragement from his mother and assistance from a helpful teacher in high school, a key point that he mentions in his motivational speeches.

According to many of Brown's speeches, he first decided to get into public radio and kept returning to the same radio station, time and time again, looking for a break. It wasn't until the on-air failures of the afternoon DJ that he got his break in radio and was hired full-time as on-air talent. Upon his termination from the radio station, he ran for election in the Ohio House of Representatives and won. After leaving the Ohio state legislature, he decided to get into television and eventually ended up on PBS. He also formed Les Brown Enterprises in order to support his newest career as a motivational speaker, and was on KFWB in California with a daily syndicated radio program from 2011 to 2012. In the late 1980s and early 1990s, he also won many local and national awards for excellence and he has one Emmy to his name.

Develop the Mindset of Les Brown

Les Brown is one of my favorite motivational speakers, and his background to triumph over his adversities is truly inspirational. I recommend that you listen to some of his tapes, along with other speakers such as Zig Ziglar, Earl Nightingale, Jim Rohn, Dr. Myles Monroe, Eric Thomas, Bob Proctor, Earl Nightengale, and Napeleon Hill and of course listen to my speeches. Les Brown's story teaches you that it doesn't matter where you come from, but if you really want something badly enough, and you're willing to fight for it, then you can achieve it. He teaches that you should only give yourself two options: either you will succeed or you will fail, and failure isn't an option. Les Brown struggled with belief in himself and it wasn't until he believed in himself that he was able to capture his dreams. I highly recommend you upload some of his speeches from YouTube and listen to his story. His tenacity is unmatched in many ways and he is a true genius.

ARNOLD SCHWARZENEGGER

Arnold Schwarzenegger was born July 30, 1947. He is an Austrian-American actor, producer, businessman, investor, author, philanthropist, activist, politician, and former professional bodybuilder. He served two terms as the thirty-eighth Governor of California from 2003-2011. He started lifting weights at age fifteen and won Mr. Universe at twenty, and he went on to win it seven times. It wasn't easy for him, but he eventually gained worldwide fame as a Hollywood action-film icon. He went on to play in a plethora of films and starred in the famous *Terminator* trilogy, with the famous line from part 2, "I'll be back."

During his childhood, his father showed favoritism to his older brother, and Arnold's upbringing wasn't one of riches. Schwarzenegger recalled that one of the highlights of his youth was when the family bought a refrigerator. His father wanted him to be a police officer, but Arnold had bigger dreams. Schwarzenegger took to visiting a gym in Graz, where he also frequented the local movie theaters to see bodybuilding idols such as Reg Park, Steve Reeves, and Johnny Weissmuller on the big screen. When Reeves died in 2000, Schwarzenegger fondly remembered him. "As a teenager, I grew up with Steve Reeves. His remarkable accomplishments allowed me a sense of what was possible when others around me didn't always understand my dreams."

In 1961, Schwarzenegger met former Mr. Austria Kurt Marnul, who invited him to train at the gym in Graz. He was dedicated as a youngster, and he even broke into the local gym on weekends so that he could train even when the gym was closed. Arnold said: "It would make me sick to miss a workout." In an interview with *Fortune* in 2004, Schwarzenegger explained the emotional gap between himself and his father by telling how he suffered child abuse at the hands of his father. Arnold refused to conform to other people's standards. He said he had a will that could not be broken. When his father used to beat him and people told him what he couldn't do, he would say,

"This is not going to be for much longer because I'm going to move out of here. I want to be rich. I want to be somebody."

During his early adulthood, he served in the Austrian Army in 1965 to fulfill the one year of service required at the time of all eighteen-year-old Austrian males. During his army service, he won the Junior Mr. Europe contest. He went AWOL during basic training so he could take part in that competition and was sentenced to spend a week in military prison: "Participating in the competition meant so much to me that I didn't carefully think through the consequences."

Arnold stated: "The Mr. Universe title was my ticket to America, the land of opportunity, where I could become a star and get rich." Schwarzenegger made his first airplane trip in 1966, attending the NABBA Mr. Universe competition in London. He would come in second place there, lacking the muscle definition of American winner Chester Yorton. Charles "Wag" Bennett, one of the judges at the 1966 competition, was impressed with Schwarzenegger and offered to coach him. Schwarzenegger had little money during this time, but Bennett invited him to stay in his crowded family home.

Staying in the East End of London helped Schwarzennegger improve his rudimentary grasp of the English language. Living with the Bennetts also changed him as a person. Arnold's training paid off and, in 1967, Schwarzenegger won the title for the first time, becoming the youngest-ever Mr. Universe at the age of twenty. Schwarzenegger then flew back to Munich, where he attended a business school and worked in a health club (Rolf Putziger's gym, where he worked and trained from 1966 to 1968). Arnold frequently told Roger C. Field, his English coach and friend in Munich at that time, "I'm going to become the greatest actor!" Arnold went on to accomplish many of his aspirations, along with so much more.

Build Your Mind Frame like Arnold Built His Body

Arnold is a great example to follow if you need a proven example for success. All of the odds were against him, and yet he was motivated and he believed in himself. Arnold's example teaches you to always give your best and to strive to be the best. Arnold wanted to be successful so badly that he broke into a gym just to work out.

Arnold wanted to be successful so badly that he risked his life and his freedom by going AWOL when he served in the military. I'm not encouraging you to break the law! I'm just mentioning his example to illustrate his level of commitment. Arnold was a foreigner, who chased his dream to get to the United States, and he took classes to work on his English, and he took acting classes after working a nine-to-five job. He literally used every second of his time wisely and he was obsessed with his dreams. Arnold stated that, when he lifted weights, it felt like he was lifting a trophy—because that's how real his dreams were to him. *Can you truly see yourself living your dream?*

Learn from Arnold's example; get your mind in shape by building mental muscles from training yourself to be the best. *Finally, you must be creative and think outside the box. Never say to yourself that you don't know what to do — because you do know what to do. In fact, simply ask yourself why you feel like you don't know what to do? Then ask yourself, "If I did know how to pursue my dreams, how would I go about doing it?"*

OPRAH WINFREY

Oprah Winfrey was born January 29, 1954. She is an American media executive, talk show host, actress, producer, and philanthropist. She is best known for her talk show *The Oprah Winfrey Show*, which is the highest-rated television program of its kind in history and was nationally syndicated from 1986 to 2011 in Chicago, Illinois. She was the richest African American of the twentieth century, and North America's first black multi-billionaire, and has been ranked the greatest black philanthropist in American history. She has been one of the most influential women in the world.

Oprah was born into poverty in rural Mississippi to a teenage single mother, and was raised in an inner-city neighborhood in Milwaukee, Wisconsin. Oprah stated that she was molested during her childhood, and early teens, which resulted in her becoming pregnant at the age of fourteen. Oprah landed a job in radio while still in high school and began co-anchoring the local evening news at the age of nineteen. Her emotional ad-lib delivery eventually got her transferred to the daytime talk show arena, and after boosting a third-rated local Chicago talk show to first place, she launched her own production company and became internationally syndicated. Oprah Winfrey overcame some intractable circumstances and she manifested her inner genius.

Develop the Mind Frame of Oprah Winfrey

I'm sure you've noticed that all of these geniuses started to manifest their gifts at an early age. So, what are the things you did as a young adult or as a child that you enjoyed? What things do you seem to grasp with ease? What are the aspirations that give you joy from just thinking about them? If you're truly unsure what your gifts are, then honestly answer the two questions previously mentioned, and it will begin the process to unlock your true genius. Oprah Winfrey teaches us that when you follow your ordained path for greatness, you'll be amazed where your gifts will eventually take you. Finally, no one can escape the adversities of life, and if you're brave enough to chase your dreams like Oprah did on a daily basis, then one day you will wake up and you'll actually be living your fantasies.

Success Leaves Clues

The universe is waiting for you to add your name to the thousands of people who have manifested their true geniuses, despite their intractable circumstances. Some of the clues left behind by the aforementioned geniuses in this chapter are: ridiculous amounts of effort; massive amounts of hard work; varied stratagems; patience; faith; self-belief; boldness; courage; flexibility; imagination. And they all knew their emotional whys. To develop the mind frame of a genius, you must know why you truly want to do what is in your heart's mind. To develop the mind frame of a genius, you must have an eclectic imagination. It's essential for you to visualize the way you want your future to be, and not the way someone else tells you it will be. You must believe in yourself and you must be willing to sacrifice your very existence in order to fulfill your destiny. Finally, this doesn't mean that you literally want to die, but a winner's mindset never seeks long-term failure, and not achieving a goal is never an option for a real winner.

Epiphany of Your Heart

"Whatever makes you feel like your life isn't worth living unless you're pursuing it is the doorway to your heart's true love." The fire that's burning inside of your heart is your true passion. If you love your dreams and you believe in your abilities, and you're willing to decry the naysayers, then you will be amazed at the things you will begin to conjure by deciding never to quit. God wouldn't give other people gifts that would allow them to become more successful than you or anybody else. James 2:9 helps us all to appreciate that God isn't a God of favoritism and that he loves us all. Acts 10:34-35 also helps us to appreciate that God is an impartial God.

So here is the simple formula for developing the mind frame of a genius: 1. Put God first and let Him guide your steps. 2. Reflect on your natural abilities and nurture them. 3. What gifts do you have that make you excited just thinking about them? 4. What are you truly passionate about? What is something that you would almost do for free because you love it so much? 5. You must use your imagination and every single day visualize yourself capturing your dreams. 6. Do massive amounts of work to get noticed and don't ever quit, no matter what. 7. You must believe in yourself and don't tell your plans to people who aren't trying to manifest their true genius. 8. Don't take on too many responsibilities unless they are associated with your dreams. 9. You must listen to motivational, inspirational, and spiritual audio programs every day. You must invest in your mind by developing a reading schedule and attending seminars/webinars that are related to your dreams. 10. Finally, you must associate with other geniuses who truly believe they are special and that everyone has a gift.

The next chapter will help you to strengthen a special part of your brain to successfully attain your dreams.

CHAPTER 11

THE PREFRONTAL CORTEX

THE PREFRONTAL CORTEX OF YOUR brain plays a powerful role in helping you to achieve your goals. You can reshape its functions to produce favorable results by using *The Limelight Spot Effect* from Chapter 5, along with the concepts in this chapter.

Prefrontal Cortex

The prefrontal cortex is a part of the brain located at the front of the frontal lobe. It is implicated in a variety of complex behaviors, including planning, and greatly contributes to personality development.

Roles of the Prefrontal Cortex

The prefrontal cortex is involved in a wide variety of mental functions, including:

- Coordinating and adjusting complex behavior
- Impulse control and organization of emotional reactions
- Personality
- Focusing and organizing attention

- Complex planning
- Considering and prioritizing competing and simultaneous information; the ability to ignore external distractions is partially influenced by the prefrontal cortex.

After reading the variety of functions of the prefrontal cortex, you can see how *The Spotlight Effect* mentioned in Chapter 5 doesn't aid in the development of the prefrontal cortex. *The Spotlight Effect* actually underdevelops the prefrontal cortex, and complicates it with too many opinions and distractions, which can potentially lead to misguided actions and misguided inactions. A misguided action always leads to misguided inactions because you will never take the proper steps if you're receiving the wrong information, even if you've convinced yourself that your plan of action is correct. So, just remember that the truth is indisputable and you must take your emotions out of the picture and view your results in life objectively. A misguided action can unconsciously discourage you from investigating another aspect of a pursuit that might interest you.

Failures are necessary but if you can knowingly avoid failures, then by all means you should. Too many failures can lead to a loss of drive to achieve your goals, especially if you haven't developed a true obsession with self-development. I'm not being contradictory, I just know that it takes time to truly become obsessed with self-development, and people develop this obsession during different stages of their lives. Only an obsessed individual can fail 1,000 times and still be motivated to keep moving forward. So, until the proper obsession kicks in, you must be cognizant of how you're directing your dreams steps, and you shouldn't be afraid to fail. But, if you can avoid failures by making great decisions, then you should by all means avoid any unnecessary setbacks along your journey. The improper use of your heart's road map, which can only happen by using someone else's GPS, should always be avoided. Most importantly, being bold and taking full responsibility for your decisions, along with believing in yourself, strengthens your prefrontal cortex. So, always put your own individual coordinates into your life's GPS. (*Refer back to Chapter 5 for the concept of life's GPS and your heart's road map.*)

Your Life's Mirror and the Prefrontal Cortex

When you use your life's mirror to properly reflect your life's stains, you will be able to notice your temporary distractions without allowing them to be reflected in your life's mirror. Chapter 5 developed this concept, and if you refer back to Chapter 5 and read it again, it will reinforce the development of your prefrontal cortex.

The Limelight Spot Effect taught you to be concerned with your heart's map, your life's GPS, and only with what you think. When you sync these three important things together, it will help you to see your life's mirror clearly. The prefrontal cortex helps you to control your emotions, and a healthy prefrontal cortex will help you to resist the temptation to react presumptuously. If you seek advice from too many people, it can lead to impulsive acts in a positive or a negative way. How can you focus your attention on your dreams if you're consumed with other people's opinions? How can you fix your life's GPS if you aren't truly following your life's coordinates? Never unconsciously program your heart's map to showcase hundreds of coordinates that belong to other people's hearts. How can you train yourself to ignore misguided competing information if you allow yourself to be consumed with what other people think? How can you win, if you allow the haters who may have already fallen, to pull you down? Remember: you are your own opponent, so use *The Limelight Spot Effect* to defeat yourself. Your weakness is you and your strength is you. You can improve your strengths by focusing on yourself and what you think. Finally, Chapter 5 helped you to appreciate that this form of thinking will elevate your belief system about yourself, along with eliminating the weakness to rely on what others think.

The struggle not to be concerned with what others think will always exist, so fight your weaknesses by strengthening your belief in yourself. You have to love yourself, so continue to take in knowledge, because knowledge about your dreams will keep you going. Some important points to remember are: when someone quits, they also aren't doing anything to keep themselves motivated toward achieving their desired outcomes. For example, if you wanted to eat better, but you quit because it's too hard, then you will never eat better. If you wanted to get in shape and you quit because it's taking too long, you will never get in shape. If you wanted to get a job, and you stopped looking because you tried 100 times, then you may never find one. Remember: rejection has strength in numbers! Make your current spot in life shine by controlling your destiny, along with accurately pursuing your dreams, so that your affect will be that of happiness. When you're working in harmony with your life's GPS and your heart's map, it will always lead you to your true destiny.

It's imperative that you strengthen your prefrontal cortex. If you do so, you will drastically increase your chances of being successful. However, I urge you to wait until you have read each chapter of this book, especially the final chapter, before you implement the exercises for the prefrontal cortex. This whole book is an exercise for your prefrontal cortex; in fact, it was specifically designed to elevate your prefrontal cortex. You have to use your brain and you have to keep training it, just like any other muscle. Just think about how powerful your abilities will become for thinking, focusing, prioritizing, considering, adjusting, coordinating, and impulse control! Just think about how exponentially your success rate will increase through positively retraining your prefrontal cortex.

The next chapter will help you implement a few concepts that are necessary for capturing your dreams. Remember this: *A clear vision of where you're headed and how to get there will always help you along your pursuit toward greatness.* The next chapter will help you to truly grasp the importance of manifesting your greatness by focusing on your efforts, and the objectivity of the numbers that are associated with your dreams.

Exercises to Strengthen Your Prefrontal Cortex

✓ Create a positive future story; optimism is associated with rising levels of dopamine which engages the brain.

✓ Follow a sleep routine. At the end of the day, choose a pleasant activity that brings your day to a peaceful end. Getting adequate sleep is connected with memory function.

✓ Avoid drama and avoid getting caught up in gossip, along with negative what-if's and negative theatrical reactions. Drama fires up the amygdala, which will keep your prefrontal cortex off of its game.

√ Move your body with sports, dance, exercise, and other active, adventurous pursuits.

√ Find ways to express your gratitude. Feeling gratitude activates your positive emotions, which helps to productively activate the prefrontal cortex.

√ Offer and receive physical contact. Give and take hugs to literally soothe the brain with calming inhibitory peptides.

√ Create silly sentences and acronyms to help you remember things. These skills call on the prefrontal cortex and the brain's executive functions to access your working memory. By integrating jokes, riddles, and puns, you can also learn to think flexibly by shifting between different meanings, and associations of words.

√ Play! Make-believe play will strengthen your prefrontal cortex, so use your imagination.

√ Be of service and volunteer. Social and mental activities send blood rushing to the prefrontal cortex, but it must involve free labor, and something that's meaningful to you.

√ Learn to juggle. Learning any new and engaging activities fires off neurons in a positive way. Some other activities that can be effective for firing off neurons are dancing, circus arts, music, theatre, and sports. Also, use your nondominant hand more. If you're right-handed, look for ways to do more things with your left hand. Finally, change your daily patterns peridorically. For example, if you brush your teeth as soon as you get up, do something different, like, read a positive section from the newspaper first.

CHAPTER 12

NUMBERS DON'T LIE

CHAPTER OBJECTIVES: TO KNOW THE importance of numbers and their relationship to your dreams. Do you know what grades you have earned performing the goal-oriented tasks necessary to achieve your dreams? Do you know how much effort you're putting into each individual goal-oriented task that's necessary to achieve your dreams? Do you know how to determine the overall performance effort of your dreams? Do you know how to calculate the overall performance percentages of your dreams?

If you graded the overall performance effort of your dreams, would you have a 100% A+ effort? How do you know if your effort is 100%? This chapter will reveal to you how much effort you're actually putting into your dreams. 100% effort is the only thing that works! Sometimes, achieving your goals will have nothing to do with your talents and skills. But it will have everything to do with your lack of giving a 100% A+ effort, which will most likely hold you back from fulfilling your dreams.

You can grade your efforts toward your dreams in the same way that mathematicians, scientists, and educators grade tests. For example, suppose you were taking an English class and the English teacher indicated exactly what you needed to do to pass the class. So technically, all you would need to do are the things indicated by the teacher in order to receive an A. Sometimes life is just like school and taking a test, and similarly, all you have to do are the things required to successfully capture your dreams.

Whether you're still in school or out of school, you're familiar with receiving an A, B, C, D, F, or an incomplete for school grades. However, the interesting thing about grades and dreams is: you always start off with a 100% A. Look at it like this: you can't injure yourself until you do something that could put you at risk of injuring yourself, so until you injure yourself, you're injury-free. All of your life's endeavors should be viewed the same way. Theoretically, goals are 100% guaranteed until you actually start pursuing your goals. It's just like a full tank of gas: a full tank of gas will remain a full tank of gas until you actually start using the gas. And an empty tank of gas will remain an empty tank of gas until you add gas to the gas tank. Here is the point: 0% and 100% value quantities are only measurable if the substances, volumes, and constructs being measured and tested are absolute. For example, if a car's gas tank was designed to only contain 16.23 gallons of gas, then that's the absolute maximum amount of gas the car's gas tank will be able to contain. If you tried adding more gas, the gas would simply flow out and spill all over you. I'm sure you've filled up a gas tank at a gas station, and once the tank was full it automatically stopped the pump, indicating the gas tank was full. So any measurable substance, construct, or volume that contains a 100% maximum value quantity will always have a 0% minimum value quantity as well. However, it's important to remember this: this is only applicable if the volume being measured has already been tested, and if the absolute maximum and minimum value quantities have been concisely measured and proven.

To help you remember the concepts of what I'm disclosing, simply think of putting gas into a car. The amount of gas a car's gas tank may contain is a 100% absolute maximum value quantity if the car's gas tank is full, but once the gas is completely used and the gas tank is empty, this indicates a 0% absolute minimum value quantity. It's important to note that a 0% absolute minimum value quantity has the exact same principles embedded in it as a 100% absolute maximum value quantity. To further illustrate: if a car completely runs out of gas, then the car would stop, thus indicating the car has reached a 0% absolute minimum value quantity, which would indicate the car needs gas. Furthermore, if the car's gas container is full, and you try to add more gas, the gas will continue to overflow, no matter how much additional gas you try to squeeze into the gas tank.

However, it's important to make a mental note of this: When comparing and contrasting the gas tank illustration with comprehension tests and performance assessments to measure your actual effort toward your dreams, you must recognize the slight differences and the relative components of each one of the individual tasks that are associated with the successful attainment of your goals. Your dreams aren't like a gas container that can only hold 16.23 gallons of gas. A 16.23-gallon gas container can only be measured between 0 and 100% absolute maximum and minimum value quantities. A container's volume has a 0% minimum and a 100% maximum quantity value, which means the construct is absolutely measurable. But theoretically, goals and dreams start off with a 100% relative maximum quantity value. The performances of all relative and unproven constructs can only be tested after the execution of each individual task. Most importantly, each individual goal-oriented task tested must be universally recognized as an essential aspect to objectively test the performance of all relative and unproven constructs.

To illustrate: a 100-point test containing fifty questions indicates that each correct answer is worth two points, and if each question is answered correctly, then the grade would be a 100% A. However, if all of the questions are answered incorrectly, then the grade would be a 0% F. So, someone's actual performance can only be measured or tested after the successful completion of the construct, or the 100-point test that's administered. So the outcome of a test results can only be measured after you've taken the test.

This illustrates the differences between possibilities and what actually may or may not happen. So before you start any measurable test, you start off with a 100% and your performance dictates the percentage you will attain. The only way you can get a 0% prior to taking a test would be if you refused to take the test, which would automatically default in a 0% because you didn't do anything, so nothing can be proven, so nothing can be measured. I'm sure you're heard this saying before: "nothing from nothing leads to nothing." So 0% input will equal a 0% output regardless of whether the constructs, substances, and volumes being tested are universally known to be relative or absolute. So, go after your dreams and be brave because no one truly knows how your life's possibilities will unfold!

To reiterate: the actual performance outcome percentages assessed for any given test can only be determined after the test has been taken. So, how can someone start off with a 0% minimum relative or absolute quantity value performance before they have even attempted to perform the test? The outcome performance of any test being measured can only be assessed after the execution of the test. So all dreams and goals are theoretically 100% guaranteed until their pursuit begins. Your dreams can only have a 0% outcome before you pursue your dreams if you decide not to do anything at all. So, even if you gave a test your all and you got every last question wrong, which would result in a 0%, is still better than not trying at all, because your effort wouldn't be 0%. Why, because only you can measure how much effort you actually put into something! Remember this: *"Repeated attempts means more effort and repetition inherently will increase your performance in numbers if you force yourself to become consciously aware of why you're failing, and then make a full committment to learning how to pass whatever test that's temporarily defeating you."* So, who really knows what's going to happen whenever they're truly chasing their dreams? You may have an idea, but you really don't know exactly how things will unfold. So until you actually start a test, you actually have a default performance value of a 100% maximum quantity value if the construct being tested has absolute maximum and minimum quantity values. The only way you can get a 0% absolute minimum quantity performance value before executing a test would be if you refused to take the test, which would automatically equate to a 0% performance grade and a 0% in positive effort! Only positive efforts produce satisfying results. Quitting is a negative conscious effort and cannot and will never produce a winner! Are you a winner? Whether you're a winner or a loser will be demonstrated through your actions!

However, if the construct that's being assessed is relative and unproven, no percentage can be measured because nothing has been proven. How can you give 0% or 100% to an unproven substance or performance? Anything that's corporeal or incorporeal will require a certain amount of effort, whether it's universally known or not. In fact, simply thinking about a matter requires effort, but how can you accurately measure the percentage of thought given to an idea? No one can accurately measure the amount of effort they put into their thoughts, so it's reasonable to conclude that the percentage of effort put into thoughts alone can't be 0% because effort is required to think. Remember this: *"Deciding not to decide is still a decision because unconscious and conscious thinking effort would still be required in order to decide not to decide. Unconscious derelictions aren't noble, it's just like driving sober or driving drunk, and if you have an accident—sober or drunk—it's still an accident."*

Capturing your dreams is always possible! All you need to do is to grade your current efforts and assess your percentages, and then do an honest self-analysis of your current efforts. If you're not giving your dreams a 100% A+ effort, simply increase your percentages until you're literally giving a measurable 100% A+ effort. Most importantly, these percentages must be based on everything that is clearly defined, and connected to the successful attainment of your dreams. However, it's important to know that new discoveries are made all the time. So all dreams must be viewed as an evolving mechanism, and your various pursuits toward your dreams always start off with you winning, if you're truly viewing it in a scientific way. An evolving mechanism simply represents a living organism or a non-living construct that has room for growth. All things are capable of being upgraded and refined, so just remember: you don't really know what's going to happen until you develop the courage to go for it! You might invent or discover something after you recognize life's possibilities for what they truly are. Life's possibilities are unlimited because all dreams are relative to a degree, and each dreamer will always have a different experience, despite any proven or unproven paths for success.

How to Implement the Concepts of Numbers Don't Lie

There are steps you need to take for all of your endeavors and you must know them. Success is never an accident, and if it is, then you won't know how to repeat it. If you cheat on tests and cheat your way through life, it will catch up with you at some point. So in order to be great you must embrace life's challenges and never seek the easy way out.

What precise steps are needed to achieve your goals? Have you asked yourself this question relentlessly? You can grade yourself accurately or relatively by looking at your efforts. Maybe you failed because although you thought you were giving a 100% effort, after conducting a personal audit your numbers show you're actually putting forth a 75% C effort. Train your mind to give 100% from this point moving forward. Do not move on to the next phase of your goals if you gave the previous phase for attaining your goals a 99% effort, because the 1% you didn't master may come back to hurt you. Your input will be your output. Suppose you were instructed by your teacher to expect twenty words on a test, and you only made sure you knew fifteen of those words. In this case, you shouldn't expect to get a 100% A+. I can promise you, the words wouldn't just pop into your head. So likewise, you will receive the grades and the percentages you've put into your dreams. Let's look at a few examples of dreams, along with the prerequisites to achieving them.

Suppose someone wanted to run a marathon and they wanted to run the marathon within a certain timeframe, without stopping. After doing extensive research they discovered everyone who ran a marathon within the timeframe they're shooting for ran 60 miles a week. Would it be reasonable for someone to run 30 miles a week, and expect to be able to run longer than someone who has been running 60 miles a week? If you only give 50% toward an endeavor, then you should only expect a 50% return. Your input is your output! You should always be interested in assessing the efforts you're putting into your goals and dreams. By doing so, this allows you to see if the direction you're headed in is congruent with what it takes to be successful in whatever dreams you're pursuing. If you apply the important concepts from this chapter toward achieving your goals, you'll officially be setting the stage for a calculated risk.

Concrete Numbers

There are twelve months in a year, 168 hours a week, 8,760 hours a year, and 8,784 hours in a leap year. Only one month out of the year has 672 hours, and that's February. If it's a leap year, February will have 696 hours. The other eleven months have 720 to 744 hours in a month. Four months out of a year have 720 hours in each month and seven months have 744 hours in each month. Once all of the hours from each one of the twelve months are added together it totals 8,760 hours or (720 x 4 + 744 x 7) + 672 = 8,760 hours in a year. As you continue to read, you will begin to see why these numbers are important.

The first thing I want you to do is to look at how you're using your time Mondays through Sundays. Subsequently, write down all of the activities you're participating in throughout the week. I want you to write down how many hours you sleep on each day. Write down how long it takes for you to get dressed and commute to and from work. Write down the total amount of hours it takes for you to eat every day. Write down how many hours you work in a week. Write down how many hours you spend watching TV each week and every day. Write down how long it takes for you to get dressed. Write down how long it takes for you to get ready for bed. Write down how many hours you dedicate toward family time each week. If you exercise, write down how many hours a week you work out. Write down how many hours you use to study and read each week. Write down how much time you typically spend talking on the phone every day. Write down how many hours you spend each week cooking. If you attend a weekly religious service to worship God, and if you're spending time in the ministry, write that down as well. Write down how many hours a week you spend cleaning up. Do not exaggerate the time you spend on these activities. After you do this, I want you to add up the total hours you spend in a month doing these activities.

I can guarantee you're noticing you have over 150-280 unaccounted-for hours. If you don't work, you may have more like 350-500 unaccounted-for hours, which are hours you aren't using doing the things that will help make you great. For example, someone who says they don't have time to exercise isn't looking at their time management correctly because there are 168 hours in a week. Suppose Jim says he doesn't have time to work out. Well, he works 40 hours a week and sleeps eight hours a day. That's 56 hours of sleep in a week, and 96 hours with work and sleep combined. That leaves Jim with 72 hours remaining in his week.

To achieve a basic fitness regimen, Jim would only need to dedicate three to four hours of his remaining unaccounted-for 72 hours. If you were to subtract four hours from his remaining 72 hours, that would still leave him with 68 hours. Trust me, the time is always there! Jim's remaining 68 hours in a week more than likely isn't being used entirely for kids, fun, and family time. The time is there, but it's just that sometimes people allow themselves not to value the importance of exercising regularly.

So even after work, sleep, and exercising, Jim still has 68 hours to do things. If you wanted to look at it on a monthly basis, Jim would have 272 hours after sleep, working out, and work, and he could use some of those hours to work on his dreams. When you audit your time, you will most likely have 150-280 or even more unaccounted-for hours after you subtract work, exercise, and sleep. One hundred and fifty hours would be commensurate with someone who probably works 80 to 90 hours a week, which is rare. If they're working this many hours in a week, they're normally getting several consecutive days and weeks off. So regardless of how much someone works, they still have the time. Even if someone is sleeping for ten hours a day, they will still have around 200 hours a month to use at their discretion.

So, never fall prey to telling yourself that you don't have time because that's the biggest lie of all time! Some people only need 20 to 50 hours of the 272 unaccounted-for hours that the average person will have in a month to achieve their dreams. However, even if someone needed to dedicate more than 50 hours in a month to achieve their dreams, that's still okay because they would still have over 200 hours remaining. However, that's extreme because you don't have to use over 200 hours a month to fulfill your dreams.

Use Your Time Wisely

How many hours does it take you to eat in a week? I can guarantee you that you use between 28 and 84 hours in a month eating food, and 84 is really pushing it; you're probably closer to 28 hours or less. Suppose someone needs 84 hours a month to eat their food. That would be three hours a day with about 190 unaccounted hours remaining in a month. Go ahead and subtract all of the other things you think you do with your time. Even if you only had 20 hours remaining, those 20 hours can be used to help fulfill your dreams. The time is there, so never make excuses for why you can't capture your dreams. The problem is sometimes we don't want it badly enough! *"When you're passionate about something you really want, you will always find the time that has always been there."*

You Don't Have Any More of Your Time to Waste

It's normal to get tired from a job you like, especially if you have eight- to twelve-hour work days. If you have this type of job, you aren't always working like that and you will have days off. If you're tired, it may be because you need to eat better and get in shape. Have you ever thought that sometimes you're tired because you aren't fulfilling your passions? Your true passion will make it hard for you to sleep a lot because you'll be too excited to sleep. You'll want to get up the next day and embark upon an exciting journey of rewarding work. So stop pursuing careers you don't like! Stop staying in relationships you don't like! Stop spending time with people who make you count every second until it's over.

Let me be frank: no one consistently uses all of their 8,760 hours on work, family time, recreation, sleep, and spiritual matters. The numbers are incontrovertible proof, so never lie to yourself. Always reflect back on the numbers when the poisonous excuse, "I don't have the time," tries to show its ugly face. Take a few minutes to write down how many hours and minutes you spend every day working on your dreams. After this, write down how many hours a week you spend working on your dreams. After this, write down how many hours a month you spend working on your dreams, and then write down how many hours you spend each year working on your dreams. What did your numbers reveal about how you're using your time?

Numbers Don't Lie if You Calculate Them Properly

Out of the average 272 hours that we all have after work and sleep, let's suppose you used three hours a day for family time Monday through Friday. That's 15 hours a week. Suppose you used six hours on Saturday and six hours on Sunday for fun and family time. That's 12 hours a week used on the weekend out of 168 possible hours for the whole week. If this scenario were true, within a month's time family, and fun time would equal 15 hours during the week and 12 hours over the weekend, to total 27 hours in a week. If I added 40 hours of work and 56 hours of sleep to 27 hours, that's 123 hours. You still would have 45 hours to work on your dreams in a week. Using this example gives you between 204-252 hours a month, minus the 160 hours used for work, 224 hours used for sleep, and 108 hours used for fun and family time. Remember, four months of the year have 720 hours in them, and these months are April, June, September, and November. Seven months out of the year have 744 hours in them, and these months are January, March, May, July, August, October, and December. February is the only month that has 672 hours. These are facts. Numbers Don't Lie!

We all have the same amount of time in a day, a week, a month, and a year. No one gets more time than someone else. The example I'm using is generous because some people aren't using 56 hours a week for sleep. Some people aren't using 108 hours a month for fun and family time. Some people aren't using 224 hours a month to sleep. So what are they doing with these precious hours? They are wasting their time and forfeiting their dreams in the process. You have the time to dedicate thirty minutes, an hour, or maybe two hours every day to work on your dreams!

The Ivy League School of Life

Have you heard of the *Ivy League School* known as *The School of Life*? Of course you have! Unfortunately, not everyone applies for the grand opportunity to study life and push through life head-on. However, you're different from everyone else and you're ready to enroll in *The Ivy League School of Life*. So, how many Degrees of *Greatness* will you earn from *The Ivy League School of Life*? How many Degrees of *Greatness* do you want to earn? The School of Life gives you the opportunity to be bad, average, good, great, or phenomenal. Which one will you be? The only way to be great is to attain one or more Degrees from *The Ivy League School of Life* each year. To be phenomenal, you must challenge yourself, and earn three to five Degrees in *Greatness* each year.

Every Year, Aim to Earn One to Five Degrees in Greatness

To receive a four-year college degree, you need 120-150 credit hours. That's about 40-50 college courses, and each course is normally worth three college credit hours. To go to school full-time normally requires twelve hours a semester. That's four classes, and the classes normally range from one to two hours in duration. However, there are classes that are three hours long, and these classes meet normally once a week. A college student who enrolls in school full-time can expect a minimum of four to six hours a week of actual core lecture time. A semester in college is about fifteen weeks. That's a total of 60-90 hours of core lecture for fifteen weeks. If you calculated only the hours of time in the classroom for the program, it would take about 600-750 hours to finish a four-year college program. However, these hours don't include studying. Here is where I'm going with this: you actually have more than enough time every year to get a four-year degree using the total classroom hours. If you took one class a semester, which would be three college credit hours, that would be 12-15 hours a month, and 27-33 hours a semester for just one class. You can work on your dreams part-time or full-time. However, similar to a degree program, part-time it will take you longer to get it. In a year you have on average 3,456 hours to work on your goals. So every year affords you the opportunity to earn a Degree in *Greatness*. Using my format from *The Ivy League School of Life* teaches you that you can earn a maximum of five Degrees a year in *Greatness*. So if you made up your mind today to put quality hours into your journey of self-development, then you will become great!

How to Attain A Degree in Greatness

I'm suggesting you aim to earn at least one Degree a year in *Greatness*. That means out of your 3,456 hours that you have each year to use in whatever ways you please, you would only need 600-750 of those hours to earn one Degree each year in *Greatness* from *The Ivy League School of Life*. On a monthly basis out of the 150-360 remaining hours that the average person has after activities, work, and sleep during any given month, only 50-63 of those hours are needed each month to study your dreams, and to develop your mind. If you invested 50-63 hours a month into developing your mind, within a year you'll earn a Degree in *Greatness*.

You can also look at it like this: if you invested two and a half days a month, or 50-63 hours a month, or 1.644-2.055 hours a day into your dreams, you would earn between one to five Degrees in *Greatness* each year. The maximum amount of core lecture hours needed to attain five Degrees of *Greatness* each year is 3,000-3,750 hours out of your 8,760 hours that you have every year. However, excluded from these hours are studying time, tests, and internships. In this illustration, the core lecture represents the hours you dedicate to learning and reading. You should take in knowledge via books, wise professional associations, workshops, audio recordings, and classes. In this illustration, your studying time represents the hours you use to practice and hone your craft. Under this format, the internship represents the hours you're applying to real-life situations using the knowledge and skills you're learning from the Degree in *Greatness* you're working on. If you subtract the minimum amount of 50-63 hours a month, every month, to earn one Degree a year in *Greatness*, you would still have about 168-240 remaining hours to use in a month for family, fun, and recreation. And of course, the number of hours depends on which month you're in and how busy your life is.

Each year you're presented with an opportunity to be phenomenal and earn five Degrees in *Greatness*. If you decided to be phenomenal and earn five Degrees of *Greatness* each year, you would still have 5,010 to 5,760 hours to dedicate to fun, sleep, work, family time, religion, traveling, exercising, eating, and leisure/recreation time every year. 8,760 hours minus 3,000 hours equals 5,760 hours, and 8,760 hours minus 3,750 hours equals 5,010, which totals five college degrees of core lecture hours, which represents 120-150 college credits times five, or 40-50 college courses times five. You can look at it like this as well: you can use some days to do more and you can take some days off, as long as you're putting the total hours in. However, before you enroll in this program of self-development, you need to determine how many Degrees of *Greatness* you want to attain within a year. If you only want one Degree of *Greatness* in a year, then dedicate fifty to sixty-three hours a month into your mind, and that's about an hour and forty-five minutes to two hours and fifteen minutes every day.

Or, you can double or triple up on your hours some days, which will give you enough time to take two to three days off a week. So really, you don't even have to actively invest into your mind every single day, if you doubled or tripled the amount of time you spent working on yourself in a twenty-four-hour day. However, I strongly recommend that you invest into your mind every day.

Finally, out of your twenty-four hours in each day that you have, invest ninety minutes to two hours and fifteen minutes of your time into your mind, and your dreams. If you do this, you will earn one Degree in *Greatness* every year.

However, I challenge you to go all out and shoot for the maximal amount of five Degrees in *Greatness* each year from *The Ivy League School of Life*. Challenge yourself and see what it leads to. Will you dedicate one and a half to five hours every day toward your goals, and earn one to five Degrees in *Greatness* from *The Ivy League School of Life*? If you do so, you will be among the prestigious graduates mentioned in Chapter 10. Whether you aim for one degree or five degrees, or somewhere in between, is up to you! Just make sure each year you're getting at least one Degree in *Greatness* from *The Ivy League School of Life*.

An Example of Applying the Philosophy of Numbers Don't Lie

Always schedule time for fun, but only after you have met your goals. However, you must determine how much fun you're worthy of having, based on an honest self-analysis of your efforts toward your goals during a particular week. For example, if my goal was to work out every Monday but I missed one out of four to five times, then that would give me a 75-80% effort and I need 100%. When you audited your activities and your goals, what were your percentages? Below is an example of how I spend my time on Mondays. Use my Monday example of how I use my time to help yourself format how you use your time for each day of the week. Also, use my example of how I use my time on Mondays to help youyourself to assess how you're using your time, and to help yourself form a schedule for how to use your time.

Monday: I get up at 4:40 a.m. and my whole Monday is consumed with various things, but I still work on my dreams!

Time	Goals/Activities for the Day	Percentages, and Y if I did it and N if I missed it
20-25 minutes	Kiss wife, eat breakfast, get dressed, read bible, pray, and visualize my dreams	Y
20 minutes	Drive to work while listening to motivational audio	Y
1.5 hours	Workout	Y
1 hour	Preach	
11 hours	Work	
1 hour	Work on book	
30 minutes while driving to appointments	Work on poetry	
10 minutes	Check websites for audition opportunities	
15 minutes	Think about business ideas for my job	
1 hour max	Eat	
4-6 hours	Sleep	
30 minutes	Read	
30 minutes to 1 hour	Watch TV and talk to wife	
10 minutes	Get dressed for congregation service	
1 hour and 45 minutes	Attend congregation service	
20-30 minute drive to congregation service	Listen to motivational speech and return phone calls	

Understanding the Process and Goal-Oriented Tasks

The example below shows you how to apply "Numbers Don't Lie" to a sales job. But you can apply these concepts to any job and it will improve your performance. However, you must know your process, and know each individual task associated with attaining your goals in order to accurately grade your performance. Similarly, you must also know the process to accurately calculate your efforts in percentages, so that you can grade your effort toward each individual task, and toward your overall effort.

Let's use a salesperson as an example: Suppose Bill is a sales representative for an insurance agency, and Bill's goal is to sell $3,000 a month in life insurance. Suppose his process for attaining this goal is to make fifty phone calls a day, send fifty emails a day, and to talk to ten people in person. Also, it's understood that he may need to exceed the company's recommendation for his daily goals in order to achieve his daily goals. Furthermore, this means that Bill probably will have to phone more than fifty people. Also, let's suppose Bill is required to start work at 7 a.m. every day. However, Bill arrives at work fifteen minutes late every day, and he doesn't start working productively until 8 a.m. If you add up the fifteen minutes that Bill is missing by being late every day, based on a work schedule of Monday-Friday he would miss 375 minutes over a twenty-five-day period, and that's minus the weekends. So, within a single week's worth of work time, Bill would have missed five hours that he could have used for attaining his work goals. That's five hours a week missed, and twenty-five hours a month missed. In this example, Bill is giving a 84.5-85% effort in the time category. That's 15.56% missed opportunities for that month. If we add up the percentages for the whole year, Bill would have 186.72% of missed opportunities in that category. Bill's work time is based on a forty-hour work week from Monday to Friday.

Suppose Bill is also required to do fifty followup courtesy phone calls a day for some of his customers, and Bill receives a thirty-minute lunch break every day. Furthermore, Bill's position also requires him to distribute fifty insurance advertising accessories during the week as well. Suppose Bill only does forty calls a day and not fifty. That's an 80% effort. Suppose that Bill only gives an 80% effort toward the emails, and the followup phone calls as well. Instead of talking to ten people a day, Bill only talks to five people. That's a 50% F in that category. Also, suppose Bill misses on average 20% of possible work from each category. These categories represent the process and the goal-oriented tasks associated with helping Bill to become successful at his life insurance agency. In this example, the agency has a process that consists of six main categories for the sales representatives to implement in order to achieve their goals.

The only way to attain a 100% effort in each category would be to meet the recommended goals, while also being willing to go beyond the company's recommendation. Remember this: sometimes the process will have intangibles you can't fully extrapolate, so you may need to put in a little more, or a lot more, effort on some days. Furthermore, if Bill averages 20% of missed work and time from each category, it'll be interesting to see how it affects his overall work performance in numbers. Bill has the possibility to give 600% overall effort every day. If you add up 100% possible effort from each one of Bill's six goal-oriented tasks, you will have a sum total of 600% possible effort. Remember: all proven measurable constructs, tasks, tests, and endeavors start off at 100%. The percentages can only drop based on the amount of effort or performance quantity value that someone actually puts into a goal, task, or test if the process is proven. Bill's work example would demonstrate an overall performance value of 480% overall effort, using the six categories that are proven, to successfully perform his job.

Let's highlight three of the six percentages and grades from Bill's work process. Bill gives an 80% effort for one of his goal-oriented tasks, which is a C effort. Furthermore Bill gives a 50% effort for another one of his goal-oriented tasks, which is an F. Finally Bill gives an 87.5% effort for another one of his goal-oriented tasks, which is a B effort. If Bill wants to guarantee the successful achievement of his goals, then he must give a 100% A+ effort in each category. In this example, Bill is giving a 480% daily effort toward his goals which is an 80% C. Bill won't become the head salesperson by giving an 80% C effort. A 120% overall daily effort to miss every day is a lot, and that's what Bill is missing. If you take out the numbers, it would appear as though Bill is doing a great job, but he still isn't attaining his goals.

The concepts contained in this chapter will always help you to expose two things: either the process needs to be revamped, or the execution of the process needs improving. For example, if a sales representative is supposed to close five sales opportunities from making forty phone calls, but they're unable to close five deals after making these calls, this could be an indication that the sales representative execution of the process needs improving. However, before you thoroughly analyze the execution of the process, you should always check the numbers to make sure 100% effort is being given toward each individual goal-oriented task.

Furthermore, once the numbers are confirmed to be 100%, then you must examine the process, and the execution of the process. Maybe the process needs to be revamped to fit the personality of the seller, or maybe eighty phone calls are needed instead of forty until the struggling seller's execution of the company's process improves. Finally, analyze the execution of the process by comparing it to a very successful person who are achieving their goals by implementing the same process. Analyze why the top achiever is able to meet their goals without revamping the current process, or changing their execution of the company's process. The sales representative who is struggling to execute the proven strategy should shadow the seller who is executing the process well. However, the struggling seller should double or triple his leads until his execution of the company's process improves. If he's making forty phone calls, he should double or triple his phone calls until he attains his goal.

You must use your dream's process along with its goal-oriented tasks to objectively examine your performance, and to grade yourself daily, so that you can get better. Use this concept at work and for all of your goals, so that you can assess your performances in life. You must be obsessed with greatness: your grades and numbers must show that you're getting better. Never judge your effort toward your goals solely based on how you feel, because that's subjective. Numbers are an incontrovertible truth that should always be used to help you assess your efforts toward your goals and dreams. If you know the process and all of the goal-oriented tasks that are necessary to achieve a goal, then you can accurately assess your efforts toward your goals.

"Numbers Don't Lie" Can Be Used for Any Goal or Dream

Here is an example of how to use the concepts in this chapter toward any goal or dream. Let's apply the "Numbers Don't Lie" philosophy to a personal goal of weight loss. Below is a weight loss example. Suppose a lady named Martha hires a personal trainer and the trainer informs Martha that she must carefully complete all of the tasks below to achieve her goals. Here are the goal-oriented tasks:

Goal-Oriented Tasks to Attain Martha's Fitness Goals

1. Do cardio 2 times a week for a duration of 1 hour.
2. Do cardio using at least 75% of your target heart rate zone.
3. Lift weights 3 times a week.
4. Eat 1,300 calories a day.
5. Use a 40/40/20 macronutrient balance.
6. Breakfast should be biggest meal.
7. Eat 6 times a day.
8. Eat every 2 hours.
9. Don't eat after 7 p.m.
10. Drink a gallon of water every day.
11. Get 6 to 7 hours of sleep each night.
12. Do not eat starches or fried foods.
13. Stay away from sweets, juices, sodas, alcohol, and dairy products.

If Martha only did cardio once a week after she was instructed to do cardio twice a week, that would be a 50% effort for her #1 goal-oriented task. If Martha used a target heart rate zone of 65% of her maximum heart rate instead of 75%, that's 0% effort for goal-oriented task #2 because the goal wasn't met. Furthermore, if Martha did weight training two days a week instead of three, that would be a 75% effort. If Martha eats 1,400 calories a day but she had been instructed to eat 1,300, that's 0% because she didn't hit the goal. If Martha used a 30/30/40 macro balance instead of the one indicated, that's 0% effort in that category. So, sometimes it's not about doing what you think will work; it's about giving it your all. If you think you're giving something your all and it still doesn't work, then you must simply do what's specifically required. If you define your goal and it gives you an exact range that's measurable, and you don't implement the exact range, then that's automatically 0%. For example, if an academic degree program consisted of forty-five courses, and each course is predetermined as far as the exact classes that are needed, and you attained forty-four of the courses, so you were only missing one class, you still wouldn't receive your degree. You wouldn't receive your degree until you finish the one class that you didn't complete. If your goal was to get a degree and if you never attained the degree, then you have failed regardless of how many courses you have taken. This is an example of giving a 100% effort and doing what's required.

Always Do What's Required

Doing what's required means you no longer manipulate the system by trying to wiggle your way to the top. Suppose 1,300 calories for Martha is the requirement for her body to respond to her diet, and her body may not respond well to 1,400 calories for weight loss. Someone could reason, "That's only 100 calories more, so who cares?" But if Martha really wants to lose the weight, she would stop trying to manipulate the system. Instead, she should do what's required. Breakfast should be her biggest meal of the day, but it isn't, and she even skips breakfast sometimes. That equals another 0% effort because either breakfast is her biggest meal of the day or it's not. The goal wasn't to just eat breakfast: the goal was to make sure breakfast is the biggest meal of the day.

People do this all the time and manipulate the system, which is why they don't get the exact results they're looking for. Imagine how many people manipulate the actual work needed to achieve their dreams. Martha was instructed to eat every two hours, but she ate every three hours. That's 0%. I know people have hard schedules, and some things aren't practical for everyone. However, regardless of our personal thoughts on a matter, the reality is: Martha still would get a 0% in that category. Failing that one goal-oriented task could stop Martha from achieving her goal in the precise way that she envisions. Numbers Don't Lie!

This doesn't mean that Martha won't ever achieve her goal, but in some situations, this could be the only category causing someone not to lose weight. Never become guilty of this: *"Are you potentially allowing one category that's necessary to achieve your dreams to hold you back?"* Never try to make yourself feel better by saying you're doing well in the other categories. Maybe the one hour that Martha misses for one of her tasks is the single culprit. Maybe the one extra hour you're not spending in a day toward your dreams is holding you back. In Martha's example, another important requirement for Martha was not to eat after 7 p.m. Suppose Martha does well four days out of the week, but she messes up three days a week. That would be a 42% effort toward that individual goal-oriented task. In some situations, this could be a 0% if she is instructed not to cheat for three weeks as an example. Another task for Martha was to drink a gallon of water every day, and suppose Martha does well in this category and achieves this goal? That would be a 100% in that category.

However, another one of Martha's goal-oriented tasks is to get six to seven hours a sleep each night. Martha achieves this goal as well, so that's another 100% effort in that category. Another one of Martha's goal-oriented tasks is not to eat starches or fried foods. Let's suppose Martha does okay in this category, but sometimes she surrenders and cheats three times a week, so that would be a 42% effort in this category. Martha's final goal-oriented task is to stay away from sodas, juices, dairy products and alcohol. Suppose Martha refrains from juices, sweets, alcohol, and dairy products, but has one soda a day. I would say that's good, but that's still only a 75% effort in that category. So, out of a possible 1300% that's calculated from Martha's thirteen goal-oriented tasks, Martha is giving a 474% overall effort. That's a cumulative overall 36.5% effort if we take the percentage of 474 out of 1300. Martha has achieved 36.5% which is an F. (100%/1300% x 474% = 36.5%). The AE or Actual Effort is represented by the 474%, and 1300% represents the TPE or Total Possible Effort. To calculate your cumulative overall effort, you must first know how many goal-oriented tasks are needed to attain your goals. In this example, Martha has thirteen goal-oriented tasks.

First identify your goal-oriented tasks, and then multiply the total number of goal-oriented tasks by 100 to get the total possible effort. Subsequently, you determine the actual effort by adding up the actual effort that's being put into each individual goal-oriented task. In this example, Martha is giving 474% overall effort for her goals, and the 474% was calculated from her thirteen goal-oriented tasks. If Martha's physique doesn't look exactly the way she wants after a certain timeframe, then she should carefully reexamine her overall effort. If you aren't fulfilling your dreams, you should painstakingly examine your overall effort.

You need to look at the individual categories associated with your dreams, and calculate your current percentages, and if your percentages don't reflect 100%, you need to fix that! Write down the individual goal-oriented tasks that you must execute correctly to achieve your goals and dreams. Make sure you write down the things that are required. Do not write down things that can be left out. Once this is done, you can determine how often you need to perform each task, which is the *frequency*. After this, you need to determine how much time you need to dedicate to each task, which is the *duration*. After this you must determine the exact amount of potency or *intensity* that's required to successfully attain your goals. This intensity represents the all or none category, which means two options for your intensity are 0% or 100%. An example of this would be someone who needs to practice for a minimum of one hour a day in order to fulfill one of their goal-oriented tasks. If they don't achieve the minimum of one hour a day, it's a 0%, even if they did thirty minutes. One could try to argue that's actually 50%, but that form of thinking will get you 50% in return. You must give all of your goal-oriented tasks a 100% effort.

Do or die! You're at war with yourself and if you train yourself to only give a 50% effort, then that will become your standard, subconsciously. After you have written down all of the goal-oriented tasks that are needed to accomplish your goals, I want you to create another category called *reflection*. In this category you're looking for *volume, order, progression, overload, types of goals* and *variation*. In the *reflection* section you will use *volume* to track the total number of everything you're putting in. Use *volume* to track the total number of books you're reading. Use *volume* to track the total number of new things you've learned. Use *volume* to track the number of referrals you get. Use *volume* for the total number of emails you send. Use *volume* in the *reflection* section for the total number of business cards you hand out. Use the *reflection* section for the total number of courtesy calls you make. Use the *reflection* section for the total number of people you refer to your website. Use the *reflection* section for the total number of new people you meet each day. Use the *reflection* section to count the total amount of times each day that you work on your projects.

After you finish the *volume* section I want you to create another section for *progression*. This section will help you to see if your numbers are improving. Also, create a section for *types of goals*, and in this section write down your short-term and your long-term goals. Use the *types of goals* section to help you to evaluate if you're internally or externally motivated. Subsequently, create a section for *variation* to track your marketing methods whenever you add a new marketing technique or a new way to develop your dreams. This will help you to see which ways are working, and if you need to add more variation. Finally, create an *order* section, and use it to check the arrangement of your goal-oriented tasks. This will help you to examine the execution of your goal's process along with its goal-oriented tasks. The *order* section is helpful for assisting you in assessing the productivity of the execution sequence you're using. There are times when you might have to change up your execution's strategy and the *order* sequence. For example, if you normally start with fifty emails, try doing the phone calls first. You may need to increase the goal amount from fifty to 100 phone calls, as a way to examine if that improves your odds of talking to people.

Peer into Your Future and Abort Your Past

"If you aren't willing to gain everything to become the person you desire to be, then it's not your true desire!" Notice I said: "If you aren't willing to *gain* everything," instead of *lose* everything. In reality, how could someone be losing by becoming the person they're in love with? Why waste your life being married to a version of yourself you don't want to be? Everyone should always aim to divorce their negative shadows with its lies and deceits. I know it's hard to change and break old addictive habits, but if you're married to your shadow, and if you have spent years together with your past, then I'm sure you

know one another very well. However, if your past doesn't involve a life of fulfillment, along with manifesting your inner genius, then I know that you don't love your shadow, and that your shadow doesn't love you. So it's time for you to amicably part ways with your past!

Doesn't it feel good, just the thought of you and your dreams finally coming together as one? The two of you, with God's guidance, will achieve things that you can't even begin to imagine. Some people live just to die. Instead, allow yourself to live by being the person you truly desire to be. If you become the person you know you were called to be, when you die the universe will never be the same. After mankind discovered electricity, has the universe been the same? After man discovered medicine, was the universe the same? What will be your divine contribution?

Your Life's Vehicle

Ignoring the "change engine oil" light when it comes on in your car won't solve the problem of your oil needing to be changed. Ignoring the light won't randomly put oil in your car, either. To the contrary, neglecting to change the oil when it's recommended will hurt you in the long run. The only way to keep the "change engine oil" light from coming on would be to change the oil *before* the light comes on. That's how your dreams are, as long as you have a brain and a heart inside your body then you will always have to maintain your dreams. Similarly, your heart and brain are the two main things to maintain for your body's vehicle to run smoothly, so never wait for your heart's oil light to come on, don't allow your heart's desires to go unfulfilled, and don't wait for your brain to communicate to you that it hates your choices in life.

Just like avoiding costly car repairs, if you want to avoid the catastrophic experience of costly life repairs, simply take care of your heart's mind by searching for ways to get better every single day. And never be guilty of taking better care of your car than of yourself! Do you invest more in your car's maintenance than you invest into yourself? Billions of people around the world take better care of their material things rather than taking better care of their heart's minds. If you don't keep up with the proper maintenance on your vehicle, it will slowly start to shut down. It's necessary to keep up the proper maintenance on your car by changing your engine's oil because if you don't, you will blow your car's engine. Similarly, you must maintain your dreams or you will be at risk of blowing your heart's engine.

In conclusion: If I audited you, would I find 40% effort here and there toward the goal-oriented tasks that are needed to achieve your goals? Or would I see a 100% A+ effort for each task associated with the process of attaining your goals? If I audited your overall percentage effort, which would include all of your goal-oriented tasks put together, would you have an overall 100% A+ effort? Or would you have a B, C, D, or an F? A 100% overall A+ effort is the only way you can guarantee that your input will give you exactly what you want the outcome to be. Remember, *Numbers Don't Lie*! So how many Degrees in *Greatness* have you earned lately? How many Degrees in *Greatness* will you earn this year? One, two, three, four or five Degrees? The choice is up to you!

Finally, it's important to remember this: you will never graduate from *The Ivy League School of Life* because life will always teach you something new every day. If you stop working on yourself every day, life will happen to you, and you will lose control of your dreams. I suggest that you keep earning as many Degrees in *Greatness* as you can, and then you will be successful. You need faith, but you also need a scientific structure to objectively assess yourself. So change your mental behavior, and manifest your greatness by using *Numbers Don't Lie* to guide your steps. The time for your ultimate experience has arrived; Chapter 13 will present *The Octagon Way*.

CHAPTER 13

THE OCTAGON WAY

The Art of Yielding and Stopping

You have traveled to the final chapter of your adventure, and this chapter will help you to finally live the dreams that are in your mind. However, it's fitting to stop, yield, and reflect before moving forward to unearthing the secrets contained in this chapter. For a moment, visualize a yield sign along with its triangular shape, and ask yourself, "What does a yield sign truly represent?"

To help you grasp the art of yielding, I'll again use driving as an example. A lot of drivers will unnecessarily come to a complete stop at a yield sign; however, a yield sign wasn't designed solely for stopping. A yield sign allows the driver to use discretion because there are times where you will have to completely stop at a yield sign to avoid a wreck. However, a yield sign mainly serves as a precautionary measure alerting you to the possibility of oncoming traffic. A yield sign was designed to tell drivers to look in the direction of oncoming traffic and to make sure it's safe, before they drive on. A yield sign doesn't require you to come to a complete stop unless the situation deems completely stopping to be necessary. However, on the contrary a stop sign always means to completely stop and its shape is an octagon. The stop sign means to come to a complete stop, and look in all directions before you attempt to move beyond the stop sign. Take a moment to visualize a stop sign along with its shape, and you will discover several yield signs that are embedded into a stop sign. A yield sign is shaped like a triangle; however an octagon actually contains eight triangles inside of its structure to configure its shape. As you continue to read, you will begin to realize the significance of the structure of an octagon.

Stop and yield signs are two universally accepted signs that are used for cueing drivers to stop for oncoming traffic or cueing drivers to be aware of oncoming traffic. Yield and stop signs are universal laws that are designed to protect you from danger. However, harm can only take place if someone decides to break one of these laws. This means you can never break a law because it's the law that actually breaks you. The possible consequences for breaking a law are already predetermined. For example, if you jump off a 100-story building without any paraphernalia to preempt gravity, then you will most certainly die. Gravity is the law and if someone chooses to defy gravity, then the law of gravity doesn't break, instead, it breaks the law breaker. All universal laws and principles already have consequences embedded into them. I'm not referring to laws that are based on biases or that lack integrity, morality, or substance. I'm referring to the laws that are incontrovertible and scientifically based. Incontrovertible laws can spring from several categories such as philosophy, psychology, religion, medicine, government, science, morality, and reproduction. A law is a universal law if it's just and objectively proven to provide obedient or disobedient adherents with the same results 100% of the time. A universal law's consequences are never affected by external or internal forces. Universal laws will function in the same way all of the time, regardless of any futile attempts to alter universal laws. For example, if you properly nurture a plant, then it will grow. The plant doesn't care if a good or a bad person waters it; because the law of sowing and reaping states that a plant will grow regardless of who does the sowing.

In order to fully grasp the laws of *The Octagon Way*, you must recognize that true success will always require you to stop and yield. As you travel to your life's success, you must always obey the laws of failure because refusing to yield or stop when necessary could easily ruin a safe travel to your dreams. If someone decides to repeatedly disobey the laws of yielding and stopping while driving, they will eventually crash at some point. All of the good things that you can think of will require several instances of yields and stops. For example, if a talented swimmer refuses to yield or stop for a breath of air, what will happen?

The Octagon Way will teach you how to know when to inherently yield and stop, whenever you're pursuing your dreams. As you develop the art of yielding and stopping it will help you avoid becoming a victim of breaking the laws of success. The laws of success require you to intuitively know how to succinctly yield and stop, or intuitively know how to succinctly stop and yield! *"If you don't train your mind to understand the significance of applying the art of stopping and yielding, then you will habitually crash into failures or your failures will consequentially crash into you."*

The Octagon Way Is Your Life's Seatbelt

The Octagon is a fitting model to symbolize how you should pursue your dreams. *"You must know how to stop and assess the potential dangers as you're traveling to your life's destiny, and you must know how to yield to the constant distractions that will ineluctably travel your way."* Stopping and yielding are the main laws of success; however, these two laws also are in constant motion throughout the universe. When you're driving, you can't control the other drivers who are driving. However, you can attempt to predict, and counter someone's actions while they're driving, but you can't directly control the decisions they make. So if someone pummels into the back of your car after you have taken steps to ensure a safe driving experience, don't take it personally. Life is similar: sometimes we take all of the precautionary measures to protect our future, and things still go wrong. Life's seatbelt represents being flexible and adaptable whenever you're dealing with uncomfortable experiences. As you're traveling on your road to success you must accept that other people may briefly, seasonally, or regularly travel on the same road you're traveling. It's important to know that just because someone is traveling on the same *road* doesn't mean they're on the same *path* as you. It's important to remember that just because people are driving for awhile on the same highway as you, doesn't mean they will continue to travel on the same highway forever.

Life's seatbelt is an analogy meaning to avoid unnecessary distractions and to be prepared to reroute whenever you're traveling to your dreams. Unfocused motivation can be dangerous toward your goals, similar to texting while driving. Driving while intoxicated is dangerous, and you can compare driving while intoxicated to pursuing a dream with a distracted mind. And it's even more dangerous for a person who is intoxicated to drive and text without wearing a seatbelt. Your life's seatbelt means that you should always avoid behaviors that will inhibit your ability to stop and yield properly. Wrecks will inevitably happen at some point in your life, especially if you drive a lot. However, you must remember that your goal is to only experience a wreck resulting from someone else's inability to obey the laws of success. For example, if someone crashes into you, they will owe you. If they run into you and don't have insurance, and if the insurance company penalizes you by increasing your premium, then the insurance company is in the wrong: so since the insurance company didn't properly yield and stop, their actions could potentially lead to the agency losing a customer because they broke the two laws of success. The laws of success create balance, and balance is connected to homeostasis, which is a stable equilibrium between interdependent elements. Yielding and stopping helps to create an appropriate balance, and these to laws are necessary for success.

Yielding and Stopping Are Universal Risks

When you're driving, you can't control if someone rear-ends you, whether the insurance company says it's your fault or not. The principle to understand is that it doesn't matter who is at fault for not properly utilizing the two laws of success. The important thing to understand is the necessity to develop an intelligent perspective regarding how the misapplication of these two laws will affect anything that's within their proximity. The misapplication of yielding and stopping tangibly and intangibly affects everything that's proximally involved, which is an unnoted corollary during the breach of these two laws. So you must always attempt to protect yourself, but you must also understand you can't always guarantee your own safety. This is a necessary perspective to grasp because you must be willing to eliminate any hesitation that will risk or possibly stop you from reaching your unique potential! *"An unwillingness to address this necessary perspective can and will automatically produce failure as a by product, if you aren't willing to eliminate the bad effects of displaying an unwillingness to take or create risks"!* Not understanding that everything is a risk is another way to misapply the laws of yielding and stopping. Deciding to yield and stop, or deciding not to yield and stop, both are risks. However, the person who truly understands they're taking a risk regardless of what they do is more likely to intuitively take more intelligent risks!

The Philosophy Behind Taking Risks

People will always get into wrecks, even if they aren't at fault, because there will always be other people who are traveling in the direction you're traveling. You can't control if there is traffic, and even if you take a shortcut toward your destination, you can't control, or fully know, whether or not you'll travel into more traffic. You can't control if another driver runs a stop sign and pummels into you. You can't control if a driver miscalculates the precision of how to properly yield. You can't control any tangibles or intangibles that would cause a driver to break the laws of properly yielding and stopping, so you must train your mind to approach the fulfillment of your life's true passions in the same way. Remember this: *"Just do what you can and always control the insatiable desire to be in control. You can't control everything, and understanding this perspective will unconsciously eliminate you as your own distraction."* The next section will begin the discovery process of the hidden treasures of *The Octagon Way.* You're getting closer to opening your eyes to a guide that will keep you motivated forever! (I will release an entire book on The Octagon Way in two to three years. The book will have eight chapters and the book will be entitled, *The Octagon Way: The Secret to Properly Reprograming the Subconscious Mind.*)

The Three Parts of The Human Mind

THE SUBCONSCIOUS MIND

The human mind has three main parts: the *subconscious*, the *unconscious*, and the *conscious* mind. It's important for you to familiarize yourself with the three parts of the mind before we discuss the true application of *The Octagon Way*.

The *subconscious* mind is something that has a huge effect on every action. The subconscious mind is a powerful layer under the conscious mind. The subconscious mind encompasses the awareness of all things the conscious mind cannot recognize. Once the subconscious mind is tapped, this unique part of the brain becomes an instrument for a plethora of different roles in your everyday life. The subconscious mind functions as a gigantic memory bank. Its capacity is virtually unlimited! It permanently stores everything that ever happens to you. Research shows that, by the time you reach the age of twenty-one, you've already permanently stored more than one hundred times the contents of the entire *Encyclopedia Britannica*.

The function of your subconscious mind is to store and receive data. Its job is to ensure that you respond exactly the way you are programmed. Your subconscious mind makes everything you say and do fit a pattern consistent with your self-concept. Your conscious mind is your master program and your subconscious mind is like an unquestioning servant. Your subconscious mind is subjective. It does not think or reason independently. It merely obeys the commands it receives from your conscious mind.

Your conscious mind can be thought of as the gardener, planting seeds. Your subconscious mind can be thought of as the garden, or fertile soil, in which the seeds germinate and grow. Your conscious mind commands and your subconscious mind obeys. Your subconscious mind is an unquestioning servant. It works day and night to make your behavior fit a pattern consistent with your emotionalized thoughts, hopes, and desires. To illustrate: your subconscious mind can grow either flowers or weeds in the garden of your life. However, what you plant depends on the mental equivalents you create. So, if you are conditioned to think negatively, then you will process positive information in a negative way. If you are conditioned to think positively, then you will figure out how to process negative information in a positive way.

The subconscious mind is connected to yielding and stopping because the subconscious mind is the preserver of balance in your life. The subconscious mind has something called a homeostatic impulse. This impulse helps to keep your body temperature at 98.6 degrees Fahrenheit. The homeostatic impulse helps you to breathe regularly and it keeps your heart rate stable. Your subconscious mind also practices homeostasis in your mental realm. *The subconscious mind works to keep you thinking and acting in a manner consistent with what you've done, and said in the past. Your subconscious mind works to keep you in your comfort zone, whether you have programmed your master program to find comfort in greatness or mediocrity."* All of your habits of thinking and acting are stored in your subconscious mind. It has memorized all of your comfort zones and it works to keep you there. Your subconscious mind is what causes you to feel emotionally and physically uncomfortable whenever you attempt to do anything new or different. Your subconscious mind goes against changing any of your established patterns of behavior. You are feeling your subconscious mind whenever you feel anxiety from trying something new. In fact, just thinking about doing something different from what you're accustomed to can make you feel tense and uneasy.

Remember this: *one of the biggest habits of successful men and women is that they are always stretching themselves or pushing themselves to get out of their comfort zones.* Successful people are alert to how quickly a comfort zone in any area can eventually turn into a rut. Successful people know that complacency is the great enemy of creativity and future possibilities. So, always remember: in order for you to grow and get out of your comfort zone, you must be willing to feel awkward and uncomfortable doing new things. You must train yourself to know, and to fully believe, that if you have something you know is worth doing, then you must know that it's worth doing poorly until you get it right. So always strive to develop new comfort zones along with an ever-higher level of competence. Furthermore, you must also look for ways to get better every day in each domain under *The Holistic Approach,* so you can positively train your subconscious mind. (Refer back to Chapter 4 to refresh your memory on *The Holistic Approach*)

THE CONSCIOUS MIND

The *conscious* mind is your objective or thinking mind. It has no memory, and it can only hold one thought at a time. The conscious mind has four essential functions. First, it identifies incoming information. This is information received through any of the five senses: sight, sound, smell, taste, and touch or feeling. Your conscious mind is continually observing and categorizing what is going on around you. To illustrate, imagine that you are walking along the sidewalk and you decide to cross the street. Suppose you step off the curb and at that moment you hear the roar of an automobile engine. So you immediately turn and look in the direction of the sound to identify it, and where it's coming from. This is an example of the first function of the conscious mind.

The second function of your conscious mind is comparison. The information about the car that you have been seen and heard immediately goes to your subconscious mind. There, it is compared with all of your previously stored information and experiences with moving automobiles. If the car, for example, is a block away, and moving at thirty miles per hour, your subconscious mind memory bank will tell you that there is no danger, and that you can continue walking. However, if on the other hand, the car is moving toward you at sixty miles per hour, and the car is only 100 yards away, you will get a danger message that will stimulate further action on your part.

The third function of your conscious mind is analysis, and analysis always precedes the fourth function, deciding. Your conscious mind functions very much like a binary computer, performing two functions: It accepts data, or it rejects data in making choices and decisions. The conscious mind can only adequately deal with one thought at a time, whether it's positive or negative. This is why you should make it a habit to read and listen to inspirational things every day. The conscious mind can only entertain one idea at a time, so keeping it occupied with uplifting material gives it the power to block negative thoughts. Positive affirmations are extremely helpful for keeping your brain occupied with pleasant and empowering thoughts or visualizations.

Positive affirmations are a way for you to continually filter through impressions, and you can decide which ones are relevant to you, and which ones are not. Let's consider an example of how to effectively use positive affirmations. I'll refer back to the automobile illustration. So, suppose you're walking across the street, you hear the roar of the moving automobile, and you see that it's bearing down on you. Because of your knowledge of the speed of moving vehicles, your analysis tells you that you are in danger and a decision is required. Your first question before you can make a decision would be, *"Do I get out of the way, yes or no?"* If your decision is "yes," then your next is, *"Do I jump forward, yes or no?"* If your decision is "no," because of cross traffic, then your next question is, *"Do I jump backward, yes or no?"* If your decision is "yes" this message is instantly transmitted to your subconscious mind and in a split second, your whole body jumps back out of the way with no additional thought or decision on your part. Remember this: *You must consciously focus on positive things every day, and every five days, look for a new way to spend at least two minutes positively applying your new information.*

THE UNCONSCIOUS MIND

The unconscious mind consists of deeper mental processes that are not readily available to the conscious mind. However, the unconscious mind is where much of the mind's work gets done; it's the repository of automatic skills, the source of traumatic experiences, intuition, fantasy, and dreams. The unconscious mind is an engine of information processing. Psychologists and psychiatrists both acknowledge that it is difficult to measure what exists in the unconscious mind. However, they do acknowledge that fleeting perceptions can leave lasting imprints on the unconscious mind long before you become aware of them. What truly lives in the unconscious mind can also leak out at any time, in various ways, such as a misspoken comment to address someone's random behaviors.

Whenever you have an unconscious mind leak, you can use it to help you to gain a clearer understanding of your inner state along with your deeper motivations. So the next time someone is correcting you or hating on you, pay close attention to how you respond. Also, question yourself as to why you want to capture your dreams, and be honest with yourself regarding why you're chasing your dreams. Train your conscious mind by responding positively to negative situations, and through repairing any character flaws that you have. You must conduct a self-analysis every five days, and look for ways to enhance the following qualities: patience, love, determination, flexibility, and giving. Now that you understand the three parts of the mind, we can move on to discussing the various features of *The Octagon Way*.

Understanding The Octagon Way

Take a moment to study the unique features of an octagon. Earlier in this chapter, I mentioned how an octagon is composed of eight triangles.

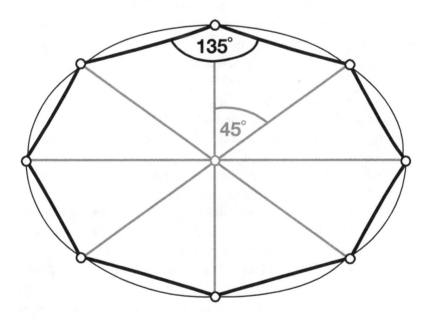

An octagon has eight vertices along with three revolutions, which indicates that the figure contains three 360-degree circles. The inner vertices of an octagon are 360 degrees, which represents a circle, and the outer vertices contain 1080 degrees. 1080/360 = three revolutions. An octagon has eight triangles with each side of each triangle containing 45 degrees. A triangle has three sides, and one vertices of an octagon is 135 degrees, so 135/3 equals 45 degrees.

The three sides of each individual triangle represents one of the three parts of the mind. The inner 45-degree angle of each individual triangle inside of the octagon represents the conscious mind. The outer 45-degree angle on the left of each triangle represents the subconscious mind. The outer 45-degree angle on the right of each triangle represents the unconscious mind.

Negative and Positive Refocuses

The Octagon Way was designed to remodel the subconscious mind, since it's the master program that will control your belief system. Your subconscious mind will dictate how you think, and if your subconscious mind is sullied with malnourished memories of mediocrity, then it will almost be impossible to maintain the proper motivation for achieving your dreams. The method I'm about to disclose is a true treasure that will help you to stay motivated. Remember, an octagon has 360 degrees on the inner vertices and 1080 degrees on the outer vertices. Furthermore, there are 365 days in a year and if you divide 360 by five you will get 72, and if you divide 1080 by five you will get 216. Most importantly, there are five points on an octagon where 72 and 216 meet. Finally, you must positively focus your conscious mind every five days in order to achieve this, and I'll explain the tangible factors of how to achieve this throughout this chapter.

Forty-five degrees represents forty-five days and every five days you must focus your conscious mind with positive things to positively condition the three parts of your mind to be positive. The numbers 0, 9, 27, 72, 144, and 216 are special numbers, and they serve a critical role for time, and motivation. Zero is an additive identity and it can be an even or an odd number. Nine represents the maximum number of cubes that are needed for the sum of any positive integer. Twenty-seven is the largest number that is the sum of the digits of its cube. Seventy-two is the maximum number of spheres that can touch another sphere in a lattice packing in six dimensions. Without a sphere, radius, center, and diameter wouldn't be possible. So the number 72 helps to center everything, and 72 is the only number that makes everything three-dimensional. So the three parts of the mind are centered every 72 days using *The Octagon*

Way. And 72 is a set pattern for 216 as the Octagon is arranged to make three revolutions for a complete rotation of 360 degrees for the inner vertices and 1080 degrees for outer vertices. The largest square in Fibonacci sequence is 144 and 216 is the smallest cube that can be written as the sum of three cubes.

There are a total of 144 possible refocuses that you can attain during a year, and 72 focuses are the total possible amount of focuses that you can attain in a year as well (seventy-two possible focuses for your conscious mind, which also represents 72 refocuses for the conscious mind). Furthermore, there are 72 possible refocuses for the subconscious mind, and 72 possible refocuses for your unconscious mind. It's important to know that you can't refocus the conscious mind without refocusing the subconscious and the unconscious mind, too. *So, this is why you're focusing the conscious mind: because the conscious mind is the only part of your mind you can focus on to help undo the negative experiences stored inside of your subconscious mind.* Also, you can't actively focus on an unconscious entity that exists as a separate function that no one can really explain. *The unconscious mind can be compared to involuntary muscle contractions, which means it doesn't require any conscious effort to create movement. So likewise, the unconscious mind doesn't require any conscious effort to create its own thought patterns.*

Days and Numbers Are Connected to Your Inner Motivation

Every forty-five days you must attain nine positive focuses for the conscious mind, and every forty-five days you must attain a combined 18 positive refocuses for the subconscious, and the unconscious minds. If you focus your conscious mind every five days you will have 18 refocuses and nine focuses to total 27. Remember, an octagon has eight triangles with 135 degrees in each triangle. If you successfully complete *The Octagon Way*'s cycle each year by not skipping one of your five days to focus your mind, then you will have successfully applied *The Octagon Way*, and you will have a positively combined 216 focuses and refocuses.

If you successfully focus your mind every five days for 45 days at a time you will attain nine focuses, and if you add nine to 45 three times, you will get this equation: 45 + 9, 45 + 9, 45 + 9. *By positively focusing your conscious mind for 45 days you automatically refocus the subconscious and the unconscious mind to be positive as well.* So 45 – 0, 45 – 0, 45 – 0 would represent a full positive refocus over a 45-day period. (45 + 9) x 3 = 162 and 45 x 3 = 135, and if you subtract 162 from 135, then that's 27. The difference of every segment of your focusing and refocusing during a 45-day period will always be 27. For example, suppose I missed all of my conscious mind focuses for 45 days, which would read like this: a positive 45 + 0, 45 + 0, 45 + 0, and a negative 45 – 9, 45 – 9, 45 – 9, or a positive (45 + 0) x 3 = 135 and a negative (45 – 9) x 3 = 108, 135 – 108 is 27. *Here is the point: every five days you can strengthen your subconscious, unconscious, and conscious mind in a negative or a positive way.* So your aim is to achieve a +27 after each 45-day segment opposed to a –27. +27 represents a positive refocus of the subconscious, conscious, and unconscious mind. –27 indicates a negative refocus of the subconscious, conscious, and unconscious mind. Either you will have –9 or +9 for the subconscious, unconscious, and conscious minds every 45 days. If you added them up it will be -27 or +27. 45/9 equals one refocus whether it's positive or negative every five days. Five represents your five senses and the extra five days that make up a year that's not included in the 360-degree circle of an octagon. You can only store, and receive new information through the activation of your five senses, and you can stimulate your five senses in a negative way or a positive way. You can condition your five senses positively to help reshape the subconscious mind, but you must focus the conscious mind positively in order to achieve this.

In case you're wondering why all three parts of the mind must be positively focused every 45 days, and reassessed to make sure the focuses and refocuses are on a positive track every 72 days to strengthen and reassess the reprograming of the 3 parts of the mind, here is part of the answer: It's known in the world of psychology that typically if you can consistently do something for 21 to 30 consecutive days, then most likely it will become a new habit. However, a thorough research study done by University College London shows that it takes longer to form a new habit. The university's portentous results demonstrated that 62 days is a better range for forming a new habit. Their research also demonstrated superior behavioral changes because a longer duration to develop new habits was proven to be what is best.

The Benefits of Studying the Components
and Numbers Contained in an Octagon

When you apply *The Octagon Way*'s format, you will have a default of a −72 or +72 refocus increase in your subconscious mind, but it's up to you whether it's a negative or a positive increase. The same applies for the unconscious mind: you will have a default of a −72 or +72 refocus increase in your subconscious mind, but it's up to you. However, the focuses are different because you have a focus possibility between zero and 72 focuses after you've completed a full 360-day cycle using *The Octagon Way*'s format. The only way to truly stay motivated is for you to attain a total of 216 after you've completed three full revolutions of *The Octagon Way*. If you arrive at 144 to 215 after a full cycle of *The Octagon Way* then you will be stoppable, but if you attain 216, and you properly focus your conscious mind every five days, then you will be unstoppable. Remember, 216 represents 72 subconscious mind refocuses, 72 conscious mind focuses, and 72 unconscious mind refocuses.

Avoid Negatively Strengthening the
Three Parts of Your Mind

Don't negatively strengthen your conscious, unconscious, and subconscious minds. On the contrary, you must positively strengthen your conscious, unconscious, and subconscious minds. Your aim is to always achieve positive focuses, and if you properly focus the conscious mind every five days, then you will attain the positive or +9 necessary conscious focuses every 45 days. You have a possible nine focuses every 45 days within each triangle of the octagon, so if you miss any focuses, you must subtract those misses from 9. For example, suppose during a 45-day period you missed three focuses, which would read like this, 9 − 3, which would represent a positive 45 + 6, 45 + 6, 45 + 6, a negative 45 − 3, 45 − 3, 45 − 3, a positive (45 + 6) x 3 = 153, and negative (45 − 3) x 3 = 126.

Your aim is to positively stimulate old positive memories, and to create new and exciting memories when using *The Octagon Way*. One of the central principles of *The Octagon Way* is that your mind is evolving into its negative or positive experiences. Either you're conditioning your negative memories, or you're conditioning your positive ones. Remember, the conscious mind can't do both at the same time. This is why you will never see someone prosper who is unconsciously growing their mind in a negative environment. However, if the person is consciously aware that their environment is negative, and they're determined to change their environment, then this person can figure out a way to win despite their negative environment.

You must focus your conscious mind every five days with stimulating seeds that consist of watering all of your five senses in a positive way. So look for ways to listen to new positive speeches every five days. Look for ways to discuss a positive topic in a new or old way with a family member or friend. Look for ways to try new things such as: a new exercise, activity, lotion, restaurant, run longer, run harder, smile more, get up earlier, go to bed earlier, and change up the order you eat your food. For example, if you normally eat your fries after your burger, switch up the order and eat your fries first, and then eat your burger. Ask your parents or close relatives about unique things that you did as a baby and as a child. Meet a new person every five days and briefly look for a way to hold a thirty-second conversation. (*You don't have to remember the person's name, and it doesn't matter if you see them again. You will be amazed how this will reset your mind.*)

Challenge your mind by engaging in complex activities, and spend five minutes every five days being honest with yourself about your fears and failures. When you implement this portion, think of someone who needs your help, and look for a way to compliment them and give them encouragement. This can be done with a simple phone call. This is important because it will focus your mind on being a giver, and it will refocus your negative memories of people not helping, or being kind to you. *The Octagon Way*'s format will also refocus any negative propaganda that you have consciously or unconsciously heard. When you were a child you heard all types of negative stuff that you can't recall, and these experiences still shape how you think, and the fears that you have. Being a loving person and helping other people out strengthens your belief that people will help you out. However, you must volunteer your time and skills freely. Hug more, smile more, and read self-affirmations every five days that start with the words "I am." Make sure you're using affirmations that encompass your five senses.

The Octagon Way Creates a Neutral Mind

The Octagon Way was designed to reset your mind to zero, so that a new form of programming can take place. The refocusing strategy must be implemented every five days and the process will require you to spend a total of twenty-five minutes every five days focusing on each one of your five senses in a positive way. *Here is the format for implementing this concept: spend five minutes on each one of your five senses every five days by focusing on each one of your five senses in a positive way.* If you successfully focus your mind every five days through strengthening your five senses, it will perpetually reset your mind, and recondition your subconscious mind. The number zero can be an odd or an even number, so if the mind is reset to zero, then the subconscious mind will be more impressionable to activate its positive zones because the mind will be in a neutral state.

Compare it to a car in neutral. A car that's in neutral can move, even if the engine is blown. A car in neutral will move by itself without any internal force, depending on the surface. For example, if you put a car in neutral on a deep slope, then it would move without any force. However, a car in neutral on a horizontal plane may require a push to move the car. Here is the point: the car will still move based on the environment it's put into. Your mind is the same way, and when your mind is set at zero, once your mind begins to move, you can control your mind's direction as it receives new data.

The Octagon Way focuses on new positive experiences, and your positive focuses help to refocus your negative experiences, which then guides your mind back to neutral once you've completed three full revolutions of an octagon, which takes 360 days. Why every five days for focuses? There are 365 days in a year and some calendars used to use 360 days. However, once we discovered that it takes the earth 365 days to orbit the sun, then the additional five days were added. If you divide 360 by five you will get 72, and if you divide 1080 by five you will get 216. The number five is unique in many ways. The number five is used in *The Octagon Way* as days of a year, and dividing five into an octagon produces a quotient of 72 for the inner vertices, and 216 for outer vertices. The numbers 72 and 216 represent where the human mind is capable of reaching a new dimension, and also represent the center of diameter where the three revolutions meet. The number 72 is a sphere and spheres create a three-dimensional figure if it contains three elements that meet up at the same points for diameter and circumference. Most importantly, the three parts of the human mind all have the number 72 attached to them when using *The Octagon Way*. The human mind is a sphere in *The Octagon Way*, so all three parts of the mind are multiples of 72, and all three parts of the mind meet up at 72 for the inner vertices, and 216 for the outer vertices to reflect one mind. (Refer back to the meaning of 72 mentioned earlier in this chapter).

If you actively focus your conscious mind, then it will meet up with your unconscious and your subconscious mind. *The Octagon Way* assists in helping the three parts of your mind to become unified and centered. So, always strive to observe obvious mental behavioral changes every 72 days. Furthermore, a neutral mind means that the mind is set at zero. Also, the mind can be odd or even at the same time. *"If you properly train yourself to constantly achieve a neutral mind, then you'll always be aware and able to control the different forms that your mind is capable of adapting to."*

You Must Fly Through Life like an Eagle and a Ruppell's Griffon Vulture

An eagle is the king or queen of the bird kingdom; however, the Ruppell's Griffon vulture flies higher than any other bird on the planet. If a Ruppell Griffon vulture witnesses another bird when it's flying its highest, that other bird will most certainly be another Ruppell's Griffon vulture. However, it's fitting to mention that eagles fly very high as well.

"Are you an eagle in a caterpillar's form? What does this mean? Before a butterfly can become a butterfly it must be a caterpillar, but if the caterpillar never progresses into a butterfly, then the butterfly will never use its true capabilities or potential. The question to ask is: is the butterfly a butterfly while it's in its caterpillar state? Yes, it is! Think about it this way: What if someone said a baby could never be an adult because the baby is a baby. Ridiculous! Babies already have the seeds for being an

adult inside them because it's in their DNA to grow, and if fed properly, babies will inevitably grow."

An eagle in a caterpillar's form means that you never reach your full potential. An eagle and a Ruppell's Griffon vulture are capable of flying the highest of all the birds; however, this doesn't mean that they will! An eagle or a Ruppell's Griffon vulture can choose not to fly at all, or to fly as low as a butterfly. So never imprison your gifts and don't fly lower than you're capable of flying. Now go, and *Just Get Up and Manifest Your Inner Genius!*

Just Get Up Keys and Treasures

1. **Yield.** Know when to yield to your circumstances, and know when to speed up and go.
2. **Stop.** Know when to come to a complete stop, and know when to cross over into the next lane of your dreams. **You must have an intuitive mind!**
3. **Believe**/have relaxed faith.
4. **Focus** your conscious mind **every five days** by positively stimulating your five senses with new experiences, information, and challenges. **A true challenge must involve a high likelihood of failure,** and you must recognize that failure is only a yield sign telling you to possibly stop or look out for oncoming traffic. Remember; **Learn from all of your failures before you move on to the next phase of your dream's adventure!**
5. Always stick with your **true passion** because it will unlock **your inner genius,** and once your **inner genius** is tapped, it will lead to **your true purpose** in life.
6. *"Don't let one stop in your life represent an eternity of No's."* —*Isaac Samuel Miller*

ACKNOWLEDGMENTS

I WOULD LIKE TO GIVE my heartfelt recognition to everyone who was a part of helping me write *Just Get Up: And Manifest Your Inner Genius.* First, I would like to thank my creator Jehovah God for bestowing me with my gift of inspiration, and endowing me with the inspired intuition of desiring to help guide people to identifying their inherent gifts of value that Jehovah God infused within every piece of flesh that has and will ever exist on this planet! *(Read Ephesians 2:10 and Romans 12:6-8)*

I would like to give a special thanks to my beautiful wife, Erika Miller, for putting up with me through this process. Everyone who knows me well will attest to the fact that when my mind is set to do something, I'm focused and I have a tendency to be abnormally obsessed, so thanks for the support, My Love, and for helping to keep me balanced. Furthermore, I would like to thank my client and friend Robert Lancaster who, one day during 2017, suggested that I download the dictionary.com app. This occurred after I apprised him that I was going to start a reading program and learn a new word every day! A few months after using the dictionary.com app, I developed an overwhelming spark to start writing poetry again, which led to me auditioning for *American's Got Talent* as a spoken word artist. Furthermore, as I prepared for my audition I decided to write a book as well, and instantly the thought crept into my mind subtly and intensely, whispering, *Just Get Up!* From that moment onward, a relentless journey of self-discovery began to imbue and I knew I had a mission to manifest my inner genius. Just seeing words displayed on my phone every day from dictionary.com reminded me of my love for writing and helped to reunite my heart's mind with my true passions in life. Robert, you will always be invaluable to me for that! Although simple, this suggestion changed my life.

I would like to thank my lovely Mom, Shareese Miller, my Dad Isaac Carter, my grandmother Bertha Miller, my brother Travis Miller, my sister Brittany Miller, Sherman Dunn, Marques Harris, Jane Byo, Jim Byo, Brent, Mike, Michelle Smith, Tyras Walker, Rita Dykes, Anthony Rollo, LeMar Clifford, Brandon Abidin, Lisa Perez, Brandon Apple, Shelby Apple, Ryan Hartley, Luke Cusimano, David Boh, Kevin Banks, Michael Francios, Micah Smith, Sue Smith, Emma Rollo, Isabello Rollo, Letita Roberts, my wonderful father-in-law Lonnie Coleman for supporting me along this journey, and everyone else who my memory may have forgotten. Thanks and I love you all. Also, I would like to give another special thanks to everyone who gave me an endorsement quote, and all of you dear readers for deciding to read my book. Finally, I would like to thank my publisher John Koehler along with my editor Joe Coccaro, and proofreader Marshall McClure.

AFTERWORD

To you, dear readers, I encourage you to read my *Just Get Up* program several times, so that the gems contained throughout my thirteen chapters will deeply sink into your subsconscious minds. Robert Sharma once said: "Everything is created twice, first in your imagination and then in reality." You can truly be and do whatever you want! Remember, everything should and must be done to bring honor and praise to Jehovah God, so don't forget to develop a daily bible reading program as well. God's word is and will always be the greatest motivational book on the planet. Remember wise King Solomon's words found at Ecclesiastes 2: 13-16 and never lose sight of Matthew 6:24 and 33. You must pursue your gifts to help others and to solve a problem. Never let money guide you as the only reason why you desire to maximize your unique potential. Remember, true success is something that you personally, intentionally, and continuously seek. You must aim to get better every day because apoptosis is real, and without a vision we perish. Proverbs 29:18 (King James Version)

Listen to my new podcast episodes on Fridays at 1:30 p.m. Central time zone. You can locate my podcast episodes on my Youtube channel: JustGetUpWithIsaac. Furthermore, I strongly suggest that you listen to episodes 4 through 7 of my podcast show. These episodes are a part of a four-part series entitled *How to Discover and Use Your True Gift of Value.* These episodes will help you to complete the process of discovering your gifts, so listen to episodes 4 through 7 several times until the episode's concepts are fully understood. If you also want to hire me for a speaking engagement, fitness training, nutrition coaching, or sales coaching, herewith are my website and my social media links. Also, I conduct free bible studies with whoever wants one, or I'll direct you to another qualified fellow sister or brother of my same faith, if my schedule doesn't permit. Preaching and teaching are my main missions in life and that's what I love to do the most. Finally, feel free to contact me for guidance and a free one-hour consultation.

Contact Information

1. Website: www.isaacsmiller.com
2. Instagram: justgetupwithisaac
3. Link: https://www.instagram.com/justgetupwithisaac/
4. Facebook: Justgetupwithisaac
5. Link: https://www.facebook.com/justgetupwithisaac
6. Linked-in: Isaac Miller
7. Link: https://www.linkedin.com/in/isaac-miller-b08103167/
8. Pinterest: JustGetUpWithIsaac
9. Link: https://www.pinterest.com/JustGetUpWithIsaac/
10. Twitter: JustGetUpWithIsaac twit: @justgetup
11. Link: https://twitter.com/justgetup
12. Email: isaacfittherapy@gmail.com

CPSIA information can be obtained
at www.ICGtesting.com
Printed in the USA
BVHW071415080321
601998BV00002B/146